The Leafs

THE
LEAFS

* *

*An Anecdotal History of
the Toronto Maple Leafs*

Jack Batten

KEY PORTER BOOKS

Canadian Cataloguing in Publication Data
Batten, Jack, 1932–
 The Leafs : an anecdotal history of the Toronto Maple Leafs

ISBN 1-55013-561-9

1. Toronto Maple Leafs (Hockey team) — History.
I. Title.

GV848.T6B3   1994   796.962'64'09713541   C94-931235-5

Key Porter Books Limited
70 The Esplanade
Toronto, Ontario
Canada M5E 1R2

The publisher gratefully acknowledges the support of the Department of Communications, the Canada Council and the Ontario Arts Council.

Design: Maher Design
Typesetting: MacTrix DTP
Printed and bound in Canada

94 95 96 97 98 99   6 5 4 3 2 1

Contents

This book is for Brad

1

Last Day of the New Beginning

THE DIRECTORS' ROOM IN MAPLE LEAF Gardens looks like your average bastion of privilege. It's tucked into a hidden corner under the Gardens' southwest stands, off a narrow hallway and behind a pair of security guards. The room is large and L-shaped, the lighting is subdued, the walls are panelled and hung with photographs of Gardens' directors dating back to the first board in 1931. The small bar in the corner of the L stocks French wines and Scotch whiskeys. And tall waitresses in chic outfits move discreetly through the room, serving drinks and urging guests to the lavish buffet table.

As early as six o'clock on the night of Saturday, May 29, 1993, ninety minutes before the drop of the puck, members of the Gardens' board and other credentialled men and women began to fill the Directors' Room. They were gathering for the most significant Toronto Maple Leaf hockey game in twenty-six years. May 2, 1967, marked the last of the good times in Toronto hockey. On that night, the Leafs beat the Montreal Canadiens at the Gardens, 3–1, to win the Stanley Cup, Toronto's fourth in six seasons. The Leafs missed the playoffs the following year and eight more times in the next quarter-century. In the sole year they made it as far as the semi-finals, 1978, the Canadiens creamed them in four straight. But the 1992–93 season brought victories and optimism to the Maple Leafs, new respect and excitement. They finished the NHL regular schedule eighth overall in league standings, and in the preliminary playoff rounds, they beat each of the Detroit Red Wings and St. Louis Blues in seven games. Now, on this historic May night, Toronto was meeting the Los Angeles Kings in another seventh game, the decisive contest in the Stanley Cup semi-finals, the winner to go for it all against Montreal in the finals. The good times were rolling again for Maple Leaf hockey.

In the Directors' Room, in an atmosphere where conviviality edged up against anticipation, retired hockey players—Ken Dryden, Larry Robinson—schmoozed with politicians—Toronto mayor June Rowlands, one-time Ontario Tory leader Larry Grossman. A former prime minister of Canada and spouse, John and Geills Turner, huddled with a publisher, Avie Bennett of McClelland and Stewart. Over here was a theatre mogul, Garth Drabinsky. And back there was the mogul of moguls, Steve Stavro. He's the proprietor of a food-market chain, Knob Hill Farms, and of a stable of stakes-winning racehorses, and as chairman of the Gardens, he was everybody's host for the evening.

And Bob Rae was on hand, the New Democrat premier of Ontario.

"You're in here, what, campaigning?" one guest asked Rae, apparently expecting the man of the people to hang out in the cheap seats, up in the greys.

"There're no NDP voters in the Directors' Room!" Rae answered. He laughed, giving it everything he had. "Shoot a cannon through here, you wouldn't hit an NDP voter!"

Terry Kelly, a lawyer and a Gardens director, was still steaming over Wayne Gretzky's clip on Doug Gilmour's face in overtime during the previous Thursday's game in Los Angeles. Gretzky's stick cut Gilmour, the star Leaf centre, for eight stitches. The referee called no penalty, and seconds later, Gretzky scored the winning goal. Kelly, a silver-haired man with a soft Irish lilt to his voice, was still browned off at Gretzky's deed.

"Gretzky could have done what no man in sport has ever done," Kelly said. "He could have taken himself out of the game. Do you follow my point?"

Kelly's audience wasn't certain it could guess at the answer.

"The referee said he didn't see Gretzky highstick Gilmour," Kelly continued. "Very well, but Gretzky knew he'd cut Gilmour. He could have stepped forward and said, 'I did it and I'll sit out the rest of the game.' That would have been the noble thing. Gretzky declined to be noble."

"Go Leafs, go!" Bob Rae said, and everyone left the Directors' Room for seats in the golds.

THE CROWD GOT INTO IT AT ABOUT THE MOMENT WHEN the two guys on the ice singing the national anthems, Michael Burgess and John McDermott, reached ". . . and the rocket's red glare . . ." The noise had been building through the introduction of the Leafs' starting players — after the requisite boos for the Kings' starters — and by the end of the anthems, into the dropping of the puck, the sound had grown huge and visceral. This, the fans were saying, was going to be a night of hockey — big time.

The players seemed to agree. From the start, it was all speed, hard hitting and skill. L.A. had the edge in speed; the Leafs did most of the hitting; and the skill, except when Gilmour was on the ice, tilted in favour of the Kings by a fairly substantial margin. Toronto players were having trouble with the puck. It kept bouncing over their sticks, skittering out of their control.

At 8:45 of the first period, the Kings took a penalty for, of all ridiculous crimes in the biggest game of the season, having too many men on the ice. Leaf expectations stepped up a notch. But those problems with the bouncing puck didn't go away, and a minute into the penalty, the Kings' Jari Kurri scooped up the puck off a Leaf bungle at the L.A. blueline. Kurri fed Gretzky, who scooted away on a two-on-one with the big L.A. defenceman Marty McSorley. Gretzky, on the left, carried deep into the Leaf end, cradling the puck, passing to McSorley on the right when the two were about twenty-five feet from the Leaf net. Felix Potvin in the Toronto goal moved to his own left, to McSorley's side. McSorley whipped a pass back to Gretzky. Potvin scrambled to greet Gretzky. He was a fraction too late. Gretzky put the puck in the corner of the net.

It was 1–0 Kings, and the score went to 2–0 before the period ended, when Gretzky set up his winger Tomas Sandstrom for a low wrist shot from the slot. Gretzky, it was becoming clear, had the power on this night to cast spells over the Leafs. Each time he appeared on the ice, he worked a couple of wonders with the puck, and the Toronto players didn't seem able to do much about it. Once or twice, away from the play, out of Referee Andy vanHellemond's sight, Doug Gilmour took a whack at Gretzky. The whacks didn't make any difference.

IN THE DIRECTORS' ROOM BETWEEN PERIODS, A VICE-president of a bank talked about Gretzky.

"Curious thing," he said. "Somebody wrote of Gretzky a long time ago that he doesn't go where the puck is, he goes where the puck is *going* to be. What's curious is that the expression has become standard in my business, in banking. We don't adapt our strategies to today's conditions. We adapt them to where the conditions are taking us tomorrow. We call it 'the Gretzky approach.'"

THE LEAFS TOOK CHARGE IN THE SECOND PERIOD. IT wasn't an exercise in superior talent. It was an outbreak of the characteristics that got the team through the season and into the playoffs — determination, drive, toughness. The first goal came fast, just over a minute into the period. Wendel Clark banged and banged at the puck in front of the L.A. net until it went past the goalie, Kelly Hrudey. Six minutes later, Glenn Anderson swooped on Hrudey from the right side, took a pass from Gilmour, and sent a wrist shot into the net.

Tie game.

The crowd in the Gardens sent up a wall of sound. It began in sheets of cheers, distinct and separated for a moment, then coalesced into one sustained monster of noise. It was exhilarating and terrifying, and for about five minutes, down on the ice, the Kings lost their poise. That was unusual. All night, the L.A. players had radiated a kind of unassailable cool. Now there was a small crack in their confidence.

Except in Gretzky's. He didn't bend. Through the incredible din from the crowd, he continued, during his shifts, to run the play. And in the middle of the period, he led the Kings across the Leaf blueline in a three-on-three. Two of the Leafs, defencemen Sylvain Lefebvre and Bob Rouse, peeled off to check two of the Kings, Sandstrom and Rob Blake. That left rookie Toronto winger Kent Manderville to look after Gretzky. It was no contest. Gretzky put a fake on Manderville that left him waving a forlorn glove at Gretzky as he skipped past and unloaded a slapshot into the net. The goal moved L.A. in front once again, steadied the team's equilibrium and sucked the noise out of the crowd.

BETWEEN THE SECOND AND THIRD PERIODS, STEVE STAVRO and Terry Kelly sat alone on the small sofa just inside the door to the Directors' Room. Kelly, leaning close to Stavro's right ear, was doing most of the talking. Stavro is dapper, in his middle sixties and, among Toronto's multi-millionaire businessmen, so shy of the limelight he makes Paul Reichmann seem as public as Honest Ed Mirvish. He's given just one private press interview in his life, to a dogged *Globe and Mail* reporter in 1978. For eyes and ears on the world beyond the areas Stavro knows best, groceries and horses, he looks often to his friend Kelly. Soccer brought the two men together thirty-five years ago. Stavro is passionate about soccer. Hockey? He knows plenty, and Kelly, informed and wise about all sports, sometimes fills in the gaps.

"It's only a single-goal difference, Steve," Kelly said, his voice low, almost a hush. "And you know the kind of fellas we have on our team. There's no quit in them, am I not correct about that?"

Stavro, staring straight ahead, nodded his head.

"There's a whole period to pull it out," Kelly went on. "More than enough the way Wendel and Gilmour and our best men are playing. Mark my words, Wendel's a man possessed tonight."

Stavro looked at his watch. It was long past his favoured 8:30 bedtime, a sensible hour to retire for an executive who's spent a life rising at 4:30 to make the rounds of his supermarkets.

KELLY WAS RIGHT ABOUT WENDEL CLARK. AT 1:25 OF THE second period, he'd scored his first goal. He got his second, making the game even, at precisely 1:25 of the third. The second goal came much the same way as the first, off a centring pass that Clark banged at until it eluded Hrudey.

The goal gave Toronto a lift, and the action on the ice pitched back and forth, a thriller of a game. But of the two teams, tied on the scoreboard, L.A. continued to look like the bunch who knew how the game would end. The Kings looked hip. They were cool, the Leafs were hot. The Kings were jazz, the Leafs were country and western.

Fifteen minutes of deadlock went by in fast, hard hockey. Each team had glorious chances to score. At about the twelve-minute mark, L.A.'s Alexei Zhitnik, coming over his own blueline, fired a cross-ice pass, left to right, intended for Gretzky. Toronto's Peter Zezel picked it off and flew away on a breakaway. He whapped a gorgeous slapshot. Hrudey got his glove on it. Crisis averted for L.A.

Four minutes later, Zhitnik involved himself in another offensive charge—Kings defencemen, especially Zhitnik and McSorley, were getting into the attack all night—and this time Zhitnik put the puck on the Leaf net. Bob Rouse got in the way. Rouse didn't stop the puck. He deflected it. The puck caromed to the right side of the Leaf goal. Mike Donnelly, the L.A. left-winger, was stationed there. At that moment, Felix Potvin was spot-welded to the left goal post. Donnelly had an empty net in front of him. He shot the puck into it.

Kings 4, Leafs 3.

Forty more seconds of play passed. The Gretzky line was on the ice for L.A., near the end of a shift. Gretzky had the puck at the Leaf blueline on the right side. He seemed to have nothing more in mind than keeping the puck deep in the Toronto end while his team changed players. He swept down the boards and behind the Toronto net. Leaf defenceman Todd Gill rode him all the way. Gretzky carried the puck on his back hand, holding himself between it and Gill. He rounded the net, a stride ahead of Gill. There were no Kings in front of the net. The L.A. guys, newly arrived on the ice on the change of players, were still skating from their own bench across the Toronto blueline. Gretzky, now ready to leave the ice himself, backhanded the puck in the direction of the Leaf net. It was the move of a player just getting rid of the puck, unloading it, maybe hoping it might cause a little trouble. The puck hit Toronto defenceman Dave Ellett's skate. Ellett didn't seem to notice the puck. Or feel it. He was busy looking up ice at the new arrival of L.A. players. And in the most heartbreaking piece of rotten luck, the puck banked off Ellett's skate and into the net.

Kings 5, Leafs 3.

In the three minutes left in the game, the Leafs didn't give up. Ellett scored a goal at 18:53, a surprise really, when he found himself about fifteen feet in front of the L.A. net all by himself, taking a pass from Dave Andreychuk and snapping a shot past Hrudey.

Sixty-seven seconds to go and the Leafs poured it on, Potvin out of the net, six attackers for Toronto, the play entirely in the Los Angeles zone.

The Leaf players looked crazed with effort and hope. They hurled themselves at the Kings, whacked at the puck. This wasn't a time for slick playmaking. This was a time for desperate guys to drive the puck in Kelly Hrudey's direction. Maybe it would hit a leg, take a crazy bounce, anything—a deflection, a fluke, a last blessing.

But in the end, the very end, the seconds flicking towards zero on the timer over the ice, the puck stayed out of the Los Angeles net. It was over. For the Leafs, it was finally over.

"GRETZKY SUCKS!"

The loud chant erupted out of the seats in the north end of the Gardens.

"Gretzky sucks!"

The L.A. players were leaving the ice through a north-end gate, and the chanters let fly a thick shower of plastic cups, programs and miniature hockey sticks. The stuff bounced off and around the Kings. Gretzky was the number-one target. A container of coffee whipped past his shoulder. It left a brown stain oozing across the ice in front of the net.

"Gretzky sucks!"

IN THE L.A. DRESSING ROOM, GRETZKY TRIED OUT HIS collection of metaphors.

"I've taken the roses and I've taken the heat," he said. "But tonight, I stood up and answered the bell."

He also said, "I have never had this much personal satisfaction from winning a playoff series."

Later he elaborated on the "personal" part. It seemed that he'd been cheesed off by something that *Toronto Star* hockey columnist Bob McKenzie had written about him. In the first five games of the series, McKenzie wrote, Gretzky played like "someone carrying a piano on his back." Gretzky clipped out the column and carried it with him for days. He read the column, reread it and grew hot under the collar.

"Maybe those kinds of things get me going," Gretzky said.

IN THE PRESS INTERVIEW ROOM, TORONTO COACH PAT Burns stood in front of the microphones and cameras and invoked a Bruce Cockburn lyric. He said, "I kept on telling the guys, you've got to kick at the darkness till the daylight comes."

Burns got off the funniest line of the night. He was discussing the Toronto fans, their loyalty, their noise in the Gardens, their numbers across Canada — 4.2 million viewers watched this night's game on CBC-TV — and he emphasized how the support helped carry the team.

"We flew back from losing the sixth game in the series against St. Louis and fans turned up to welcome us at the airport," Burns said. "When I coached in Montreal, if we'd come back from the same loss, they'd have sent up two fighter planes to shoot us down."

IN THE DIRECTORS' ROOM, THE MOOD WAS SOLEMN. PEOPLE got drinks from the bar and murmured consoling words among themselves. A group of directors entered the room in a bloc, Stavro, Kelly and the others. They'd come from the Leaf dressing room.

"Some very long faces in there," Kelly said.

Bob Rae asked for everybody's attention.

"I'd like to propose a toast," he said. "This is to Steve Stavro and to the people in the Leaf organization and what they've done for all of us this year. The way they've worked, the way the players have worked, Pat

Burns, everyone, that kind of work is symbolic of many things. It's symbolic of the kind of thing we want to teach our children. It's symbolic of the very best. It's meant a great deal to all of us, to all of Canada."

Rae raised the glass in his hand. His words, a balance of gracious tribute and corny schmaltz, had hit the right note in the room. Other glasses were raised.

"To Mr. Stavro," Rae finished.

"Mr. Stavro," the others answered.

Stavro, in a group of four men to Rae's right, stepped back, reluctant, looking as if he were trying to lose himself in the small crowd. For a moment, he said nothing. Then he spoke, but it was only to call on the other directors to take a bow. His voice trailed off.

Rob Prichard ended the instant of awkwardness. He arrived in the Directors' Room at this moment, the president of the University of Toronto, a tall, stylish man in his mid-forties. He had on a blue work shirt open at the neck, a sweater tied around his shoulders. The casualness broke the room's jacket-and-tie rule, but nobody was objecting. Prichard gripped Stavro's hand and told him what a "fabulous" thing he'd done for Toronto and hockey. The rest of the people in the room, relieved, letting Prichard take care of Stavro, went back to their personal laments of the game they'd just watched.

"It's a wonderful night when you see someone like Gretzky play at his best," Ken Dryden said, not lamenting. "That's just tremendous hockey."

A couple of others in his circle mumbled something that sounded like agreement, but most of the people in this crowd were too intrinsically connected to the Leafs to concede anything to the Great One. Maybe tomorrow, not tonight.

"I'll tell you what," Terry Kelly said after a while. "I'll tell you what this bunch of Leafs got accomplished. They took us back to a better time for hockey in this city. They took us back"—here he pointed at the wall near the bar where a photograph hung of the Gardens' builder and the Maple Leafs' founder—"to Conn Smythe himself."

2

Conn Smythe

CONN SMYTHE WORE SPATS.

Perhaps he wore them as a fashion statement. He dressed in the conventional big-shooter-Toronto-businessman mode of his period. He favoured grey suits tailored with enough fabric to make the pants billow and the jackets hang like tents. Then he added extra sartorial fillips. His fedoras came in a sharp off-white shade, and he always had the spats. They were eye-catchers.

Or maybe the spats operated as one more indicator that Conn Smythe was the original character-about-town. Smythe stood out, not so much in the physical sense, since he was a little guy, about five-feet-seven, in businesses—hockey and construction—that you associate with big men. But he stood out in the size of his ambitions and the thoroughness of his accomplishments; in his temper and his expression of it; in the flavour and noisiness of his views; in his ability to make enemies, hold grudges and to stab his opponents, though never in the back. Smythe was up-front. He was the feisty martinet in the pearl grey spats.

As a family man, Smythe made a flinty father. That may have been because he had peculiar models in his own father and mother. They were a mismatched pair. His father was an unworldly, devout innocent. His

Kent Manderville, here in action against the Hawks in the 1994 playoff series, emerged that season as a tough young forward on the rise.

Mike Eastwood, another up-and-comer on the front lines, beats Belfour in game five against the Hawks.

Never mind, guys. The Hawks' Tony Amonte may have hit for the hat trick in Game three of the Toronto-Chicago series, but Leafs prevailed, four games to two.

Ooooh, says Doug Gilmour after popping one on the San Jose net during the 1994 series between the Leafs and the Sharks.

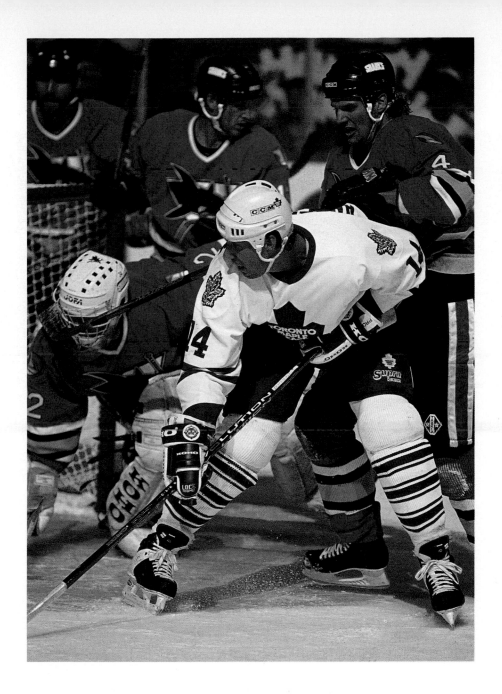

Felix Potvin is known as "The Cat," but, as he shows here in a scramble against the Sharks, "Mr. Cool" is also apt.

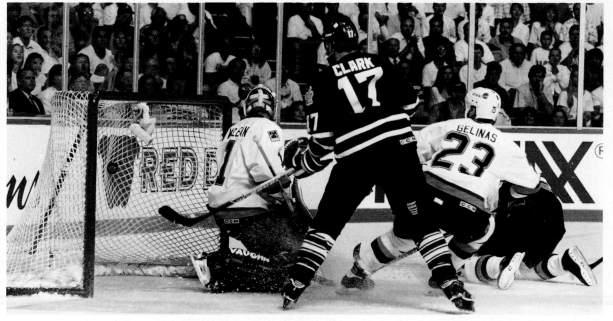

A few weeks after Wendel Clark watched this Mike Eastwood shot get past Kirk McLean in Toronto's losing semi-final to Vancouver in May, 1994 he was traded to Quebec.

mother was a jolly, promiscuous alcoholic. He came from Ireland, she from England, and they were married on a ship carrying them to Canada in the late 1880s. Once on land in Toronto, they seem to have rarely lived together. This unlikely union produced two children—first, Mary, then, four years later, in 1895, Constantine Falkland Cary. Conn resented Mary. He thought his father favoured her over him, and he didn't much mourn when Mary died of a horrible thyroid ailment at age twelve. From then on, Conn and his dad lived in a series of tiny houses and cramped apartments. Conn's mother dropped in from time to time. She was often drunk. Drink killed her in 1906 when she was thirty-eight and Conn was eleven. Conn grew up in what would be called today a dysfunctional family.

His father earned his small living as a reporter for the *Toronto World*, covering every beat from the racetrack (where young Conn began his lifelong love affair with horses) to symphonic music (it didn't take with Conn). But Smythe senior's most consuming passion was his religion, theosophy. The Theosophical Society was a discipline founded by a nineteenth-century, Russian-born mystic named Elena Petrovna Blavatsky. She knocked about the world for many years—India, Tibet, Texas—before lighting in New York City. Out of her travels, she put together a religion that emphasized reincarnation and the brotherhood of man. It attracted about 100,000 followers worldwide. Conn Smythe's father was one of them, for years the president of the Theosophical Society's branch in Canada.

"My dad taught me theosophy, and I'm a theosophist today," Conn Smythe told this writer in an interview in the late summer of 1977. "Very straightforward religion. Just believe in the basic things—The Golden Rule; As ye sow, so shall ye reap. Things like those two. Cast your bread on the waters! That's the best one. Cast your bread! Great truth in it. But I'll tell you what it all comes down to in theosophy, the reason I've stayed a theosophist all my life: it's because theosophy teaches that you can't get away with anything in this life anyway."

SMYTHE DIDN'T LET HIS RELATIVELY PUNY STATURE GET in the way of his love of sports. The kid was a tiger on any playing field.

Hockey took first place in his affections. He was a scrappy player, always sticking his nose into places where it was likely to get banged. But he must have had a bit of a touch with the puck because he frequently scored winning goals. And he must have had some presence about him because he kept getting chosen captain of his teams.

Some of his hockey, for a year and a half in his early teens, was played for Upper Canada College. His father had to scuffle to meet the school fees, and often young Conn suffered the humiliation of handing in payments to the UCC registrar in weekly packages of quarters, half-dollars and crumpled bills. The elder Smythe thought an upper-class education might be good for his son. Conn loathed the experience of being the poor boy among the sons of Toronto's swells. In later years, when Smythe was a huge success with hockey, his attitude to the city's Establishment was ambivalent. He took pride in welcoming the nobs to the red seats at Maple Leaf Gardens. But he liked rubbing it into them with his financial triumphs. Odd, too, that he sent both of his sons to Upper Canada College.

SMYTHE WROTE IN HIS 1981 AUTOBIOGRAPHY THAT "THE two qualities I admire most are guts and loyalty."

Loyalty? Well, loyalty to him, Smythe liked that, but it wasn't necessarily a two-way street. He was hardly loyal to Jimmy Thomson, a player who won Stanley Cups for him in the 1940s and '50s but who had the nerve to set about organizing an early players' union. As punishment, Smythe traded Thomson to Chicago in 1957. And loyalty didn't come into it when he dumped Hap Day in the same year. Day had been with Smythe from the late 1920s, winning Stanley Cups as player, coach and assistant general manager, but when Smythe decided to move his son Stafford towards Day's job, it was, what have you done for me lately, Hap? Day was gone.

But guts, in the sense of physical courage—Smythe came up big in that department. He put himself in places of danger and death in both of the century's World Wars. In March 1915, he enlisted as a gunner in the 25th Battery, Canadian Field Artillery. He fought in mud and gas and terror at the Somme in the fall of 1916 and at Vimy the following winter.

On a February 1917 day at Vimy, Smythe went a little nuts and charged a German trench position, armed only with his revolver. He winged a couple of German soldiers, scared some others and escorted two back to the Canadian lines as prisoners. The army gave Smythe a Military Cross for that escapade.

In the spring of 1917, Smythe transferred to the Royal Flying Corps. He got his pilot's wings and drew an assignment as an airborne artillery observer. His job was to fly over the German lines and pick out targets for the Allied guns. On a mission in October 1917, an enemy machine-gun burst clipped his plane. It crashed, and Smythe was taken prisoner. He sat out the rest of the war in POW camps. It was one of the few times in his life that Smythe was forced to keep still and stay silent. He didn't appreciate the experience.

Back in Toronto after the war, Smythe took care of unfinished business. He completed his engineering degree at the University of Toronto and got into the sand and gravel business with a company, C. Smythe For Sand, which would eventually make him a millionaire. He continued his romance with a young woman he'd met when he was sixteen, Irene Sands. By all accounts, she was, and remained, uncommonly sweet, gentle and patient; when she and Smythe married on March 10, 1920, both, according to Conn, were virgins. And Smythe resumed his hockey career, not as a player, but as a coach, manager, scout and all-round bird dog for good players.

Most of his hockey associations were with teams from the University of Toronto or with teams of ex–Varsity players. He coached and managed intercollegiate champions, one finalist in the Allan Cup for the best senior team in Canada, and, in 1927, an Allan Cup winner. His hockey activities, which were non-paying, took him to much of the rest of Canada and into the United States. Word began to get around in professional-hockey circles that this young Smythe fellow seemed like a real comer in the game.

AT THE END OF THE 1925–26 SEASON, THE NATIONAL Hockey League, which had been formed in 1917, consisted of four Canadian teams — the Ottawa Senators, Toronto St. Patricks, Montreal

Maroons, Montreal Canadiens — and three American teams — the Boston Bruins, New York Americans, Pittsburgh Yellow Jackets. During the spring and summer of 1926, three new franchises, all American, were admitted to the league: the New York Rangers, Chicago Black Hawks, and Detroit Cougars. A Manhattan blueblood named Colonel John Hammond was in charge of the Rangers, and he retained the new kid on the block, Conn Smythe, to put together a team for him.

Smythe did a honey of a job. In less than three months, by scrolling through his mental databank of good players he'd encountered on his travels, he produced a team that included many future Hall-of-Famers: Lorne Chabot in goal, Ching Johnson and Taffy Abel on defence, Frank Boucher at centre between the remarkable Cook brothers, Bill and Bun. This Ranger team was so instantly competitive that it won the Stanley Cup a mere two years later, in 1928. But Smythe wasn't around for the triumph. In fact, he wasn't around for the drop of the first puck in the Rangers' first game. Hammond, perhaps jealous of the accomplished young whippersnapper, perhaps offended by the Canadian's intransigent ways, fired Smythe six months after he'd hired him.

"I knew I wasn't gonna last in New York," Smythe said in the 1977 interview with this writer. "When I was young, I could smell a rotten deal a mile away. There was something rotten in New York, and sure enough, Hammond let me go before that first season started. Gave me the gate!"

SMYTHE HAD HAD A TASTE OF THE NHL, AND HE WANTED another. He got it at home in the winter of 1927 when the Toronto St. Pats, a team in last place in its NHL division and drawing flies at the gate, came up for sale. Smythe talked his way into a deal. A wealthy mining man named Jack Bickell, who already had a large share of the St. Pats, agreed to leave $40,000 in the club if Smythe could round up the investors to kick in another $160,000 to make the total purchase price of $200,000. Done, said Smythe, and on February 14, 1927, he became the new manager and occasional coach of an NHL team which he renamed the Maple Leafs two months later. Smythe had worn the maple leaf on badges and insignia during the war, and if it was good enough for his country, it was good enough for his hockey team. Similarly with the colours of the new team's uniforms: Smythe switched from St. Pats' green to the blue and white he'd worn at the University of Toronto. If it was good enough for his school, it was good enough for his hockey team.

It wasn't much of a hockey team. By the time Smythe had finished cleaning house of the old St. Patricks, a process that took three or four years, he had only two St. Pats players left, Hap Day on defence and Ace Bailey at forward. To fill in the blanks, Smythe went to a variety of sources. He traded with the Rangers to get the goalie, Lorne Chabot, whom he'd originally signed for New York. He bought Baldy Cotton, a winger, from Pittsburgh. He picked up another forward, Andy Blair, from the minor pro league out west. And in the most spectacular money transaction in hockey up to that time, he paid the Ottawa Senators $35,000, an astronomical sum—not to mention a nervy gamble for a financially strapped franchise—for the small, brave and clever defenceman King Clancy.

But the core of Smythe's young players came out of the junior operation he acquired, the Toronto Marlboros. The man at the head of the Marlies was Frank Selke, an electrician by trade, a hockey man by avocation. Selke, who joined the Leafs in 1929, turned out to be a genius at hockey organization, on the scale of Smythe himself. That ultimately led to a parting of the ways for the two; Smythe said it was over the issue of "loyalty," but the true cause of the split may have been his envy at Selke's skill in sussing out winning players. In the late 1920s, however, the separation lay many years in the future, and in the meantime, Selke groomed a bunch of marvellous Marlboro Juniors for Smythe's Maple Leafs. They included such players as the rough defenceman Red Horner and the high-scoring forwards Charlie Conacher, who was big and hard skating, and Busher Jackson, a man with a glorious repertoire of tricky moves. These young guys had the stuff of Stanley Cup champs.

SMYTHE WAS FAR LESS EFFECTIVE AS AN NHL COACH THAN as an NHL manager. He was keen on pre-game discussions of strategy with his players. But he wasn't deft at orchestrating it in the heat of battle. During one game, a referee called four penalties against the Leafs in less than a minute. Under the old rules, there was no such entity as a delayed penalty, and Toronto had to play with just two players, Lorne Chabot in goal and Andy Blair in front of him. Blair, who had a stammer and a wicked sense of humour, skated over to the boards for a conversation with Coach Smythe. Smythe leaned over from the bench, intent on Blair's question.

"W-w-w-w-well, C-Conn," Blair asked, "what's the s-s-strategy n-n-now?"

Smythe discarded himself as coach, and eventually settled on Dick Irvin, the former Chicago coach, as the right man for the job in Toronto. This was in late November 1931. At the time, the Leafs were in the basement. It was imperative that they get out of there and start to play winning and crowd-pleasing hockey: the team had just moved into a brand-new sports arena with 13,000 seats that needed filling.

THE LEAFS, AND THE ST. PATS BEFORE THEM, HAD PLAYED in the Mutual Street Arena. It was a rude, chilled, homely building which accommodated about 8,000 fans. Smythe wanted something both bigger and grander, elegant even, an arena where "people can go in evening clothes, a place that they can be proud to take their wives and girlfriends to."

The first miracle was that Smythe built Maple Leaf Gardens at the bottom of the Depression, and the second was that he built it so fast, in a mere 155 days. He always insisted that the explanation for the speed lay in a mutual brain wave that he and Frank Selke came up with—to offer the men who erected the building partial payment in Gardens stock. That, so Smythe's thinking went, encouraged bricklayers, carpenters, plumbers and electricians to set records in getting a move on with the construction.

Smythe was probably right, but the actual construction was preceded by his own slick and righteous selling job. Didn't this guy know the floor had just dropped out of the money markets? Not Smythe. He talked the Bank of Commerce into financing his vision of a great hockey palace, talked Sun Life into bankrolling him, talked the T. Eaton

Company out of some cash, persuaded large and small investors to back the Gardens to the tune of about a million and a half dollars. Smythe also had the good taste to hire an architectural firm, Ross and MacDonald of Montreal, that had a special vision of its own. Ross and MacDonald, using a rather advanced cantilever form, designed an airy, pillarless interior which gave every Gardens customer an unobstructed view of what was happening on the ice. When the Leafs played their first game in this beautiful new building on November 12, 1931, preceded by the combined bands of the 48th Highlanders and the Royal Grenadiers giving a rousing rendition of "Happy Days Are Here Again," 13,542 Torontonians turned out to marvel at Conn Smythe's sports arena. Some of them wore evening clothes.

DICK IRVIN, THE NEW COACH, PUT HIS FINGER ON ONE crucial problem with the Leafs. It was simple. They were out of shape. Irvin was a cool and cerebral hockey type, but he had his fiery side, and he lashed the Leafs into condition. Somewhere in the lashing process, the players became believers — in Irvin, in themselves, in the chances that they could win a Stanley Cup. The season caught the Leafs in one of those moments that all great sports teams experience, a moment when they know they're good, that they're destiny's choice.

Individually, the Leafs made a neat mix. The Kid line of Jackson, Conacher and the smooth puck-handling centre, Joe Primeau, handled the scoring; they finished the season with a total of seventy-five goals. Clancy, Day and Horner constituted a complementary trio of defencemen, Clancy essentially a rusher and the other two stay-at-home operators. Lorne Chabot was steady in the net. And the rest of the team included stylish Ace Bailey; speedy Bob Gracie; Baldy Cotton, who was Mr. Dependable; the peppery Andy Blair; and the steady old veteran Frank Finnigan. They blended into a cohesive bunch.

FROM 1927 TO 1938, THE NHL WAS SPLIT INTO TWO divisions, the Canadian and the American, and in this season of 1931–32, the Leafs recovered from their slow, pre–Dick Irvin start and finished with fifty-three points, a close second to the Montreal

Canadiens (fifty-seven points) in the Canadian Division, and third overall behind Montreal and the Rangers (fifty-four points).

The Leafs began the playoffs in a mild state of jitters and lost the first game of the two-game total-goals quarter-finals to Chicago, 1–0. But by the second game they were rolling and took a 6–1 victory. Similarly, in the semi-final against the Montreal Maroons, Toronto dithered to a 1–1 tie in the first game before asserting themselves for a 3–2 win in the second, the deciding goal scored by Bob Gracie.

That set up a best-of-five final that offered all Smythe could ask in the possibilities for revenge. Toronto's opponent was the New York Rangers, the team Smythe had put together six years earlier, the team that rejected him, the team headed by Colonel John Hammond who symbolized for Smythe everything "rotten" in Manhattan.

"I couldn't have written a better script myself," Smythe said.

But he wouldn't have dared to write the finale that his team produced.

Game one: the Leafs rushed to a 5–1 lead, then hung on through a Ranger counterattack to win 6–4.

Game two: with the score tied two-all, King Clancy scored a short-handed goal. It broke New York's spirit, and the Leafs cruised to a 6–2 win.

Game three: at home in Maple Leaf Gardens, Charlie Conacher came up with the shot that shifted the balance of play. It wasn't a goal. It was a rocket that caught Ranger goalie John Ross Roach under the heart and left him shakey and vulnerable to Leaf scorers. Toronto whipped New York 6–2, and took the series in three straight games.

How sweet it was for Conn Smythe in 1932, a victory over his old enemies, a Stanley Cup, a gorgeous new arena. There was just one catch—Smythe's beloved Maple Leafs would not win another Stanley Cup for ten more years. If Smythe had known this in 1932, he might have given it all up—the Gardens, the Leafs, hockey, even his spats.

3

Red

THE MEDAL WAS ABOUT THE SIZE OF A LOONIE, it was gold, and it had the words "Toronto Maple Leafs," fading now, engraved in the centre.

"They gave everyone on the team one of those when we won the Stanley Cup in 1932," Reginald "Red" Horner said on a late June day in 1993, pointing at the medal hanging in the frame on the wall in the foyer of his Toronto condominium. "It was a great team, 1932, and that medal, well, you don't see many of those around any more."

Not many of those medals? How about none? Horner's may be the last of the medals in the hands of its original recipient. The giants, Hockey-Hall-of-Famers who played on that '32 team—Charlie Conacher, Joe Primeau, Busher Jackson— were gone now. King Clancy, Baldy Cotton, Ace Bailey— all dead. And it was left to Horner, a Hall-of-Famer himself, one of hockey's most intimidating bodycheckers, to bear witness, to carry the torch for the champs of '32.

On this 1993 June day, Red Horner was eighty-four and appeared good for at least another decade. He looked younger than his years (still with plenty of hair in the colour that gave him his nickname), thought younger, talked younger, played golf younger (he shot to an eighteen handicap at Rosedale, the fifth-oldest golf club in Canada and one of the most exclusive). Horner had made himself a wealthy man since his Maple Leaf days. It was clear that he lived comfortably, the condo on the fourteenth floor of a handsome building in mid-Toronto, a winter place in Naples, Florida. And as he sat talking in his living room, he exuded an embracing sense of contentment, nothing showy, just the modest satisfaction of a man who'd always got the job done.

HORNER SAID, "I ALWAYS ENJOYED THIS STORY, THE ONE about how I started with the Leafs." And he proceeded to tell it.

It was a Saturday afternoon in mid-December 1928. Horner was nineteen years old. He had a job as a clerk on the Standard Stock Exchange in Toronto. It paid twenty-five dollars a week and was intended to train Horner for a career in the brokerage business. On Friday nights, he played hockey for the Toronto Marlboros, defenceman and captain, and every Saturday afternoon, he played for the Solway Mills club in a league made up of teams sponsored by four brokerage firms. On this particular Saturday afternoon, after the game at the Mutual Street Arena, Conn Smythe showed up in the Solway Mills dressing room.

"Red," he said to Horner, "you've had enough of this amateur hockey. I want you to come with the Leafs."

"That's very flattering, Mr. Smythe," Horner answered, "especially when you consider I've only seen two pro games in my entire life."

"I want you to play tonight."

"Tonight?! But I played last night and this afternoon. You just saw me play this afternoon."

"I'll pay you $2,500 for the rest of the season."

Horner thought about the offer.

"Let's do it this way, Mr. Smythe," he said after a while. "Why don't you pick me up on your way to the game tonight. I'll take you in and introduce you to my parents. If everything's all right between you and them, we'll drive on down to the arena and you can introduce me to the rest of your team. We'll take it from there."

Sitting in his living room in 1993, thinking back to that Saturday afternoon sixty-five years earlier, Horner smiled a wondering smile. "Life was simpler in those days," he said.

Horner played for the Leafs against the Pittsburgh Yellow Jackets on the December night in 1928. "I don't recall any problems," he said of the game. The problems came in Horner's second game, on Christmas Eve against the Montreal Maroons. "I was checking the Maroons' players quite heavily," Horner remembered. "They didn't like that, and one of them, Nels Stewart, slashed me across the hand. He broke the hand. I was out five weeks."

By then, Horner had quit his clerk's job at the stock exchange. He recovered from his injury and played twelve seasons for the Leafs. In the last two—his pride in this was immense—he was captain of the Toronto Maple Leafs.

HOCKEY PEOPLE WITH EXTREMELY LONG MEMORIES HAVE said Red Horner was the game's greatest bodychecker.

"That's a talent you're born with, bodychecking," Horner said, looking grave about it. "Everything else in hockey I had to work hard at, my skating, my passing. But bodychecking came naturally to me. I don't believe you can train a bodychecker. A player is one or he isn't. I was one."

There's a fine line between bodychecking and actions that referees give penalties for, and Horner crossed it many times. He led the NHL in penalty minutes for eight consecutive seasons.

"That's a misleading statistic," Horner said, speaking more quickly. "People look at it, eight years of the most penalties, and they say, well, how can this guy be in the Hockey Hall of Fame? What they don't understand is that when I went to the penalty box, I usually took a player from the other team with me. I didn't leave my own team short-handed. In fact, it wouldn't surprise me if, over my whole career, players from other teams got more penalties from run-ins with me than I got."

PROBABLY THE MOST HORRENDOUS INJURY IN NHL history happened at the Boston Garden on the night of December 12, 1933. The injured player was Ace Bailey of the Leafs. The player who inflicted the injury was the Bruins' all-time, all-star great defenceman Eddie Shore. Bailey came out of events on the ice with a cut in his scalp that needed sixteen stitches to close, a terribly fractured skull, five weeks in hospital, and a hockey career that had ended. Shore got suspended for sixteen games. Those are the certain facts. Piecing together the rest of the story is a *Rashomon*-like exercise. Everybody remembered what happened on the ice that night just a little bit differently. But, by default, because Red Horner was the last of the principals in the tragedy still living, his version may have become definitive.

"To start with, Eddie Shore was having a very frustrating night," Horner said in his living room. "He was playing a great game, but it wasn't getting him or the Bruins anywhere. They couldn't score on us, we were in front 1–0, and Eddie was uptight about the whole situation. This was still in the first period, and all of a sudden, the referee gave us two quick penalties. Our coach, Dick Irvin, sent out King Clancy and myself on defence and Ace Bailey up front to kill off the penalties. Bailey was a very expert stickhandler, and he ragged the puck for a while. Kept it away from the Bruins. Well, eventually Shore got his stick on the puck and made a nice rush deep into our end. I was playing right defence, Clancy was on the left. Shore came down my side, and I gave him a very good hipcheck. Knocked him down in the corner. The puck went over to Clancy, and he rushed it out of our end. When he did that, Ace Bailey dropped back into Clancy's position on left defence. That was the Leaf system, to have a winger fall back when a defenceman rushed. In the meantime, Eddie Shore picked himself up from the corner where I'd dumped him. He was in a fury, and he charged into Bailey. Now"—here Horner moved forward in his chair and became very deliberate—"what I've always believed is that Shore thought he was attacking me. He wanted to get even for the check I'd just put on him. He thought Bailey was me. He charged into Bailey on an angle from the side. You have to remember that Shore was exceptionally strong. He hit Bailey at this side angle and flipped him in the air. Just like a rag doll. Bailey landed on his head. That happened just a few feet from where I was standing. Bailey hit the ice, and he went into some kind of convulsion. I thought to myself, well, that's the end of Ace. Eddie Shore, my gosh, Shore skated away in a very nonchalant fashion. I wasn't going to let him get away with that, so I went after him, gave him a punch and flattened that son of a gun. By this time, everybody in the building realized something serious had happened to Ace Bailey. Half the crowd got awfully silent. The other half was yelling at me for socking Shore. The whole situation got more frantic and confusing before we carried Bailey off the ice and on the way to medical help."

Horner paused, sat forward in his armchair.

"The part I can't forget," he said, "is that Shore probably thought he was hitting me. It might have been me and not poor Ace whose hockey life was all over that night."

THE MAPLE LEAF PLAYERS OF THE 1930S CAME AS CLOSE as Canadians get to matinee-idol status. They were good-looking, virile young guys, a colourful bunch, amazingly gifted at the country's favourite sport. They drew crowds to hockey arenas and on the streets. When Hap Day got married in 1937, 3,000 uninvited guests showed up to gawk at the groom; at his best man, King Clancy; and at his ushers, Ace Bailey, Baldy Cotton and Red Horner. And the Leafs were the centrepieces of probably the period's most wildly successful advertising promotion—mail in two labels from cans of Bee Hive Golden Corn Syrup and receive a black-and-white glossy of your favourite player.

The fame of these Leafs spread out of Toronto and across Canada, winged along the way by the radio broadcasts of their games by Foster Hewitt. From his perch fifty-six feet above the Gardens ice on the west side, a perch named "the gondola" because it resembled the control compartment underneath a 1930s dirigible, Hewitt's flat, nasal tone became one of the most instantly identifiable sounds in the country.

"Your Imperial Oil hockey broadcast, bringing you Foster Hewitt," the radio announcer said at five minutes after nine on Saturday nights (Leaf home games began at 8:30, and the broadcasts caught the end of the first period).

"Hello Canada and hockey fans in the United States and Newfoundland," Foster began, and a million Canadians, and a few thousand foreigners, grew a little excited, a little tense and a lot pleased. The Leafs, the objects of all this emotion, were heroes.

There was just one thing out of whack—the Leafs couldn't win the damned Stanley Cup. They won practically everything else. From 1933 to 1941, they finished first in the NHL's Canadian Division four times, first overall in two of those years. They reached the Stanley Cup finals no fewer than six times, but emerged with six runner-up prizes. All they showed was a remarkable talent for spreading around their generosity, allowing the Rangers to take the Stanley Cup from them twice, in 1933 and 1940, four other teams to win it once each: the Montreal Maroons ('35), Detroit Red Wings ('36), Chicago Black Hawks ('38) and the Boston Bruins ('39).

What accounted for the failure of the Leafs at the climax of those six seasons?

"I think I know the reason," Red Horner said in June 1993. "Some of our players, once we got into the playoffs, they knew they were going to get a bonus, knew they'd already earned it, so they didn't take care of themselves as carefully as they should have. They didn't pay attention to their conditioning. They let themselves go just enough that it made the difference between winning and losing by the time we got to the finals."

Which players?

Horner wasn't saying. He was too much the gent, too nice to smudge the reputations of men now dead, his old comrades.

Conn Smythe had no such reluctance.

"Conacher and Jackson were never half as good as they were thought to be," he said in his autobiography. "They wanted Joe Primeau to do all the work, and they'd score the goals, which they were pretty good at. But you have to play hockey in three spaces: your end, the middle, and their end. They didn't do it."

Especially, Smythe went on, they didn't do it in the playoffs. And wild times were part of the reason. "Conacher and Jackson," Smythe's book complained, "never did feel very interested in getting in shape. They were too busy driving their new cars and chasing women." Not to mention drinking booze. Poor Busher Jackson was a particular victim of the demon rum. His life stumbled after hockey, and Smythe, unforgiving, made Jackson pay for his transgressions by using the Smythe clout to keep Jackson out of the Hockey Hall of Fame. Conacher was elected to the Hall in 1961, Primeau in '63. Jackson, with Smythe relenting, finally made it in 1971. That didn't do Jackson much good. He had died five years earlier, without a job, money, a home, honour or self-esteem.

RED HORNER'S OFF-SEASON ACTIVITIES IN HIS EARLY hockey years seem, at the remove of more than a half-century, quaint. In the first summers of his first two seasons as a Leaf, following Smythe's warning that he needed more heft than his 170 pounds, Horner took a job as a counsellor at Camp Wanapitei on the lake of the same name north of Sudbury. So, Red Horner, budding star of the Toronto Maple Leafs, already famous, taught little kids to swim, led older kids on canoe trips and gathered everyone around the camp fire for evening sing-songs. He put on six pounds per summer. The next summer, he carried hod for bricklayers who were constructing the Robert Simpson ware-house on Mutual Street. And during another summer, part lark and part hard competition, he was half the added attraction on the professional wrestling card at the Gardens, Red Horner versus Hap Day, two out of three falls to a finish. The ladies in the crowd went wild at the sight of two hockey heroes in their briefs.

By the mid-1930s, Horner got serious about planning a life after hockey. He took a job in the office at the Elias Rogers Coal Company for the last summers of his hockey career. When he left the Leafs at the end of the 1939–40 season—42 goals, 110 assists, 1,254 minutes in penalties—he stayed on at Rogers for thirteen years. Then he switched to Canada Coal, a company he ended up owning and eventually selling for a swell profit. In retirement, he built a villa on a golf course in Por-tugal's Algarve. That was good for seven years until, concluding that Por-tuguese medicine might be a trifle primitive for a guy in his seventies, he transferred to Florida and another place near a golf course.

When it was pointed out to Horner, in the living room of his Toronto condominium, that all of what he'd done over his years as a Leaf and in the years that came after appeared to add up to a complete and satisfying life, the thought took him not entirely by surprise.

"It's been pretty good," he said, nodding. "It still is—golf, bridge, sitting out there on the balcony for a drink before dinner. Pretty good all right, but one thing for sure, it was a darned shame, when you consider all the talented fellas we had on the Maple Leafs, we didn't win two or three more Stanley Cups in the 1930s. Just a darned shame."

4

The Big Comeback of '42

IN THE SUMMER OF 1940, LESS THAN A YEAR AFTER Hitler launched the Second World War, a month after the British forces escaped the Germans at Dunkirk and prepared for the Battle of Britain, Conn Smythe mailed this memo to all of his hockey players:

"It is my advice, no matter what your age or your position as a family man, that you sign up immediately with some non-permanent militia unit and get military training as soon as possible. The advantages are obvious. In case you are honored with a call to the Canadian forces, you will be ready...."

Some players may have paused over the "honored" part, but twenty-five of them immediately enrolled in a militia unit. It was probably either that or suffer a quick trade to the oblivion of the New York Americans, perpetual last-place finishers and ultimately dismantled in 1942. If Smythe, Anglophile and patriot to a super degree, asked much of his players, he chose more for himself. He was forty-five, the father of four children, but he lusted after battle. He persuaded the Canadian Army to let him form the 30th Battery as part of the 7th Toronto Regiment, Royal Canadian Artillery. Smythe dubbed it the Sportsmen's Battery because he attracted to it athletes, sports writers and others who liked to rub shoulders with sports guys. Smythe intended to take the Sportsmen's Battery overseas.

This put him on dicey ground at the Gardens. Though Smythe built the place, put the Leaf team together, held the title of managing director and made virtually every significant hockey decision, he remained a Gardens employee. He owned stock in the Gardens, but not enough to make him a major player, and there were some around the building whom he'd rubbed the wrong way, directors and others who wouldn't weep if Smythe were out of the picture. In November 1941, Smythe shipped out to the army camp at Petawawa for a course that would give him the rank of major. That's when his enemies at the Gardens licked their lips. Principal among these were two directors, Ed Bickle and Bill MacBrien, and Smythe's assistant, Frank Selke. In Smythe's absence, those three took over management of the Gardens and the Leafs. Smythe suspected the three meant treachery. He had more confidence in the team's coach, Hap Day.

HAP DAY PLAYED STUPID JOKES ON TEAMMATES. THAT WAS his only vice. He didn't smoke or drink or cuss. He was never late for the job, never known to utter an untrue word. But hand him a pair of scissors and put him in the vicinity of Charlie Conacher's tie, and it was clip, clip, clip. Or what about the time in the hotel room when King Clancy, nude, was showing off his rippling physique? Day pushed Clancy on to the outside balcony and locked the door. Pretty funny, right, King?

In all other dealings in hockey and in life, Day was absolutely straight-arrow and relatively humourless. (Well, there was the unfortunate slip of the tongue at his wedding, the one attended by the 3,000 uninvited guests. The groom began his speech, "Now that the marriage has been consummated. . . .") Day was born in Owen Sound, Ontario, and intended to remain there as the town pharmacist. It was pharmacy he was studying at the University of Toronto when the people running the Toronto St. Pats noticed what a large, strong, smart hockey player he was. They signed him to a contract in 1926. He was a forward. Conn Smythe's first player move after taking over management of the team two years later was to switch Day to defence. He stayed in the position, a rock of reliability, for the rest of his fourteen years in the NHL, the last season with the New York Americans to whom Smythe traded him (a trade to the Americans meant either punishment for some sin or a broad hint that your career was over; with Day, it was the latter).

In 1940, Smythe decided that Dick Irvin had taken the Leafs as far as he ever could. Smythe knew the Montreal Canadiens coaching job was coming open and he steered Irvin into the vacancy (where he would win three Stanley Cups). For the new Leaf coach, Smythe turned to a colleague at C. Smythe For Sand. That was Hap Day. He had worked in the Smythe sand and gravel business since the late 1920s and eventually became a minority owner. Smythe figured Day had the organizational sense and hockey brains to guide the Leafs. Smythe was right. Day compiled one of the most remarkable coaching records in NHL history, five Stanley Cups in ten years.

He was a coach who elevated defensive hockey to a new, if sometimes boring level. "It's defence that wins hockey games," he always said, and he elaborated on that philosophy in a conversation with this writer in 1974:

"Coaching offensively is too hard. A centre goes down the ice, he doesn't know what he's going to do with the puck. It depends on where his wings happen to go. You can give them a plan of attack, and then the situation for the plan may never come up in the game. But defence, now, think of all six men on the ice doing the job on defence. I told my players if they worked as hard coming back as they did going down the ice, we'd be okay. Of course, you had to have the proper type of player to handle that approach—or make them into the proper type."

THE TEAM THAT HAP DAY TOOK OVER BORE NO RESEMblance to the team he had played on just a few years earlier. Gone were the glamour guys—Conacher, Jackson, Horner—the matinee idols. The team of the early 1940s was essentially younger, though sprinkled with veterans. The young players tended to be home-grown products, kids who had come up through the Toronto system or had been scouted by Selke and Smythe. The vets arrived almost exclusively by way of trades in which Smythe, in a pattern he perfected over the years, gave up a batch of four or five players he could spare in return for the one player he couldn't live without.

Sweeney Schriner, a left-winger, and Lorne Carr, a right-winger, were two of the latter. Both came from the favourite Smythe dumping ground, the New York Americans, Schriner in 1939 for five players (including the unfortunate Busher Jackson) and Carr in 1941 for four players. Carr had a seamless, self-effacing style, the invisible man on the ice until he put the puck in the net, something he did 204 times in his career. Schriner looked like the heavy who ran a 1930s speakeasy. He wore his black hair parted in the middle and Brylcreamed flat to his skull, he had a world-weary expression, and his dark eyes were the kind that never missed a trick. As a player, his touch with the puck was possibly unrivalled in the late 1930s and early '40s. He led the league in points in 1936 and '37, and finished his eleven years in the NHL with 201 goals and 204 assists. Smythe called him "the best left-winger ever to play, better than Harvey Jackson, Bobby Hull or Frank Mahovlich." With the Leafs, Schriner and Carr had Billy Taylor for their centre. Taylor was small, blond, quick, clever and cocky. It was the cockiness that later got him in trouble with the league—for gambling—but it was the quick and clever attributes that complemented his old-pro wingers and made the Taylor–Carr–Schriner line so aesthetically pleasing.

On defence, Hap Day worked mainly with hard-edged stylists. Bingo Kampman and Reg Hamilton were like that, a couple of sock-those-other-guys types. Bucko McDonald, purchased from Detroit in 1938, was bulky and rather immobile, but he bodychecked so well as to suggest he might have dipped into the Red Horner gene pool. That left the lad of the group, Wally Stanowski, twenty-three years old, as the designated rusher. The loopy creativity of his puck-carrying probably gave Day the willies, but Stanowski had speed and strength, and rarely lost the puck in embarrassing circumstances.

Behind the defencemen was Turk Broda, the goalie Smythe picked up from Detroit in 1935, a steal at $8,000. Never mind that Broda was none too bright, that he was much put upon, the butt of practical jokes; that his later life disintegrated in booze and lost opportunities—he was still a master goaltender, cool, able to shrug off bad games almost instantly, at his best in the most critical circumstances, with a 2.08 goals-against average in 101 playoff games over his career. He was the ultimate last line of defence.

Up front, Day had plenty of forwards who were receptive to his defensive ideas. There were the Metz brothers, Nick and Don of Wilcox, Saskatchewan, and Bob Davidson of Toronto, players who seemed older, beyond their years, in the serious virtues, in honesty, team work, selflessness. Pete Langelle was the exception, a player with a dipsy-doodle style, a flakey kid from Winnipeg who skated like the wind. But the team included such other honest pluggers as Hank Goldup, and John McCreedy, who must have had thoughts beyond hockey since he ended his later business career as president of International Nickel.

And then, among the forwards, a right-winger, there was Gordie Drillon. He was tall, he was handsome, he was the pride of Moncton, New Brunswick, the pride of the entire Maritimes; he scored goals, winning the league points title in 1938; and he was officially a gentle-man, winning the Lady Byng Trophy as the most gentlemanly player in '38. So what was not to like about Gordie Drillon? Ask Maple Leaf fans of the day. They treated Drillon to more calumny, gave him more boos and nasty gestures than probably any player in Leaf history received. When a photograph appeared in the newspaper of Drillon serving as a pallbearer at a funeral, one fan sent Drillon a ripped-out photo with the words scribbled across it, "Is Drillon carrying his share of the load?" Maybe that was it. Maybe the fans thought Drillon was a one-dimen-sional player who shone on offence but didn't do his duty, carry his share, on defence. Or maybe Drillon suffered from comparison with the centre on his line. Anyone would pale in that matchup. Drillon's centre was Syl Apps.

APPS SAID OF DRILLON, "HE WAS THE BEST FELLOW TO put the puck in the net I ever saw." But then Syl Apps would only be generous in his spoken view of every person. Apps was strong, virtuous and true, stainless, flawless and kind. Consider this: in his entire NHL careeer of 423 league games, all with the Maple Leafs, he had only 56 minutes in penalties. Less than an hour in ten seasons. And he wasn't any lollipop. He scored 201 goals in those ten seasons, was voted to the First All-Star Team twice and the Second Team three times, won the Calder Trophy as best rookie and, naturally, the Lady Byng as most gentlemanly. He was the fastest skater in hockey, by contest the fastest. The contest took place during a benefit night at the Gardens in 1942 for a man named Moose Ecclestone, a popular Toronto fastball player who had been injured. As part of the festivities, each of the NHL teams sent their speediest player, Doug Bentley from Chicago, Lynn Patrick from New York, Flash Hollett from the Bruins, and so on. Each raced individually around the rink, along the boards, with stick and puck, winner determined by stopwatch. Apps had the best time. He was the fastest. He was the best at practically everything.

Apps had more to do with the image of the Leafs in the 1940s as Canada's team—the good guys, the very good guys—than any other player. He looked so dashing on the ice, all that speed and skill. And off the ice, he was the last word in pure vessels, a teetotaller, a non-smoker, a Baptist steeped in moral propriety, the model team captain. So what if he was emotionally inscrutable? Fans didn't look to this handsome athlete, a college graduate too, for jokes and tears. They wanted him only to be upright. On that, Syl Apps delivered, and, by extension, the rest of the Leafs—drinkers, carousers, practical jokers included—shared the shiny image.

THE LEAFS WOULD PROBABLY HAVE FINISHED THE 1941– 42 season in first place if they hadn't encountered a run of injuries early in the schedule. By mid-January, Don Metz had missed twenty games with a broken ankle, Stanowski had been out for fourteen games, Apps for ten, Nick Metz for nine. Carr had played with a sore shoulder, Schriner had been bugged by a series of pains, and at one point, Day had been down to three defencemen. That's when he called up a pair of rookie defenders from the minors, Bob Goldham and Ernie Dickens. Still, Toronto made it a close race with New York and Boston, and squeezed into second place between those two, the Rangers first with sixty points, Leafs second with fifty-seven, Bruins with fifty-six.

In the first playoff round, in a custom of the time that challenged logic, the first- and second-place teams met, Rangers versus Leafs. The series was a tremendous defensive affair from the beginning, Broda sensational in the Toronto goal, Sugar Jim Henry the same in New York's net. Broda had the early hot hand, beating the Rangers 3–1 and 4–2 in the first two games at Madison Square Garden. Sugar Jim shut out the Leafs in the third game in Toronto, 3–0.

Before the fourth game, Conn Smythe put in an appearance, just down from Petawawa to see his first hockey game in weeks. The way Smythe later told it, it was his pre-game pep talk in the Leafs locker room that fired up the team. Whatever, the Leafs won the game, which was more relentless than fiery, by the score of 2–1. Rangers took the fifth in New York 3–1, and the teams returned to Toronto for a sixth game, which produced a most unlikely hero scoring a most crucial goal.

The game was tied at two apiece, the clock winding down to zero time in the third period. Nick Metz carried the puck over the New York blueline. This was Nick Metz, the defensive specialist, on a line with two of Toronto's sharpest offensive operators, Apps and Drillon. To be sure, Metz scored 131 goals over his 538 NHL games plus 19 more in 61 playoff games. Not too shabby, but the odds were that Metz, in the circumstances of the sixth playoff game, all tied, the Leafs with one more chance on the Ranger goal, would pass off. He didn't. He surprised everyone. He surprised the Ranger defencemen; the goalie, Sugar Jim Henry, his linemates, Apps and Drillon. He shot. And the puck went past all of those surprised parties into the New York net. The time on the clock showed 19:54, and the Leafs were off to the Stanley Cup final, where they would make a stunning piece of hockey history.

THE DETROIT RED WINGS WERE TORONTO'S OPPOSITION in the final. On the surface, that seemed strange. Detroit had finished way back in fifth place in the regular season. (What was even stranger was that six out of the seven teams in the league qualified for the playoffs, meaning that the forty-eight games per team in the schedule eliminated only the Brooklyn Americans, as the New York Americans were renamed in their last, hapless season.) The secret to Detroit's success in reaching the final lay in the new offensive system that Red Wings coach

Jack Adams introduced that year—shoot the puck into the other team's end, then forecheck like crazy. The system is so old hat today that it's hard to conceive that someone had to invent it. But the inventor seems to have been Jack Adams, and the simple new system had the Leafs buffaloed in the first three games of the Stanley Cup final.

Actually, the story is slightly more complicated than this. During the regular season, Hap Day counteracted the Red Wing technique somewhat by directing his players to adopt the same methods—to fire the puck into the Detroit end and chase after it. But when Smythe, on a visit from Petawawa, saw what the Leafs were up to, he directed Day to cut it out. "Smythe," Day said many years later, "didn't like any system that involved giving the puck away." Thus, playing the traditional offensive style, carrying the puck over the Red Wing blueline, Toronto lost the first three games of the final, 3–2 and 4–2 at the Gardens and 5–2 at the Detroit Olympia.

At this point for the Leafs, down three games to zip, in a position from which no team had ever progressed to a Stanley Cup, or ever has since 1942, a number of factors, both tactical and emotional, came into play.

First, on the tactical front, Day told his team to adopt once again the Detroit offensive method of shoot-and-chase. This change was made with Smythe's approval. Indeed, in a rare admission of error, it may have been Smythe who suggested that the Leafs revert to the strategy that he had once countermanded. At the same time, Day introduced a fresh defensive technique. Bob Goldham, a nineteen-year-old rookie defenceman in 1942, later described the change this way: "Day had the answer in time for game four. When Detroit fired the puck into our end from centre, which was a new wrinkle, we'd simply fire it straight back out, which was also a new wrinkle."

To handle these adjustments, Day made two lineup changes, putting in younger, swifter players for older, slower, possibly weary, possibly injured players. So it was Ernie Dickens for Bucko McDonald and Don Metz for Gordie Drillon. This was goodbye for Drillon as a Maple Leaf. Toronto traded him to the Montreal Canadiens that summer. How incredibly melancholy it was—a fine player booed, then benched, then discarded. At least in Montreal, under his old coach, Dick Irvin, Drillon had one last splendid season: twenty-eight goals, twenty-two assists, and no jeers.

For emotional incentive, Day read a letter to his players a few minutes before the face-off in the fourth game. It was a letter from a fourteen-year-old girl, a Toronto fan who now lived in Detroit and who expressed heartbreak at the downturn in Leaf play. "I never sensed such tension in a dressing room," Day said of the mood after his letter-reading. Day was right about the tension but possibly mistaken about the explanation for it. Something other than the letter may have been motivating the Leaf players, something that Syl Apps spoke of in a 1975 interview with this writer: "I remember sitting in the dressing room, waiting for the fourth game to start. The only thing on our minds was, we can't go back to Toronto if we lose this game too. We were thinking we couldn't lose four straight and face the people back home." Syl Apps would say something noble like that.

The Leafs won the fourth game, but it was a near thing. They had to come from behind twice, get the winning goal at 12:45 of the third period — another pressure score by Nick Metz — and hang on for the 4–3 victory. The game was so hectic that Jack Adams lost his cool — in truth, Adams, a man given to volcanic outbursts, hadn't much cool to lose — and crashed the referee's changing room after the game. He was enraged over a couple of calls that the referee, Mel Harwood, made against the Wings, a ten-minute misconduct to Eddie Wares for arguing and a team penalty for having too many men on the ice. Adams expressed himself with such clarity and venom that the league president, Frank Calder, suspended him.

Back in Toronto, Hap Day made one more lineup alteration, Gaye Stewart in for Hank Goldup. This completed a season-ending upward spiral for nineteen-year-old Stewart, from playing on a Memorial Cup junior team to an Allan Cup senior team, to a Stanley Cup–finalist NHL team. In the game that followed, the Leafs blitzed the Red Wings 9–3. Almost every Leaf had a hand in the scoring. Don Metz had the biggest hand, with three goals and two assists.

The sixth game, at the Olympia, turned into the Turk Broda Clinic.

He shut out the Red Wings. The Leafs got three goals, with the first, coming fourteen seconds into the second period, qualifying as the winner. Guess who scored it? Don Metz. The guy got into the series as a fourth-game substitute, a player who scored a grand total of twenty-seven goals, regular season and playoffs, in his entire seven-year career, and he emerged a hero in the biggest group of games of his life.

April 18, 1942, was the date of the seventh game of the final. It was at the Gardens, 16,218 people crammed into the building, the largest crowd to attend a hockey game in Canada to that date, and it looked as if the Red Wings might cheat them out of a celebration. Detroit's players, give them credit, had no intention of rolling over. They led Toronto 1–0 at the end of the second period, and it seemed Detroit goalie Johnny Mowers might have in mind doing to the Leafs what Broda had done to the Wings in the sixth game—shutting them out.

Smythe visited the Toronto dressing room between the second and third periods. He wrote in his autobiography that he felt apprehensive, that he probably showed it. "What are you worried about, Boss?" Sweeney Schriner is supposed to have said to Smythe. "We'll get you some goals." It makes a good story. It may even be true. What is recorded fact is that, at 6:46 of the third period, Sweeney Schriner scored a goal to tie the game. The reason Schriner got the goal probably lay in the particular situation. It was the third period of the seventh game, the players were tiring, the pace of the hockey was slowing. That was just the ticket for a line of smoothies like Schriner, Lorne Carr and Billy Taylor. Their puck-control style prospered at the more sedate speeds.

But no member of that line scored the next goal. It came from a player who, like Don Metz, didn't leave behind a legacy of big numbers in the scoring column. This was Pete Langelle. Just past the nine-minute mark of the third, he was chasing the play as it crossed into the Detroit zone. John McCreedy took a pass from Bob Goldham. He shot at the Detroit net. Johnny Mowers stopped the puck on his pads. It bounced to Langelle, who had just arrived at one side of the Red Wings goal. Mowers was on his knees at the other side. There was nothing between Langelle and most of the net except air. This was reflex stuff. Langelle shot the puck into the net. (How many goals did Pete Langelle score in his four years of NHL play? Twenty-two in the regular season, five in the playoffs.)

Schriner popped another goal at 16:13, Carr and Taylor assisting, making the score in the end 3–1, and with the win, the Leafs had completed a comeback in the Stanley Cup final, from three down to victory. It still remains the precedent for such a glorious facing-down of calamity. No other team has managed the feat in the last series of the Stanley Cup playoffs, though, as we'll see, three years later, in 1945, a team almost pulled it off at the Leafs' expense.

5

The Young Reliable

O N THE CONCLUDING DAY OF 1993'S SUMMER, Bob Davidson took his memory back to the spring of 1945, to the sixth game of the Stanley Cup semi-finals, Leafs versus Canadiens at the Gardens. Almost a half-century earlier? No problem for Davidson. The events of the last couple of minutes of that game, particularly one vital sequence, are videotaped in his brain.

"Nobody expected us to be where we were, beatin' Montreal. That's the first thing you gotta consider," Davidson began, settled in the living room of his home in the Leaside neighbourhood of Toronto. "Montreal finished the season way out in front in first place. Us, we were about thirty points back in third place. But in the playoffs, we surprised the bunch of them. We went ahead three games to two, and in the sixth game, it was 3–2 for us with less'n two minutes left. The Kennedy line was on for us: Teeder at centre, me on left wing, Mel Hill on right. Montreal had their big guys out there—the Rocket, Elmer Lach and Toe Blake. Those three'd finished first, second and third in the league scoring. Jeez, Richard had fifty goals in fifty games. That's the calibre they were. Anyway, Blake had the puck in his own end. He was their left-winger, but it was Teeder who went after him. I took the Rocket on my wing, and Mel Hill had Lach over on the far side. Teeder got pretty much beat by Blake. Hill and me stayed with our guys, and Blake sailed right through everything. He came to our defence; Elwyn Morris and Babe Pratt and those guys never even put Blake off his stride. He just kept goin'. Right about there, I left my winger and went to Blake. So did Mel Hill. But, jeez, Blake was practically walking in on Frank McCool in our net. All I could think was the game was gonna get tied up and we'd be finished after that. Well, I don't know how it happened, but Blake's shot ended up hittin' the side of the net. By then, me and Hill and everybody else piled into the picture, and there wasn't a player left standing. Everybody was sprawled all over the ice. But the puck never went in the net. If Blake had scored, I think Montreal'd have beat us in that game. Then we would have gone back to the Forum for the seventh game, and there's no way we could've won that one. So I think you can say the key moment to us eventually winnin' the Stanley Cup in 1945 came in the sixth game of the semi-finals when Toe Blake didn't score."

OF THE EIGHTEEN PLAYERS WHO WERE MORE OR LESS regulars on Toronto's 1942 Stanley Cup team, a mere six played for the Leafs during the 1944–45 season. Most of the others, including such irreplaceables as Syl Apps and Turk Broda, were in the armed services. A couple of others had retired. Another couple had been traded. Even the figure of six needs qualifying. One of the six, Sweeney Schriner, retired at the end of the 1942–43 season, then unretired to play half the regular schedule in 1944–45 and all of the playoffs. And another of the six, Wally Stanowski, began the season still in the service and returned to the team only in mid-season.

Apart from the six, some of the team's regulars played rather irregularly. Two players, Jackie McLean and Ross Johnstone, were taking classes at the University of Toronto. They didn't see much ice time. Tom O'Neill, nicknamed Windy, enjoyed more renown as a piano player, a budding lawyer and an all-round gadabout than as a goal scorer (two in thirty-three games). And Art Jackson, who came over from Boston during the season, played with style, but was essentially running out the string in the last season of an eleven-year NHL career.

So it was just your average ragtag wartime team, raw kids and past-the-limit old guys filling in for the real article while the latter were away at war. It could have been worse for the Leafs. It could have been the New York Rangers. Pitiable New York—Stanley Cup champs as recently as 1940, first-place finishers in 1942, they hit a nadir in 1943–44, not just last place but last place with mortification. How bad was the Rangers' season? So bad that they allowed 310 goals, won only 5 games and finished 25 points behind the next-worst team. How really bad was their season? So bad that the team's coach, Frank Boucher, came out of retirement to suit up. Forty-two years old, and he got four goals and ten assists in fifteen games. Good for Boucher, bad for the team.

The Leafs had at least the benefit of a few players they could count on, players of skill and leadership and craft. Principal among these were Babe Pratt, Teeder Kennedy and Bob Davidson.

Pratt had an aversion to defensive hockey. That made him something of a hockey oddball since he played defence.

"Babe used to be paired with Elwyn Morris," Bob Davidson remembered. "And when the other team brought the puck into our end, Babe'd point to the puck, and he'd holler, 'Mo, Mo, over there!' The puck'd bounce into the other corner. "No, no, Mo, over that side.' That was Babe on defence, a guy directing traffic."

But on offence, Pratt was a smooth operator. Over his career, a dozen seasons in the NHL, he had 83 goals and 209 assists, very impressive numbers for the era. He turned in his single-most-spectacular season in 1943–44. That was the year after Toronto traded to get him from the Rangers, Pratt for Hank Goldup and a kid named Red Garrett who played twenty-three games for New York, then got killed in the war. Pratt scored seventeen goals for the Leafs that year, assisted on forty others, made the First All-Star Team, and won the Hart Trophy as the league's most valuable player.

Pretty terrific, but according to a story that Windy O'Neill always insisted was the gospel truth, Pratt's sensational numbers led to a year of disenchantment. Make that a half-year of disenchantment. It seemed that Hap Day refused to give Pratt the raise he figured he'd earned with his Hart Trophy year. Okay, Pratt told Windy, if they're only paying me enough for half a season, I'll only play for half a season. And so Pratt stayed on idle until Christmas. Then, in O'Neill's description, "I never saw a player stand the league on its ear the last four months of a year the way Babe did in '44–45."

Pratt scored eighteen goals and got twenty-two assists for the season. The large majority came in the second half. In your eye, Hap Day.

WHEN YOU COME RIGHT DOWN TO IT, IT WAS PROBABLY homesickness that cost the Montreal Canadiens a shot at keeping Ted Kennedy. In the autumn of 1942, the Canadiens hustled Kennedy, a child of sixteen, out of his home town, Port Colborne, Ontario; installed him at the Queen's Hotel in Montreal; enrolled him at Lower Canada College; and prepped him for a season with the Montreal Royals Juniors. Kennedy rebelled.

"I didn't like the environment," Kennedy said many years later, explaining his sudden exit from Montreal. "I just told them I was going home."

Back in Port Colborne, Kennedy fell under Nels Stewart's spell. Stewart had been the NHL's greatest goal scorer in the pre–Rocket Richard period, and now he was coaching the Port Colborne Seniors. "Nels taught me how to operate in front of the net," Kennedy once recalled. "Something basic—take a look before you shoot the puck. Don't rush. Coming from Nels, I never forgot the lessons."

Stewart did something else helpful to the young Kennedy—he tipped off the Leafs to his protégé's talents. Frank Selke arranged a deal, the swap of Montreal's rights to Kennedy in exchange for Toronto's rights to a young defenceman named Frank Eddolls. Eddolls was a particular favourite of Conn Smythe's, and Selke later maintained that the trading away of Eddolls without Smythe's approval—Smythe, remember, was off saving the free world—played a key part in the later Selke–Smythe split. Smythe denied that. He said Selke left the Leafs simply because he was a disloyal little weasel. Frank Eddolls, meanwhile, went on to a reasonably decent NHL career. Ted Kennedy became possibly the all-time definitive Maple Leaf player.

He stuck with the team as a regular in the 1943–44 season,

twenty-eight goals, twenty-three assists. Wartime hockey, sure, but Kennedy was a babe of eighteen when the season began. Next year, 1944–45, he upped his figures to twenty-nine goals, twenty-five assists.

"What made Teeder so good was determination," Bob Davidson said in his living room, thinking back. "He worked and worked at hockey. Jeez, he really worked. And in a game, he never quit. He was a guy who didn't smoke or drink, but could he ever swear! Sittin' on the bench, if something went wrong on the ice, Teeder'd blast away, and the wives in the vicinity, the lady fans, they'd have to cover their ears."

And Kennedy was special in attracting the most uniquely vocal one-man fan club in the history of the team. The man was John Arnott, a Toronto garage owner who had a season ticket in the second-row blues in the southwest corner of the Gardens. As long as Kennedy played, close to 400 home games, Arnott would lean forward four or five times per game, picking his moments, waiting for a lull, often just before a face-off, and he would let loose a simple cry that carried across the ice, upwards through the reds, blues, greens, greys to Foster Hewitt's gondola.

"Come on, Teeder!"

ON THIS LAST SUMMER DAY OF 1993, AS BOB DAVIDSON skipped back in recollection of his career, he projected a quality that was at first hard to put a finger on. He was eighty-one years old, slowing by a pace or two maybe, but sharp in all his faculties, a generous host and raconteur. He talked about growing up in the east end of Toronto, about playing junior hockey for the Toronto Canoe Club, about working as an office boy in a meat-packing plant ("Seven dollars a week, but the place was on the Don River and I could walk down and back from home"), about moving up to the Marlboro Seniors ("I was leading the league in scoring at Christmas, but I got a ruptured appendix, and that finished me for the season"), about trying out at the Leafs' training camp in the fall of 1935 ("I was gonna get sent down to Syracuse, except at the last moment Buzz Boll tore the ligaments in his knee, and I got asked to stay, which I did until I quit playin' twelve years later"). And eventually, as Davidson talked, reminisced, showed his shy and rueful smile, the quality about him that seemed elusive became clear. The quality was serenity.

Bob Davidson gave off a sense of calm, of equanimity, and it was no doubt this serene air that had sailed him through the vicissitudes of his life. Humble beginnings, injuries, the odd case of hard luck, the long wearying haul of his career as the number-one scout for the Leafs from 1951 to 1978, his abrupt leave-taking of the scouting job just before Christmas of '78—Davidson seemed to have absorbed them all in his even, temperate way.

That last breaking of his connection with the Leafs must have hurt terribly, his end as a scout. Davidson had a hand in funnelling super players into the organization—Dave Keon, Frank Mahovlich, many others. And he'd accomplished marvels in the 1970s, when Harold Ballard had become the owner and insisted that scouting operate on a minuscule budget. But in December 1978, when Davidson was sixty-six and looking forward to his forty-fifth year at the Gardens, as player, minor league coach and scout, he discovered on one shocking pay day that Ballard had cut his salary by two-thirds. There was no explanation, no formal acknowledgment that his career had apparently run its course. Just a cruel hint. Davidson resigned without fuss. He was a grander man than Harold Ballard.

As a player, Davidson was principally a checker. He filled that role on Syl Apps' line for several seasons, on Ted Kennedy's for a few more. He was steady, indomitable. The kind of player he was is reflected at least partly in the statistics—490 league games, 94 goals, 438 minutes in penalties. He took care of the stars on his line, particularly of Apps. A reliable guy, that was Bob Davidson, and he was the player, a young thirty-one, whom the Leafs named as captain in the two seasons, 1943–44 and 1944–45, when Apps was away. So it happened that Bob Davidson led the team to the Stanley Cup in 1945.

BY THE TIME THE LEAFS STARTED THE '45 PLAYOFFS, HAP Day was using a roster pared down to twelve players:

Frank McCool in goal. Here was a curio, a goalie so nervous that he needed long gulps of milk between periods to soothe his ulcer. "Sometimes," Bob Davidson recalled, "we had to take him a drink of milk when he was in the goal." Nevertheless, McCool, a Calgary man who found his way to the Leafs on Lorne Carr's recommendation, had a lovely season, playing all fifty games: four shutouts, a 3.22 goals-against average, winner of the Calder Trophy as rookie of the year.

On defence: Babe Pratt and Elwyn Morris, Wally Stanowski and Reg Hamilton.

One forward line: Kennedy, Davidson, and Mel Hill, a good veteran purchased from Boston the previous season.

A second forward line: Sweeney Schriner and Carr centred by a sweet young player from Fort William, Ontario, Gus Bodnar. Bodnar broke in with the Leafs in 1943–44, only nineteen years old, in the splashiest possible way. Fifteen seconds after the referee dropped the puck in Bodnar's first NHL game, October 30, 1943, he scored a goal. He kept up the pace, twenty-two goals, forty assists that season, winner of the Calder Trophy. In 1944–45, he sloped off in goal scoring, but he fed the passes to his wingers in fine fashion, helping to set up twenty-two goals for Schriner, twenty-one for Carr.

And one utility forward: Nick Metz, who relieved Kennedy and Bodnar, killed penalties and scored goals — a career-high twenty-two of them.

At one point or another, all twelve chipped in their two bits' worth in beating much-favoured Montreal in the semi-final.

Game one: McCool shut out the Canadiens. Bill Durnan in the Montreal net almost shut out the Leafs. Kennedy scored with twenty-two seconds left in the third period for a 1–0 win.

Game two: Kennedy, Carr and Metz got goals, and the Leafs hung on, 3–2.

Game three: Montreal did what it was supposed to do in the series — dominate. The Canadiens won 4–1 and made it appear easy.

Game four: it seemed as if the Canadiens were going to dominate some more when Lach and Richard scored goals in the first couple of minutes of play. But the Leafs, gamers all, recovered to send the game into overtime, which was when Gus Bodnar produced a wizard piece of work. There was a face-off to the right of Durnan, twelve minutes into the first overtime period, and off the drop of the puck, Bodnar, in a remarkably crisp and fluid move, cradled the puck, drew his stick back no more than two feet and zipped a shot past Durnan's right pad into the net.

Game five: Richard scored four goals. That would have been enough to beat the Leafs since, collectively, they scored three. But the entire Montreal team was in an offensive state of mind, and the final score was 10–3.

Game six: Toronto took the series when Toe Blake broke clear with a couple of minutes left in the third period but shot the puck into the side of the net.

THE FIRST THREE GAMES OF THE STANLEY CUP FINAL against Detroit went this way, all in favour of the Leafs: 1–0 (goal by Schriner), 2–0 (goals by Kennedy and Elwyn Morris) and 1–0 (goal by Bodnar).

On the face of it, this seemed crazy. During the regular season, the Red Wings had thrown a blanket over the Leafs; in ten games, Detroit won eight, outscored the Leafs forty-four to twenty-four and finished fifteen points ahead of them in the standings. But in those first three games, with Frank McCool playing like the second arrival of Georges Vezina, the Leafs took an insurmountable lead on ferocious defensive hockey.

But was the lead really insurmountable?

Shades of Toronto's own magnificent comeback against Detroit in the 1942 final, the Red Wings set themselves to match the feat. Detroit took the fourth game 5–3, with rookie Ted Lindsay scoring the winner. Game five saw the Red Wing goalie steal McCool's thunder; the goalie was eighteen-year-old Harry Lumley, destined for a tremendous NHL career which would take him, among other stops, to Toronto, and in this fifth game, he shut out the Leafs 2–0. Game six was more of the same, another Lumley shutout in a contest that didn't end until the fourteen-minute mark of the first overtime period when Eddie Bruneteau scored.

Did the Leafs panic at this point? Tremble at the thought of giving up their three-game lead? Expect the worst, another loss in the seventh game?

"Oh nah, not at all," Bob Davidson said in 1993 in the comfort of his living room, Captain Serenity himself. "One thing, that goal Bruneteau got in the sixth game was just an awful piece of good luck for the Red Wings. The puck was back of the net, and when it came out front, it was screened, and McCool couldn't see the thing. And anyway, all we needed to be ready for the seventh game was a good night's sleep. The game we lost, the sixth, was on a Saturday night at the Gardens, and the seventh was Sunday night at the Olympia. We jumped on the train Saturday, and went right to bed. I slept really good. So did the other guys. We were all feelin' okay by Sunday."

The good-night's-sleep theory seems as sound as any other, particularly when it's propounded by the team captain. And, sure enough, the Leafs came out in fast form in the deciding game's first period. Ted Kennedy set up Mel Hill for a goal. The 1–0 lead held into the third period when Murray Armstrong tied it for the Red Wings.

That brought the game down to a case of breaks and mistakes and — who knows? — to which team had the better sleep the previous night. It was Detroit's Syd Howe who made the mistake. He cross-checked Gus Bodnar. That presented the Leafs with the break in the form of a two-minute power play.

With the man advantage, Nick Metz carried the puck into the Detroit zone and put a shot in Harry Lumley's vicinity. Lumley tried to smother the puck. It wouldn't stay smothered. It kept on the bounce. Kennedy took a swipe at it. He missed. Davidson had his try. He missed too. Now here came Babe Pratt — lousy defence, smooth offence — waltzing in from the blueline. He swung twice at the puck. He connected on swing number two. The puck slid past Lumley. The time was 12:14, and Pratt's goal stood up as the one that brought perhaps Toronto's least-expected Stanley Cup.

6

Down and Up

ONN SMYTHE GOT HIS SPORTSMEN'S BATTERY to France on July 9, 1944, thirty-three days after D-Day, the Allied invasion of Europe. The Sportsmen's Battery took up position outside the small city of Caen a few miles inland from the English Channel. At that stage of the invasion, this was a fairly strategic point. It was close to two bridges over the Orne River. The bridges were a key crossing point for the invading forces.

On the night of July 25, bombers from the *Luftwaffe* flew over Caen. They were intent on knocking out the two Orne bridges. A flaming splinter from a German bomb set fire to a tarpaulin which covered an ammunition truck belonging to the Sportsmen's Battery. Smythe led the effort to yank the tarpaulin off the truck before the ammunition exploded. While he was at it, something struck him in the lower back. A bomb fragment? A piece of bursting ammunition? Whatever it was, it hurt like hell.

The fragment had penetrated Smythe's bowel and urinary tract. His next months passed in a haze of operations, hospital beds, wheelchairs. Doctors thought he had maybe five years to live. They were wrong about that. But for the rest of his life, Smythe suffered. He needed a daily enema. One of his legs was out of kilter with nerve damage, shrinking tendons, toes that turned under. Every day brought its hits of pain. The pain affected his personality. If he was hard-nosed and demanding before it, he added crankiness to the mix after it.

He found plenty to be cranky about back at the Gardens in the spring of 1945. As he had feared, Ed Bickle, with the support of fellow Gardens director Bill MacBrien, was manoeuvring to show Smythe the door. Look how beautifully the operation had run without Smythe, Bickle pointed out, two Stanley Cups and no aggravation. Frank Selke may have been partial to the Bickle cause too. With Smythe brushed aside, Selke would be his logical successor in the managing director's office. Selke played things close to the vest, committing himself to neither side.

"You can't be neutral," Smythe told Selke. "You're either with me or against me."

Selke shrugged.

One day in the spring of 1946, Selke left the Gardens at noon for lunch. He came back to find a memo from Smythe on his desk. From now on, the memo instructed, don't leave the building unless I give you permission.

Selke wrote a memo of his own.

"Lincoln freed the slaves in 1865," it read. "I'm gone. Goodbye."

That summer, Selke signed as general manager for the Montreal Canadiens, where he produced six Stanley Cup champions in seventeen years.

To beat off Ed Bickle, Smythe launched a campaign to make himself president of the Gardens. He needed shares to give him a position of strength from which to operate. He got them through his old pal on the Gardens board, Jack Bickell, and through Percy Gardiner, a stockbroker friend of Bickell's. Gardiner had gathered a large block of Gardens stock over the years. He sold Smythe 30,000 shares at ten dollars per share. Smythe didn't have the cash on hand to pay Gardiner the full amount. Give me something down, Gardiner told Smythe, and the rest when you're in funds. As far as Gardiner was concerned, Smythe deserved to be the main man in Maple Leaf hockey.

In November 1947, the Gardens board of directors elected Smythe its president. After almost twenty years, the man who named the team and put up the building was in unqualified charge of both.

ON THE ICE IN THE 1945–46 SEASON, THINGS WENT wrong for the Leafs. They weren't supposed to go wrong. The team had high expectations. That wasn't because Toronto was coming off a Stanley Cup season. The Cup was nice but, well, possibly a fluke. Besides, the players who were exuding all the confidence about the new season hadn't been with the team in 1944–45. They'd been in the army, navy, the air force. Now they were back—Syl Apps, Bob Goldham, Gaye Stewart, Don Metz, Billy Taylor, ten or more proven NHLers, stars even—and they were in a mood to win.

"There was a feeling among us," Syl Apps said many years later, "that, what with all the veterans returned, we were going to be home free in the league."

Wrong.

Trouble started in goal. Frank McCool wanted a raise. Smythe, the penny-pincher who hadn't been around to see McCool overcome nerves and an ulcer in such gallant fashion, turned him down. McCool stayed home in Calgary. Hap Day wasn't certain anyway that McCool had the stamina for an NHL season in which the great players, back from the war, would be firing at him. He started a pair of journeyman goalies, Baz Bastien and Gordie Bell. McCool signed. Day started him. At last Turk Broda got out of the service. Day started him. But none of the goalies was solid, none recorded a shutout all season, none had a goals-against average lower than Broda's 3.53, which was considered rather high for the times.

More trouble: Ted Kennedy and his tendon. Kennedy later recalled the season this way: "I didn't play well. Very poor. I thought I was coming out of it in a game at Christmastime. I scored a good goal, but in the same game, someone hit me and severed a tendon in my leg. I was finished for the year."

Still more trouble: Babe Pratt and his gambling. For all his imposing size, Pratt was a sweet and funny man. He loved late nights, noisy times, drinks and a couple of bets. He made his bets with George Meade, the old gent who sold papers down the street from the Gardens, at the northeast corner of Carlton and Yonge. Meade served as an agent for bookies in Montreal who set the betting line. Was there a problem here for Pratt? Yes, because he was betting on hockey games. In his favour, it was said that Pratt never actually threw a game (if a defenceman could throw a hockey game) or even that he bet on games in which his own team was playing. Still, when Red Dutton, the NHL president, got wind of the gambling in January 1946, he suspended Pratt. The suspension was for sixteen games, later cut to nine.

All of these misadventures created a malaise around the team, but probably a bigger contributor to the Leafs' slide into disappointment during the season was something Syl Apps later put his finger on.

"What everybody forgot at the beginning of the year," Apps said, "was that it took the players coming out of service half a season to get their bearings again. That's the way it was with me. I'd hardly been on skates for the two years I was away, and I had a terrible time settling down."

Alone among the Leafs, Gaye Stewart had a season to brag about, a league-high thirty-seven goals and selection as the All-Star left-winger. But the team as a whole dropped off to fifth place in the standings and out of the playoffs.

BRING ON THE ROOKIES, SMYTHE SAID. AND FOR THE 1946–47 season, on came the rookies.

To make room for them, Smythe had to get rid of the old guys. No problem. Sweeney Schriner, Lorne Carr and Frank McCool retired. Smythe sold Babe Pratt to Boston. And he traded Billy Taylor to Detroit for Harry Watson, who fit in beautifully on Syl Apps' left wing.

Billy Taylor's post-Leaf career was a grim story. He had one moment in the sun with the Red Wings, getting seven assists in a game against Chicago on March 16, 1947. That was an NHL record, and Taylor held it alone until 1980, when Wayne Gretzky matched the record, then matched it twice more, in 1985 and '86. But nobody much remembered Billy Taylor's seven assists, not after the events of a year later, March 1948.

Taylor had always been a swell, a sport, always had more money in his pockets than his teammates. It came from betting. Taylor was good at picking winners. Unlike Babe Pratt, Taylor bet on hockey games featuring his own team. Worse, he bet against his own team. That information surfaced in a public way when Detroit police put a wiretap on a local bookie's telephone. The word was passed to the NHL. It banned Taylor from all associations with hockey forever. Taylor had known nothing else in his life except hockey since he'd been a junior whiz with the Oshawa Generals, leading them to two Memorial Cups, since earlier when he'd been a twelve-year-old stick boy for the Maple Leafs. And now, only twenty-nine years old, still a colourful guy in the game, he got himself banished. He went away, a marginal figure, the cute blond kid growing fat and bald. The hockey ban was lifted in 1970. Taylor got a job scouting for the Pittsburgh Penguins.

When the Leafs opened the 1946–47 season, they had six rookies in the lineup plus one more player, the ace bodychecking forward Bill Ezinicki, who had played only thirty-two NHL games. The rookies included three defencemen—Garth Boesch (he was the one with the moustache), Jim Thomson and Gus Mortson—together with the forwards Vic Lynn, Howie Meeker and Joe Klukay. Six was a huge number in the era of the six-team NHL when rookies were eased into a lineup with caution. But among the Leaf freshmen, not all were rookies, in the wide-eyed sense of the word. That's how Hap Day looked at it. "Some of these men weren't real rookies," he said years later. "Boesch, Meeker, some others—they'd matured in the army. I knew they'd measure up. They'd been through real battles."

Many of the Leafs, rookies and otherwise, looked on this moment in their careers, 1946–47, as an occasion for battles of a personal sort. There were things to prove, reputations to be rescued.

"I had to re-establish myself as an NHLer," Ted Kennedy has said of that time. "And I was goddarned determined. It was the same with Howie Meeker—he was out of service and desperate for a job. Vic Lynn had come up from the American League team in Buffalo, and he didn't want to go back. We were very eager people."

The team shook down fairly smartly. Turk Broda was the goalie, the only goalie; he played all sixty league games, recorded four shutouts and had an excellent 2.86 goals-against average. Kennedy, Meeker and Lynn formed one line. Apps, Ezinicki and Harry Watson made another. For a third and a fourth line, Day shuffled among Gaye Stewart, Joe Klukay who'd been promoted from Pittsburgh, Bud Poile, Gus Bodnar, and the two Metzes, who were frequent and effective penalty killers. On defence, Garth Boesch paired with Wally Stanowski, and Gus Mortson and Jim Thomson made a second twosome. Bob Goldham filled the role of defensive sub, though he suffered a serious injury, a broken leg, and in his place, Smythe introduced a seventh rookie for nineteen games, the ebullient Bill Barilko.

Mortson and Thomson were authentic rookies, at least by age, twenty and nineteen respectively. But their play, which was consistent and mature, didn't suggest any first-year tentativeness. Neither did Mortson's personality. He was, inoffensively, tart-tongued and funny. He didn't mind looking at life and hockey as jokes to be laughed at. He could even kid himself.

"Humorous how I made the Leafs," he recalled many years after he retired. "In the fall of 1946, I was in training camp with Pittsburgh over in Niagara Falls, and we had an exhibition game against the Leafs in Hamilton. I got my skates sharpened for the game. I went over to St. Catharines, where the Leafs were training, because I wanted Tommy Naylor, the Leaf sharpener, to do the job. The other Pittsburgh players waited and had the guy at the Hamilton rink do their sharpening. Well, the Hamilton guy buggered up the blades on the other players' skates. These players kept falling down on the ice, and when they stood up, they couldn't move. So I played about fifty minutes in the game and must've looked like an All-Star compared to everybody else. After the game, Hap Day came up to me and said, 'Never mind going back to Niagara Falls. Just get on our bus.' I climbed on, and I wasn't out of the NHL for the next twelve years."

Mortson figured his arrival set in motion the final event that solidified the Leaf team.

"At the time they brought me up," he said, "they had Harry Watson playing defence. They changed him to left wing on Apps' line and put me on defence in partners with Jimmy Thomson. That's what jelled the team. Everything came together, and we had a hell of a club."

IT MAY HAVE SURPRISED HAP DAY, OR MAYBE MIFFED HIM, that the Leafs of 1946–47 led the NHL in offence. They scored 209 goals, 16 more than the second-highest-scoring team, the Chicago Black Hawks, who didn't really count because they allowed 274 goals and finished in last place. More to the point, the Leafs scored twenty more goals than the first-place Montreal Canadiens. Even more to the point, the Leaf scoring was generously distributed among eight players who scored twelve or more goals, Ted Kennedy leading with twenty-nine, while Montreal leaned heavily on Rocket Richard, who scored forty-five times. On defence, Montreal had a big edge, allowing only 138 goals to Toronto's 172. No doubt the presence of all those rookies on the Leaf defence accounted for the difference—in Bill Barilko's debut game, the Canadiens blew out the Leafs 8–2—but the kids on defence tightened up over the season. They were tough. The team had all kinds of players who rejoiced in a solid hit. Ezinicki, Barilko, Mortson, Watson—with these guys on the prowl, other teams learned to keep their heads up. The Leafs could be scary. In a game on February 7, Montreal's Elmer Lach ran into an honest Don Metz check. Oops, fractured skull for Lach. Toughness and scoring, and Turk Broda in the net, kept Toronto on Montreal's nerves all year, and the Leafs finished in second place, just six points back of the Canadiens.

IN ONE STANLEY CUP SEMI-FINAL, TORONTO KNOCKED off Detroit, four games to one. That set up a final against the Canadiens, who beat Boston in the other semi-final. Dick Irvin, Montreal's coach, made much noise about the final as a revenge series, getting even for what Don Metz did to Elmer Lach. The revenge angle seemed to work in the first game, which Montreal won easily 6–0. Too bad for Montreal that goalie Bill Durnan didn't keep his mouth shut after the game. "How did these guys get into the playoffs?" he said to Elmer Ferguson of the *Montreal Herald*, "these guys" being the Leafs.
Big mistake.

Day used the newspaper quote to spur his players. Maybe they didn't need a spur. Maybe they needed only to settle down. Either way, spurred or settled, they came out fast in the second game. Kennedy and Vic Lynn each scored a goal early in the first period, and the Leafs ran off to a 4–0 win. That was the game in which Rocket Richard blew his top. Top-blowing was something that occurred frequently in Richard's career, perhaps understandably when one considers how ferociously he was checked throughout that career. In this particular playoff game, Richard slashed Lynn in the first period. The referee gave him a major penalty. Later, Richard conked Ezinicki over the head with his stick. The referee gave him a match-misconduct for that offence. After the game, the new league president, Clarence Campbell, thought over Richard's conduct and suspended him for the third playoff game.

Back in Maple Leaf Gardens for the Richard-less game, Toronto got a 4–2 win, which was closer and more desperate than the score might indicate. The fourth game was even more arduous. It was tied at one-apiece at the end of regulation time. The two goalies played as if they were joined in personal combat, Broda versus Durnan. In the first over-time period, the Canadiens drilled thirteen shots at Broda. He stopped each one. So there, Bill Durnan. Durnan was just as unyielding until 16:30 of the period, when Harry Watson passed to Syl Apps in front of the Montreal net. It was a shot, a goal, a Leaf win.

In Montreal for game five, the Canadiens remembered that they were supposed to be winning the series for Elmer Lach. They outscored the Leafs 3–1. That brought the teams to the Gardens on the night of Saturday, April 19, and it looked as if the Canadiens intended to pick up where they had left off in Montreal because the Montreal centre Buddy O'Connor popped in a very fast goal at the twenty-five-second mark of the first period. After that, the Leaf defence shut the Canadiens down. In fact, Montreal had only twenty-one shots on Broda all night. Offensively, the Leafs tied the game early in the second period, when Vic Lynn scored. For a guy who held mainly a checking position on the Kennedy–Meeker–Lynn line, Lynn was coming through with some significant goals in the series. The same line got the winning goal at 14:39 of the third period. Howie Meeker set it up, and the man who put it in,

the man who led the Leafs in almost everything all season, the man who
"re-established" himself as an NHLer, was Ted Kennedy. It was 2–1 for
the Leafs — and a Stanley Cup.

Smythe and Day had torn the team apart at the beginning of the
season, had gone with the rookies, and the gamble, if that was what it
was, paid off. This Leaf team was the youngest to that date to win a
Stanley Cup, and there was a feeling around the Leaf offices that just
maybe these young players could do it again.

7

The Best?

IMAGINE FRED ASTAIRE ON SKATES AND YOU'VE GOT Max Bentley. Like Astaire, he was slim, quick and graceful. Swift of foot, he was a dancer on the ice, master of the stutter step, the feint and the shift. Of course, one shouldn't carry the Astaire comparison too far. A key point of difference is that, for all of the appearance of spontaneity in Astaire's dance routines, every glide and tap was rehearsed and practised. Bentley, on the other hand, was an improviser in his movements, in his hockey. While he had certain set patterns, he was more often skittish and unpredictable, a couple of qualities that confounded linemates who had less talent for free-form play than he. But Bentley and Astaire were alike in character, both decent, shy and modest. And, for what it's worth, both were small men who wore their dark hair in the same slicked-back, elegant style.

Bentley was born on March 1, 1920, in Delisle, Saskatchewan, a farming community twenty-five miles southwest of Saskatoon. He was the youngest son in a family of six boys and seven girls. The closest brother in age to Max was Doug, four years older. Doug made it to the NHL with the Chicago Black Hawks in 1939. Max followed to the same team a year later. When the two brothers were combined with another little guy, Bill Mosienko, the NHL had one of its most creative lines of all time: Max at centre, Doug on left wing, Mosienko on the right.

To all appearances, these three players were plugged into one central nervous system. They moved themselves and the puck in ways that seemed uncanny and instinctive. A large part of that perception was true. They did have amazing anticipation for one another on the ice. But they also used orchestrated pieces of business. Mosienko preferred that Max—who was possibly hockey's most elusive stickhandler—pass him the puck before Mosienko hit the other team's defence, whereas Doug liked Max to dump the puck between the two defencemen, allowing Doug to swoop around the defence and pick up the puck.

"We used to talk about all kinds of ideas," Max once explained. "Mosie was very conscientious for talking. I had to keep all the ideas in my head, but I knew I'd be all right because those two, Doug and Mosie, were the best and fastest I ever saw."

The three men had enormous personal success. Doug led the NHL in points in 1943, Max in 1946 and '47. Mosienko finished in the top ten in points in four consecutive seasons. Doug was a First Team All-Star in three different seasons. Max was the All-Star centre in 1946, the same year he won the Hart Trophy as the league's most valuable player.

Alas, their individual success didn't translate into team success. Chicago finished out of the playoffs three times in the early 1940s, and in the only year they made a respectable showing, 1944, the Montreal Canadiens swept them in four games in the Stanley Cup final.

Max Bentley thought he knew the reason for Chicago's failures. "There was no ice to practise on in Chicago," he said many years after he retired. "Most of our guys couldn't get in good condition. We'd be ahead at the end of the first period or second period in games, then we'd fade right out and lose. The only guys who were okay for condition were me and Doug and Mosie. That's because we played at least half of every game all by ourselves."

All of which helped to explain why Chicago's president, Bill Tobin, agreed in November 1947 to a trade that, for sheer stunning impact, probably wasn't equalled until Edmonton peddled Wayne Gretzky to Los Angeles in 1988. Tobin reckoned that he couldn't have all his eggs in one basket, all the good players on one line. He needed more bodies, and he was willing to sacrifice Max Bentley to get them. Conn Smythe had designs on Bentley for two reasons; it would give him strength on all three forward lines, and it would protect him against the day fast approaching when Syl Apps, thirty-two years old going into the 1947–48 season, chose to retire.

So the trade: Max Bentley plus an obscure winger named Cy Thomas (who played six games for Chicago and would play eight in Toronto) for one complete forward line—Gaye Stewart, Gus Bodnar and Bud Poile—and one defence pair—Bob Goldham and Ernie Dickens. These were no stiffs that Smythe was giving up. The players included two Calder Trophy winners (Bodnar and Stewart), three certified goal scorers (Bodnar, Stewart and Poile) and a strong, intelligent defenceman (Bob Goldham, the guy in the trade Smythe most hated to lose). The five produced splendidly for Chicago, particularly Poile and Stewart, who were Second Team All-Stars in the year of the trade. What the five couldn't manage was to yank the Black Hawks out of the cellar. The team finished in last place in four of the next five seasons and didn't make the playoffs until 1952–53. That's why Bill Tobin came to regret the trade; last place was better with Max Bentley than without.

In Toronto, Bentley felt lonesome for a couple of months. He missed Doug. That was both on and off the ice. His Leaf linemates were Joe Klukay, a hard-working if unimaginative right-winger, and, as Max put it, "umpteen rookies on left wing." Sid Smith was one of the umpteen that first year, and he later explained the sense of disarray an ordinary man could experience playing alongside Max Bentley.

"I was a straight, driving sort of skater," Smith said. "But Max was different. He'd go dipsy-doodling. He'd head out of our end, then all of a sudden he'd whip to one side of the ice, and by that time, I'd be all the way down the rink."

Nevertheless, especially after Bentley got over his lonesomeness off the ice—Turk Broda, he always said, was the biggest help in that depart-ment—he brought a dimension to the Leafs that Toronto never had before. Even in the relative strait-jacket of Hap Day's defensively ori-ented system, he presented the team with invention and brio. He glit-tered. As strategy, Bentley playing the point when Toronto had a man advantage meant the Leafs had the most effective power play in the league. And even with rookies and other pedestrians on his wings, he remained a consistent twenty-goal scorer in his six Leaf seasons. Max Bentley kept the game alive and magical. He was an original. Others skated, he danced.

THE LINE WITH BENTLEY AT CENTRE OPERATED AS Toronto's third line. Talk about depth! The Apps line was the first, Ted Kennedy's was the second.

For Apps, Harry Watson played left wing, another of those solid-citizen types in the Bob Davidson mould—patrol the wing, check diligently, pop in goals almost as an afterthought (a lot of goals in Watson's case, 236 of them over his whole career). Bill Ezinicki on right wing exuded charisma. A medium-sized man, he had an erect skating style, powerful legs and much muscular development in his upper body, something he acquired through weightlifting. He had a knack, on the defensive, for skating full tilt parallel to the other team's puck carrier, then spinning laterally in a loop that put him right in the puck carrier's face. Ezinicki would flatten the poor guy. It was an electrifying manoeuvre, one of many in Ezinicki's catalogue of intimidating tricks.

On Kennedy's line, the responsibilities were simple. Howie Meeker and Vic Lynn skated—both had excellent strength and speed—and Kennedy passed. "Kennedy wasn't a skater, didn't have the legs," Meeker once said. "But he was very competitive and a great, great passer. He kept Lynn and me in the league." On defence, all three worked like demons. "Vic'd cut you ear to ear if he had half a chance," Meeker said. And on offence, it was Kennedy feeding the other two for shots on goal and, often enough, stuffing the rebounds in the net.

Turk Broda played goal—all the goal in all sixty games in 1947–48. Jim Thomson and Gus Mortson continued as one defence pair, Wally Stanowski and Garth Boesch as the other. With Bob Goldham traded, young Bill Barilko took over the swing man's role on defence. He was the Kid, as in "Don't worry about me—they're not chasing the Kid out of the big time," which was Barilko's announcement when he joined the team. Nobody minded the bravado. Barilko was a likeable Kid, big on ribbing the other guys, in many ways the most popular Leaf among his teammates. He was courageous and durable, a premier hipchecker and a major contributor to what may have been the best Leaf team of all time.

THESE LEAFS OF 1947–48 HAD CONSISTENCY. NONE OF the regulars suffered an injury that cost serious time off skates, though Meeker stepped on somebody's stick at a Boxing Day practice and broke his collarbone. Five players—Broda, Ezinicki, Kennedy, Lynn and Nick Metz, the penalty killer—played all sixty games, and nine other players appeared in fifty-three or more games. That included Meeker, whose busted collarbone kept him out of only two games. Night after night, the same guys showed up.

These Leafs had discipline. That's discipline as in the group mindset to carry out Hap Day's grinding defensive scheme. Other editions of the Leafs possessed that discipline. This one had it in spades. It was the nature of the Leafs' dedication to the purpose that it began away from the ice. Smythe, who was as much an army man as a hockey man, demanded that his players function in lock step. So, at training camp every player had to turn out for golf at precisely 2:30 in the afternoon. You didn't play golf? Okay, you caddied. Work or play, you stuck with the team. On the road, players slept in Pullman-car berths according to the numbers on their sweaters. Ezinicki wore twelve, therefore he slept in berth twelve. No detail was too tiny to be overlooked. Also on the road, players gathered at 3:30 sharp for the pre-game meal, always steak, always one vitamin pill at each place. At home or away, players arrived in the dressing room at the designated time, dressed at the designated time, put on skates at the designated time. "The discipline," Bill Ezinicki said, "I loved it."

And these Leafs had talent. The team had the best goaltending in the league that season, five formidable defencemen, the NHL's most effective collection of backchecking forwards, four twenty-goal scorers (Apps, Kennedy, Bentley, Watson), and most of all, it had three fabulously gifted centres. Dick Beddoes, the sportswriter and broadcaster, once suggested that Wayne Gretzky would have been the fourth centre on the Leaf team of 1947–48. Beddoes might have been right.

THE LEAFS DIDN'T RUN AWAY WITH THE LEAGUE CHAMPI-
onship that year. One team stuck with them. The team wasn't the Montreal Canadiens, the NHL first-place finisher the previous year. The
bottom fell out for the Canadiens in 1947–48. Toe Blake, Montreal's
captain and heart, even if he was thirty-five, fractured his ankle in a collision with the New York defenceman Bill Juzda, and the rest of the
team, disintegrating without Blake, folded into fifth place. No, it was
Detroit that challenged Toronto, a Red Wings team featuring the
emerging stars Ted Lindsay and Gordie Howe.

All season long the two teams hung close until the schedule came to
the last weekend, Toronto in front by one point and two games remaining, Detroit at the Gardens on Saturday night, Toronto in the Olympia
Sunday night. Here, it seemed, was terrific drama, the two best teams in
the league by far—Boston, in third place, was more than a dozen points
back—going head to head at the climax of the entire season.

The drama, as it developed, was muted. The Leafs did the muting.
In the Saturday game, two of Toronto's three great centres came up big.
Ted Kennedy scored two goals. So did Syl Apps. And the Leafs had a
5–3 win in a game that was more of a walkover than the score revealed.
That wrapped up first place for Toronto, with a victory that was more
anti-climax than climax.

Still, Sunday's game, meaningless as a factor in the final standings,
held potentially wondrous things for two Leafs, Syl Apps and Turk Broda.

Apps' retirement had progressed from speculation to certainty. He
was quitting at the conclusion of the season. To add piquancy to the end
of his hockey life, he went into the weekend series with 196 career goals.
Two hundred would give him tremendous satisfaction. Saturday's two
brought the count to 198. In the second period on Sunday, Harry
Watson had an irresistible chance to score. He resisted it and passed to
Apps. Apps got the goal. Later in the same period, Ezinicki sent Apps a
centring pass in a crowd at the front of the Detroit net. Apps put his
stick on the puck. Another goal. In the final period, leading the Leafs to
the win, he added a third goal for a career mark of 201. "Two hundred
goals wasn't bad in the 1940s," Apps said years later, modest but realistic.
"Now everybody gets 200."

As for Broda, he and Harry Lumley of the Red Wings entered the weekend having allowed 138 goals each, the lowest totals in the league. Whoever delivered the goods on Saturday and Sunday would win the Vezina Trophy. Broda permitted three and two goals in the two games, while five went by Lumley in each. Turk Broda got the Vezina.

THE TWO WEEKEND WINS OVER DETROIT SENT THE LEAFS on a streak of invincibility that was interrupted by only a single loss. That came in the semi-final series, which Toronto took from Boston by four games to one. The series was a breeze for the Leafs, the high point—perhaps more accurately the low point—coming in the third game, played in the Boston Garden, when a check Bill Ezinicki laid on the Bruins' Grant Warwick precipitated an all-in brawl that involved most players, some fans and a few policemen. The feature bout had two heavyweights squaring off, Harry Watson versus Boston's husky defence-man Murray Henderson. Watson prevailed on a TKO when Henderson retired with a broken nose. The Leafs, having let the air out of the Bruins, won the game 5–1.

In the Stanley Cup final, Leafs against the Red Wings, Toronto established two truths: that Detroit was a team in waiting for greatness, that Toronto was a great team now arrived at the peak of its powers.

The Leafs built as the series progressed. They fought for close wins in the first three games—5–3 and 4–2 at the Gardens, 2–0 in the next game, played in the Olympia—then exploded in the fourth, also in the Olympia. This last game represented an exercise in sublime hockey superiority.

On defence, the Leafs allowed Detroit a mere nineteen shots at Turk Broda. Two of them got by him, one in the second period when Toronto was already up by three goals, another with seventy-two seconds left in the third period when everything was over except speculation on whether this was or wasn't the best Leaf team of all time.

Toronto's offensive thrust in the game served as a demonstration of its all-round strength with the puck. Ted Kennedy got the first goal. It came on a power play, Max Bentley at the point, Bentley setting up Kennedy. Kennedy's line scored one other goal, Kennedy potting it on a pass from Vic Lynn. The Apps line got three, one by the captain, two by Harry Watson. Bentley's line scored one. Bentley did the work, earned the assist, but the fellow who got the goal was another of Max's umpteen rookies on left wing. This was Les Costello, twenty years old, green as grass, called up from the minors in March that year to play six playoff games, never having appeared in an NHL uniform until then. Nor was he destined to spend much time in the big leagues, just fifteen games with the Leafs the following season. After that, he left hockey for his true vocation as a priest in the Catholic church. But he left behind a line in the record book: "Wednesday, April 14, 1948. Game four. Third period. Toronto, Costello (Bentley) 14:37."

There was one more goal for Toronto in the final game, making the score 7–2, and the goal was a rarity. Garth Boesch scored it on a break-away. Garth Boesch, the most defensive-minded of the Leafs defence-men, a guy who seldom ventured beyond the opposing team's blueline, who scored a grand total of eleven goals in his complete career of 225 regular-season and playoff games — this unlikely player got a goal. Maybe this is the clinching statistic regarding the status of the Toronto Maple Leafs of 1947–48, that when a player of Garth Boesch's type, a player of his strictly defensive bent, scores a breakaway goal in the Stanley Cup final game, he must surely be playing on the best team in the Leafs' history.

8

Two More

FORTY-FOUR YEARS LATER, IT STILL GRIPED CAL Gardner. He made jokes about it, but the memory of the damned headline in the Toronto newspaper—he'd forgotten which one—on April 22, 1949, continued to fester away and pop out and bug him all over again. This happened especially when hockey guys got together to talk about the old days and the great games and the famous goals. Well, that goal of his was famous, wasn't it? It won a third-straight Stanley Cup for the Leafs. Darn right, it was a big goal. The Leafs versus the Red Wings in the 1948–49 final, the Leafs up three games to none, and in game four, the score was tied at one-all near the end of the second period. That's when Gardner scored, at 19:45 of the second. Later on, in the third period, Max Bentley got another goal for the Leafs to make the final score 3–1. But the one that counted, the goal that kept the Cup in Toronto, was Cal Gardner's. So what did the headlines read next day, in extra-large print?

"BENTLEY SCORES CLINCHER."

And underneath, in tinier print:

"GARDNER GETS WINNER."

"When I read that in the paper, I couldn't get it out of my mind," Gardner said in his North Toronto home one vivid autumn morning in

1993. "Still can't, as a matter of fact, the big print for Max, small print for me."

GARDNER PLAYED CENTRE, AND HE HAD COME TO THE LEAFS for a specific purpose—to replace the retired Syl Apps. Nobody could precisely take Apps' place, but Gardner had the tools to keep the old Apps line—Harry Watson on left wing, Bill Ezinicki on right, now Cal Gardner at centre—more than respectable.

Gardner was a western guy, born in Transcona, Manitoba. He played on a fine Winnipeg Rangers junior team that won the 1942 Memorial Cup, served three years in the navy, got scooped up by the New York Rangers, and played three years in New York before Conn Smythe chose him as the Leaf centre of the immediate future. Smythe gave the Rangers Wally Stanowski and in return received Gardner, Bill Juzda and Rene Trudell. Trudell didn't stick with Toronto. Juzda, nicknamed "The Honest Brakeman" because he worked on the railway out west in the off season, was a short, blocky man who provided the Leafs with four years of obstinate defence. Gardner was the main guy in the trade, good at both ends of the ice, a centre who took pleasure in handing out a body-check, not a prolific scorer but a sweetheart of a passer.

Gardner did the job for the Leafs in 1948–49. He skated miles, laid the body on Milt Schmidt and Elmer Lach and the other big-name opposing centres, kept feeding passes to Harry Watson, who ended the season with a career-high twenty-six goals. Gardner had twenty-six assists, which tied him with Max Bentley for most on the team that year. Not bad for the new guy.

The trouble with the season was that, after two consecutive Stanley Cups, the other Leafs suffered a collective case of fat-cat syndrome. "We started thinking we were some shakes as hockey players," Howie Meeker said many years later. Injuries didn't help either. Meeker himself missed thirty games and scored only seven goals all season. Ted Kennedy operated with a creaky back and endured fourteen straight games without a goal. Even Max Bentley, Twinkletoes himself, went through a bad patch, a dozen consecutive games and not a single goal. And Max didn't have an injury to lay the blame on. Disaster all around, and as late as

February, Toronto was deep in fifth place and headed out of the playoffs.

Still, according to Meeker, the Leafs—Smythe and Hap Day excepted—had an Alfred E. Neuman attitude: What, me worry? "Ahh, none of the players got concerned that year," Meeker said. "The fans did, and management and the writers. But we didn't really doubt we'd come out smellin' sweet."

Sure enough, the Leafs put on a sufficient end-of-the-year push to ease comfortably into fourth place, seven points up on fifth-place Chicago. Toronto drew the Bruins in the Stanley Cup semi-final, and that's when the real Leaf team showed up, when they began a run of nine games, playoff games, that brought eight wins and one loss.

The first two games of the semi-final against the Bruins were played in Boston, and the Leafs won both, 3–0 and 3–2. In each, Harry Watson got two goals. Thanks Cal, Watson said four times to his new centre, thanks for the swell passes.

Back at Maple Leaf Gardens for game three, the Bruins beat Toronto in overtime, and the loss brought about a mini-drama within the Leaf family. The previous year, Sid Smith had played thirty regular-season games with Toronto and a couple of playoff games before a check from Boston defenceman Pat Egan tore the ligaments in his knee. In the dressing room, moments after Smith came off the ice in excruciating pain, Smythe ordered the Leaf doctor, a man named Galloway, to freeze the knee and send Smith back into the game. Galloway refused. In fact, he quit the team over the incident. Smith worked hard all of the following summer on rehabilitating the knee, riding the streetcar twice a day from his Toronto home to Wellesley Hospital for therapy. By September 1948, the knee was sound, but the Leafs ignored Smith. No invitation to training camp, no acknowledgment of his summer of dedication, just a ticket to the American League farm team in Pittsburgh. Smith burned up the AHL— fifty-five goals, fifty-seven assists. Now the Leafs couldn't ignore him, and after the Bruins won the third playoff game in overtime, after Smythe blamed Vic Lynn for the loss, Smith took Lynn's spot on left wing with the Kennedy line. And, oh lovely redemption, in Toronto's 3–1 victory in game four, Smith scored two of the goals and assisted on the third.

"Lovely redemption?"

Well, something like that.

"I can't picture exactly how I got either of those goals," Smith said some twenty-five years later. "What I really liked about the goals at the time was me sticking it up management's ass for the screwing around they gave me the year before. That was the nice part."

The Leafs polished off Boston in the fifth game, and proceeded to the final against the Red Wings. Detroit had finished first in the regular season, carried by the great line of Ted Lindsay, Gordie Howe and Sid Abel. But the Wings may have been running out of gas by playoff time. Or out of oxygen; throughout the final, the team positioned an oxygen tank next to the bench for sluggish players to take a hit of the pure stuff between shifts.

Oxygen didn't help. Toronto won the first game, 3–2 in overtime on Joe Klukay's goal. Game two brought more joy to Sid Smith's heart; the score was 3–1 in favour of the Leafs, and Smith scored each of the three goals. Abel, Lindsay and Howe played forty minutes of game three. All that got Detroit was one goal and three very tired stars. Leafs scored three goals — by Kennedy, Ezinicki and Gus Mortson — and won 3–1. That set the stage for game four and Cal Gardner's big moment.

"The scoring of the goal itself, as I remember it, came off a routine kind of play," Gardner said on this 1993 autumn morning, looking out the window of his home at the bright reds and yellows of the maple trees, concentrating, thinking back on the game. "The score, yes, it was one-all, and we must've been in a line change at the time. I can't place Harry Watson in the play right then. He'd probably already headed for the bench. Jimmy Thomson started the play. He head-manned the puck out of our zone to Bill Ezinicki. That was Hap Day's style, head-man the puck, get it up the ice as fast as you could. So Ezzie had the puck in the Detroit zone. Ezzie didn't like to carry the puck too much at any time. He passed it quick over to me on the left side, and I took my shot. It wasn't a wrist shot, and of course we didn't have the slapshot in those days. This was what we called a windup shot that I used. I just brought my stick and the puck back and let it go. The key thing was that the Detroit defenceman was screening Harry Lumley in the net. I can't remember which defenceman it was. Leo Reise? Jack Stewart? One of those fellas. Whoever it was tried to block my shot. He missed it, and Lumley didn't have time to recover and make the stop. The puck went in the net. And that turned out to be the goal that won the Stanley Cup."

THE LEAFS GOT OFF TO ANOTHER ROTTEN START IN THE 1949–50 season. Smythe insisted that excess poundage was at fault. Too many players were overweight. Lynn, Watson, Smith, Garth Boesch—all were too heavy to play at their best. And Turk Broda?! Ugh, Porky Pig! The Fat Man! Smythe made a big public deal over Broda's weight. Broda was 197 pounds, and Smythe announced in late November that Broda wouldn't play until he hit 190. Gil Mayer was called up from Pittsburgh to fill in as goaltender, and Smythe bought another goalie, Al Rollins, from the Cleveland Barons of the AHL. In truth, the weight issue seemed to have more to do with publicity than hockey, and if Smythe's idea was to place the Leafs in a prominent spot in the newspapers during a period when sports fans had Grey Cup football and other matters on their minds, he succeeded. Photographs of Broda adorned the sports sections and front pages, Broda in a steam box, Broda conferring over menus with Mrs. Broda, Broda nibbling on a salad. On December 1, he registered 8 ounces under 190 pounds. On December 5, he shut out the Rangers. And everybody stopped talking about his weight. The episode had been an instance of Smythe the headline-grabber at his most dextrous.

THE SLIMMED-DOWN LEAFS FINISHED THE SEASON IN THIRD place and met the first-place Red Wings in the playoff semi-finals. It was a series that, as things developed, turned principally on propaganda, and this time, in the manipulation of events, Conn Smythe came up second-best.

The matter at issue surfaced in the very first game, which was played at the Detroit Olympia. Toronto won 5–0, but the score was almost forgotten in the furore over an injury to Gordie Howe in the third period. Howe, trying to check Ted Kennedy near the boards, somehow ended up in a crumpled, bleeding heap on the ice. Bones were broken in Howe's face and skull, and before he recovered, he needed a ninety-minute operation and a long rest in a hospital bed.

What happened that led to Howe's horrible injuries?

Here is how Kennedy answered the question in a 1975 conversation with this writer: "Everybody saw that Howe ran himself into the boards. For heaven's sake, George Gravel, the referee, had his hand up to signal a charging penalty to Howe, and when Howe missed me and hit the boards, he almost landed in Clarence Campbell's lap. He was sitting right there and saw everything, the president of the league."

But it was Kennedy who came under sustained and vicious attack, physically from the Detroit players, verbally from the Detroit fans, and in print from the Detroit press.

Why?

Here again is Kennedy: "Jack Adams, the Red Wings general manager, was so emotional. He was from the old school of letting your emotions run away, and he stirred up a fuss, blaming me for Howe's injury. People listened because James Norris, Sr., the old man, was still alive then. He was very influential. He owned the Red Wings, owned most of Chicago, had some ownership of Madison Square Garden, so when he made waves, you felt water all over the league. At any rate, the guys on our team were very upset over the criticism of me. It took a lot of starch out of us."

Still, Detroit had to use all seven games to beat the Leafs. Kennedy always insisted that Toronto should have won, pointing out that the Red Wings were missing their best player, Howe, and the thirty-five goals he'd scored during the regular season. But the Wings had vengeance on their side. Win one for Gordie, Jack Adams kept repeating. And the Wings had luck too. Leo Reise won the fourth game in overtime when he bounced a long shot off Gus Mortson's leg into the Leaf net, and the same guy, Reise, scored on a similar shot, a ricochet off somebody's anatomy, for the only goal in the seventh game.

After that, Detroit went on to defeat the Rangers in the Stanley Cup final.

THE LEAFS MADE MAJOR CHANGES FOR THE 1950–51 season. Traded Ezinicki and Lynn to Boston for the tough defenceman Fern Flaman. Moved Meeker to right wing on the line with Watson and

Gardner. Called up Tod Sloan from the minors and created a line of Sloan, Kennedy and Smith. Alternated goaltenders, thirty games for Broda, forty for Al Rollins. Moved Hap Day into the assistant general manager's office and appointed Joe Primeau as coach.

Primeau, Toronto's smooth centre of the 1930s, had coached in the Leaf organization for many years, a Memorial Cup winner with the St. Michael's College Juniors, an Allan Cup with the Toronto Marlboro Seniors. He was a more passive soul than Day—"Gentleman Joe" was his nickname—but he followed Day's essentially defensive system, and the players needed no adjustment to the new coach's ways.

Indeed, as a team and as individuals, the Leafs thrived that season. They showed more wins, forty-one, and more points, ninety-five, than any Toronto team to that date. It should be kept in mind, though, that this was the second year in which each NHL team played a seventy-game schedule, up from sixty games. Hence, more wins and more points for good teams. But not much more money for the players. "When they bumped up the schedule," Cal Gardner recalled, "the owners decided they'd pay each guy one hundred bucks for each extra game. Ten games, a thousand bucks. Boy, somebody was making a profit, but it wasn't us players."

The Leafs finished a close second to Detroit on the season, and several Toronto players racked up excellent statistics. Max Bentley, twenty-one goals and forty-one assists, finished third in the league scoring. The combination of Rollins and Broda had the lowest goals-against total, with Rollins, having played more games than Broda, receiving the Vezina Trophy. Gardner had his best-ever season, twenty-three goals, twenty-eight assists, and Smith and Kennedy developed into such a compatible pair—thirty goals for Smith, forty-three assists for Teeder—that both were elected to the Second All-Star Team.

One other Leaf made the Second All-Stars, Jim Thomson, and there, in Thomson, was a fine Leaf player whose talents tended to get overlooked. Maybe it was because he lacked flash and sparkle that fans forgot Thomson and sang the praises of the more flamboyant Mortson and Barilko. Thomson was tall and bulky, not particularly swift on skates, not a harumphing bodychecker. He belonged more to the clutch-and-grab school of defence. Thomson immobilized any opposing forward who came within arm's reach. And he was a superb passer. His defence partner, Gus Mortson, loved to lug the puck. Thomson preferred to pass it, which was why he played one point—Max Bentley was at the other point—on Leaf power plays. Thomson led the entire Toronto team in assists in 1947–48, 29 of them, and over his thirteen-year career, he had a total of 215 assists. Great numbers for a defenceman on a defensive team.

Cal Gardner remembered that Thomson also possessed a bizarrely effective shot. "It was all arms," Gardner said. "No body motion. It looked pretty strange. Jimmy hit a golf ball the same way, all arms, no body, and he'd drive his tee-shot a mile."

Thomson came to a grim end with the Leafs, another casualty of Conn Smythe's narrow definition of loyalty. This happened in 1957. Thomson had been a Leaf since 1946, starting out as a kid of eighteen. Never a complainer, the good soldier, solid service to the organization. Was he respected? He must have been—he was named the Leaf captain in 1956. But at a meeting of NHL owners in Palm Beach, Florida, in February 1957, talk got around to the Players' Association, the union, that some players within the league were attempting to organize. (This was in the pre–Alan Eagleson period.) It seemed that Jim Thomson was a vice-president of this group of radicals. Smythe told the other owners he'd handle Thomson. And he did. Forget Thomson's twelve years of loyal play. Never mind his captaincy. Smythe put Thomson up for grabs and allowed him to be claimed by Chicago, putting him far from potential influence over other Leaf players who might consider joining the damned union.

"We isolated the Association," Smythe later wrote with smug pride. "And it was nearly ten years before it became effective."

Thomson played one season in Chicago, and retired. He went to work for his father-in-law at McKinnon's Fuels in Toronto, later rising to the company's presidency and ownership. He was a sharp investor in the stock market, and when Jim Thomson died in the early 1990s, he departed a wealthy man.

IN THE 1950–51 STANLEY CUP SEMI-FINALS, THE LEAFS wiped out Boston in one series, Montreal upset the Red Wings in the other. That brought about a final series in which each game would go into overtime. Sid Smith scored the overtime winner in the first game, 3–2. Game two had the same score, 3–2, but Montreal won on a Rocket Richard goal. In game three, 2–1, Kennedy knocked in the winner. Leafs won again in the fourth game, 3–2, Harry Watson doing the honours.

Game five gave every indication that it, too, would be decided by a single goal—in regulation play, not in overtime. The game was played at the Gardens, and with less than a minute left in the third period, Montreal had a 2–1 lead. Joe Primeau pulled Al Rollins from the net and went with an extra forward. What happened next was described many years later by Max Bentley:

"I had the puck in the Montreal end, and I could see two of our guys beside the net, Sid Smith on one side, Tod Sloan on the other. All the Montreal guys were behind the three of us, behind me and Smitty and Sloanie. I don't know how that came about, but it did, no Montreal defencemen or forwards between us and their net. Anyhow, Butch Bouchard, their defenceman, rushed at me, and I flipped the puck over his stick to Smitty. Their goalie—Gerry McNeil, wasn't it?—he turned to Smitty, and Smitty slid the puck to Sloanie. The net was wide open for him to tap it in. Tie game. The fans hollered so much I think the noise lasted fifteen minutes. I never heard anything like it. It seemed like they must've kept up right through the intermission before the overtime, that loud, loud crowd noise."

BILL BARILKO HAS BECOME A FOLK HERO OF SORTS, THE subject of a mini-cult. Among all the great Leafs over the years, it was Barilko—not Conacher or Apps or Kennedy—who was the second player (after Ace Bailey) to have his number (5) retired after his career ended. Later, Barilko had his number attached to a banner that was, in a touching little ceremony before a Maple Leaf game in the early 1990s, raised high alongside a Bailey banner for permanent display just below the Gardens' ceiling. And it was Barilko whose name was immortalized after a fashion in 1993 by the rock band of the minute, The Tragically Hip. The members of the band were genuine hockey fans from Kingston, frequent occupiers of gold seats at the Gardens, and their tribute to Barilko in the song "Fifty Mission Cap" was heartfelt. But these guys weren't alive when Barilko played hockey. Whatever they've absorbed of the Barilko story has come very second hand. The lyrics to "Fifty Mission Cap" make that clear; after reciting the barebones facts of Barilko's life, the lyric confesses that "I stole this from a hockey card."

So how come? Why is Bill Barilko celebrated in song and banner, a player who had only four and a third seasons in the NHL, won no individual trophies, made election to no All-Star teams?

Easy answer: he scored a spectacular goal that won a Stanley Cup and, four months later, he died in a way that was tragic and, for a while, mysterious.

THE BARILKO GOAL CAME EARLY IN THE FIRST OVERTIME period of the fifth game in the 1950–51 final against Montreal. The time was just short of the three-minute mark. Gardner, Meeker and Watson came on as forwards for the Leafs, Barilko and Boesch on defence. The puck was in the Montreal zone. Meeker had put it there. Meeker, always a player of hustle and speed, chased after the puck behind the Montreal net and to the right of the goalie, Gerry McNeil. Tom Johnson, Montreal's tall defenceman, fought Meeker for the puck. Meeker won. He popped it in front. Harry Watson, to McNeil's left, took a crack at the puck. Nobody's certain whether Watson's shot forced McNeil to make a save or whether the puck bounced off a post or off another Montreal player. What is sure is that, in the next millisecond, McNeil went down, diving to the left corner of the net, while the puck caromed in the opposite direction, in front of the goal to the right side. It was at this point that Bill Barilko seized the moment. He was never noted as an offensive opportunist, not a goal scorer, twenty-six of them in 252 league games, five in 47 playoff games. He wasn't supposed to score, or to crash the net. He was supposed to bodycheck guys into oblivion. But this time, Barilko came in a storming rush all the way from his spot at the left blueline. He had his eye on the caroming puck. He and the puck met exactly at the top of the left face-off circle. Barilko's stick swept at the puck. In the days before slapshots, this might be called a modified swingshot. Gerry McNeil was still down in the Montreal net, trying to raise his bum off the ice, trying to get his right hand, the one holding the goalie stick, in the way of Barilko's on-coming shot. McNeil was too little and too late. The puck whipped into the corner of the net to his upper right. Barilko, meanwhile, continued on his headlong rush and appeared to catch the skate of his teammate Cal Gardner, who was crossing from right to left in front of the net. For an instant, Barilko was entirely airborne, both skates off the ice, both gloves preparing to stave off the downward thump. Not that Barilko cared about a hard landing, not right then. His eyes and mind were on the goal he'd scored, the one that had just meant another Stanley Cup for Toronto.

ON AUGUST 26, 1951, BARILKO WAS FLYING HOME TO Timmins from a fishing trip on James Bay. There were just two of them, Barilko and his friend Henry Hudson, a Timmins dentist. Hudson was the pilot. The plane was a Fairchild 24, single engine, pontoons. Some-where between Rupert House and Timmins, the plane vanished. For years, despite a concerted search, no trace of the plane turned up. That got rumours circulating; Barilko, of Russian descent, had defected to the Soviet Union, where he was teaching the art of bodychecking to young Russian defencemen. The rumours ended in 1962 when a bush pilot came across the wreck of a Fairchild 24 about sixty miles north of Cochrane. Barilko got a burial at home in Timmins, and The Tragically Hip had the material, thirty years later, for a song.

CAL GARDNER TOOK SOME HEAT FROM CONN SMYTHE OVER Barilko's goal.

"Cal," Smythe said in the dressing room after the game, "you should've got that goal."

Years later, in 1993, Gardner said Smythe had a point, but that he had missed the more important point.

"Sure, the puck came real close to me," Gardner explained. "But if you take a look at the famous photograph of the goal, the one that shows Barilko flying through the air, you'll see me skating in the direction of a Montreal player. It was the Rocket. I had my attention on him, not on the puck. The thing was, Barilko had left his defence spot open, and if he

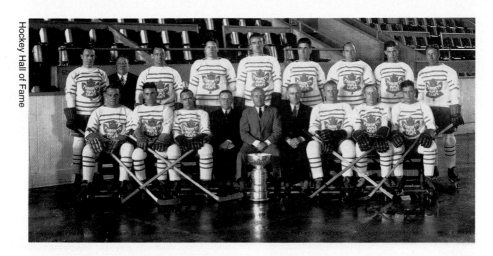

Conn Smythe — front row, middle — won the Maple Leafs' first Stanley Cup
with this 1931-32 squad.

Toronto's Kid Line of the 1930s: Charlie Conacher (left) and Busher Jackson
(right) popped the goals on slick setups from Joe Primeau.

Red Horner may have been the
NHL's premier bodychecker of the
1930s. That skill got him 1,254
minutes in penalties and a place in
the Hockey Hall of Fame.

Training camp 1930s style: the old
pyramid routine was great for
strengthening shoulder muscles.

Conn Smythe shares hockey strategy with his coach of the 1930s — and later the Montreal Canadiens coach — Dick Irvin.

Hap Day succeeded Irvin as coach and laid on his team the message that defence wins games.

When the Leafs won the 1941-42 Stanley Cup, Conn Smythe (in military uniform) was fighting two wars — one against the rest of the NHL, the other against the Nazis.

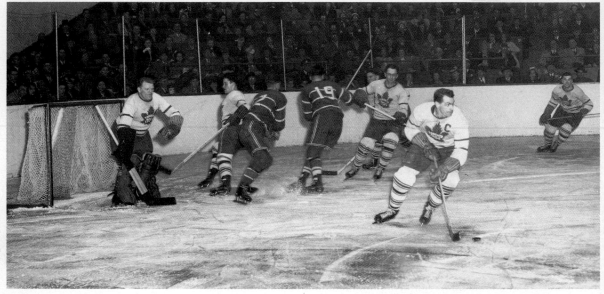

Toronto whirls back to the attack in
this early 1940s game against
Montreal. Syl Apps has the puck.

One of the splendid Leafs, Bob
Davidson, a team player, captain of
the 1945 champions and, later, an
astute Toronto scout.

Possibly the three finest centres to grace one team at one time: Ted Kennedy,
Max Bentley and Syl Apps of the 1947-48 Leafs.

Bill Barilko takes a long dive after scoring the thrilling overtime goal that brought the 1951 Stanley Cup to Toronto.

hadn't scored, the puck could easily have come out to Richard. Without Barilko in position, the Rocket could've been on a breakaway. So I was just doing my job, putting a guard on Rocket Richard."

Gardner smiled as he spoke. He was coming up to his seventy-third birthday, a good-looking man, full head of grey-brown hair, trim physique. After he ended his hockey career, after twelve NHL seasons and 154 goals, he had worked in the transport business, then in radio around Toronto. He was retired now and not liking it much. He was too full of energy just to sit around. He played plenty of golf, took in a few hockey games, kept in touch with his two sons. Both of them had played in the NHL, seven years and 75 goals for Dave, seven years and 201 goals for Paul. Dave was working for Molson's in Toronto. Paul coached the Washington Capitols farm team in Portland, Maine. Cal the father was proud of them. He was content, except now and again when he thought about the newspaper headline in the tiny print—"GARDNER GETS WINNER"—on April 22, 1949.

9

The Changing of the Guard

S UCH A LOUSY DECADE FOR THE LEAFS, THE 1950S. The 1980s would be worse, but they were worse with a footnote. The footnote pointed the finger at Harold Ballard. Under his ego-centred presidency, any franchise would have sunk to the depths. Ballard was a one-man hockey disaster area. But the 1950s, in all their horror for the Leafs, represented a group effort.

For the record, in the years between 1951, when the Leafs won the Stanley Cup, and 1958, when Punch Imlach seized the team tiller, Toronto never rose higher than third place in the league standings, finished out of the playoffs in three seasons, finished dead last in one of the three (first time that had ever happened), and lost in the first round of the playoffs in the other four seasons. Maybe the single statistic that shows best to what a low estate the team had fallen in the 1950s is this: in five of the seven seasons from 1952 to 1958, the Leafs allowed more goals than they scored. So much for the organization that was built on defence.

To be sure, the product on the ice wasn't unalloyed dreck. Good moments happened, exciting games, players with gifts, other players who at least tried hard. A highlights film from those years, admittedly not enough to constitute a two-hour feature, would show the following:

Sid Smith scoring goals by the ton, usually on setups from his regular centre, the nonpareil Ted Kennedy. Smith got 22 goals in 1953–54, 33 the next season when he was named the All-Star left-winger, 154 goals over six years. A gent on the ice too, twice winner of the Lady Byng Trophy.

Kennedy being voted the Hart Trophy as the NHL's most valuable player in 1954–55. It seemed a curious year for sportswriters around the league, the people who chose the prizewinners, to take note of Kennedy. For years, he'd been the captain of Stanley Cup teams without anyone voting him to anything more than the Second All-Star Team. Talk about scraps from the table. Then, in a season that was, by Kennedyesque standards, medium good—ten goals, forty-two assists—for a team that played straight .500 hockey and disappeared meekly in the playoffs, he got the Hart. Maybe it was a Lifetime Achievement Award. Or a Sportswriters' Guilty Conscience Prize.

Harry Lumley playing the best goal in the league in 1953–54 and close to the best in 1954–55. Lumley came to the Leafs in a 1952 trade with Chicago for Al Rollins, Gus Mortson and Cal Gardner, a lot to give up, but Lumley's numbers with Toronto were divine. In 1953–54: 69 games played, 13 shutouts, a 1.85 goals-against average, the Vezina Trophy. In 1954–55, 69 games, 8 shutouts, 1.94 average, runner-up to Detroit's Terry Sawchuk for the Vezina. This was the stuff of the Hockey Hall of Fame, a place Lumley entered in 1980.

There were other Leafs worthy of a spot in the 1950s highlights film. The tough little forward with the good scoring touch, Tod Sloan, was one. So were two younger guys who would be essential in helping the Leafs out of the wilderness later on—the man of muscle on defence, Tim Horton, and Frank Mahovlich, the Big M, the dream who played left wing. But, bottom line, the Leafs were feeble in the '50s.

RESPONSIBILITY FOR THE MESS BEGAN AT THE VERY TOP. Conn Smythe wasn't precisely the first to admit he made mistakes in 1950s hockey, nor did he ever own up to the extent of his errors. But it was at least a sign of nagging remorse that he offered reasons to explain why he might have goofed without actually acknowledging that he did goof. One of the reasons he advanced for possibly losing his hockey edge was that he was absent from Toronto for much of each winter, hoping the sun of Palm Beach, Florida, would bake the miseries out of his body. Then, too, he was devoting increasing amounts of time to his stable of racehorses. Smythe loved horses. "They're an inspiration to man," he once said. Maybe, in his later, pain-wracked, increasingly bitter years, he loved horses more than people, even more than hockey players. And, among other reasons he mentioned for his slipping grip on hockey, he worked with consuming generosity at raising money for crippled children and later for deaf children and adults. Perhaps Smythe felt, in his labours on behalf of these charities, that if he had to love human beings, he'd confine the love to those who were victims.

There was another pressure on Smythe. It came from below, from his elder son, Stafford. Unlike the other Smythe son, Hugh, who became a prominent medical man, specializing in rheumatism and arthritis, Staff went into the family industries, gravel and hockey. He put in long hours at C. Smythe For Sand, and much of the rest of the time, he handled the hockey end—Harold Ballard ran the business end—of the Toronto Marlboros organization. The Marlies Junior A team experienced success, a Memorial Cup in 1955. Staff wanted to move up to the big show. He bugged his dad for a promotion. He had ideas about the Leafs. He thought their defensive style was retrograde. He thought zippy offensive hockey should have its turn. He thought he should have his very own turn. He thought Hap Day was an old fart, though for the time being he kept his mouth shut about that.

Given all of the above—Conn Smythe's declining hockey acumen, his interest in horses and charities, his son's ants in the pants—Conn yielded some turf. Effective February 1, 1955, he stepped down as the Leafs' general manager and moved Hap Day into the post. To break his son into the organization, he adopted Staff's idea that a group of young Gardens directors be constituted a hockey advisory committee. The group was seven in number and included Staff and John Bassett, the publisher of the Toronto *Telegram*.

For some of the group, the Glee Club as they were first called, then

the Silver Seven, the committee seemed an opportunity to sow whatever wild oats they had left over from adolescence. Going on the road
with the team became a synonym for party on! "It was girls, booze and
frolic," said Harold Ballard, a latecomer to the Silver Seven, invited to
replace the Gardens' lawyer, Ian Johnstone, as one of the group in
November 1957. Nevertheless, the Silver Seven gave Staff a platform
from which to pepper his dad and Hap Day with notions for rescuing
the foundering Leafs.

MAYBE THEN IT WAS TOO MANY COOKS SPOILING THE
broth, too many voices — Conn's, Hap Day's, Staff's, any Silver Seven
person's, even Ballard's for pete's sake — chiming in with an opinion,
making a hockey decision. Certainly there was a conspicuous lack of consistent focus in choosing Toronto's coaches. That's coaches, plural. In the
mid-1950s, the Leafs went through three of them in five years, a shocking number for a team that cherished stability behind the bench.

The run on coaches began in 1953 when Joe Primeau retired.
Nothing wrong with that. Primeau was a worry-wart, "too nice a guy to
coach," in Howie Meeker's view, and he owned a Toronto cement-block
business that was flourishing in the house-building boom of the 1950s. It
needed Primeau's full attention. He left hockey.

King Clancy succeeded him as Leaf coach. Clancy is a hard one to
figure. Was he a genuinely intelligent hockey man? Or was he a good-
natured jokester with an infallible instinct for telling people at the
Gardens what they wanted to hear? Whatever the answer, after coaching
the Leafs from 1953 to 1956 and getting bounced out of the job, he
landed in the Leaf front office with a shifting assortment of duties. Fore-
most among them were providing laughs, advancing agreeable advice,
and fetching coffee, plane tickets, clean shirts from the laundry. In the
role of court jester–cum–gofer, Clancy outlasted Conn Smythe in the
Leaf organization; outlasted Punch Imlach, Staff Smythe, sundry
coaches, Imlach again; and might have outlasted Harold Ballard if his
own death hadn't intervened. This history makes Clancy sound rather
like a less malevolent Iago figure who stayed the course.

Howie Meeker was the choice for coach after Clancy. He was young, thirty-two. Staff Smythe liked that. He had grown up under Hap Day's defensive system. Day liked that. Conn Smythe appears to have liked nothing about Meeker as coach. "All theory and no practice," he later said of Meeker. "If he had a team of Rocket Richard and four more like him, he couldn't win." In Meeker's one year on the job, Toronto finished out of the playoffs. After this performance, Staff came around to his father's view of Meeker as coach. So long, Howie.

Staff seems to have had the largest influence in choosing the next coach. He was Billy Reay, a guy who had a ten-year playing career with Detroit and Montreal, then went into the Canadiens' front office. With the Leafs, Reay didn't make himself a players' favourite.

"He was all the time telling us how Dick Irvin coached Montreal," Sid Smith has said of Reay. "We didn't want to know how other people ran their team. We wanted to know how Reay was gonna run us. He never said. Awful coach."

It was Reay who led the team to its last-place finish. That got him fired on November 28, 1958.

WHILE COACHES WERE COMING IN THE DOORS AND GOING out the windows, it was another departure from the Leafs that constituted a watershed event in Toronto hockey history. It may have been a dismissal. It may have been a resignation. The facts remain murky. What is for sure is that Hap Day, fifty-seven years old in 1957, a foundation stone of the franchise, was gone.

The episode began when Conn Smythe, travelling north from Florida in late March 1957, about the time it had become evident that Howie Meeker's Leafs were going to miss the playoffs, stopped off in New York City. He spoke to Toronto hockey writers, whom the Leafs had brought to the Big Apple for the occasion, about his plans for the team.

"I haven't lost confidence in Hap Day," Smythe said. "He's my general manger, and he'll be asked if he's available to carry on."

In Toronto, Day picked up on the poisoned adjective in Smythe's statement.

"It's odd that I should be asked if I was 'available' after thirty years," Day said. "But since I was asked, I don't want the job any more."

"Oh my," Meeker said, "Smythe gave Hap an awful dart."

There are two schools of thought on whether or not Smythe intended the dart. Smythe maintained over the years that he did, that he had thought about the phrasing of his New York declaration, that "available" was the word he had arrived at as a means of dismissing Day. Consistent with this version was the increasing intensity of Staff Smythe's campaign to have his father rid the Leafs of Day's approach to hockey, which Staff perceived as that of a fuddy-duddy. On the other side of the argument, one wonders why Conn appeared so inept and graceless in administering Day's firing. Smythe had been graceless before, as he was here, but inept? Never until now. Perhaps, in some secret place, he didn't really want to lose Day. Perhaps the terrible word, "available," slipped unsummoned from his lips. That would explain the phone calls Smythe made in later years to Day in St. Thomas, Ontario. Day and his son ran a business there manufacturing wooden handles for axes and hammers. The way Day read the phone calls, Smythe was hinting that he wished Day would return to the Leafs, that he wished it was like the old days around the Leaf offices. No Silver Seven, no Staff to badger him, no girls, booze and frolic. Just a couple of good old boys, Conn and Hap, winning Stanley Cups. Day knew it was too late, knew his time had passed. He thought Smythe's time had passed too.

DAY'S SUCCESSOR AS GENERAL MANAGER WAS, AMAZING as it seems, Howie Meeker. Leaf bosses, meaning Conn and Staff Smythe, apparently deemed Meeker unfit to coach but just right to general-manage. The illogic of this dawned fairly quickly on Staff, and he ensured that Meeker wasn't around long enough to see the ice freeze on a new hockey season at the Gardens. Staff fired Howie within four months of his appointment.

Meeker's view of his own dismissal, expressed almost twenty years after the fact, seems at least partly instructive on the subject of the shifting power balance in the Leaf offices. "I'd feel bad if they'd let me go because I was no good at my job," Meeker said in a 1975 interview with this writer. "But I didn't have much chance to make my own moves. Stafford and Ballard just walked in and cleared out just about everybody who'd come up through Conn's system."

Meeker probably overrated Ballard's authority. Harold hadn't yet begun to show his best muscle around the Gardens in the late 1950s. But Meeker was right about Stafford Smythe. Staff, stepping out front, certainly way ahead of the rest of the Silver Seven, was coming on strong. His father remained as president and put the official stamp on most major Leaf steps, but Staff, at the Gardens while Conn was at Woodbine or in Florida, was the man who tended to the day-to-day operations.

One chore Stafford faced, after Meeker's departure, was to hire a new general manager, get in someone to make hockey decisions. Clancy held the title of assistant general manager, but the only decisions he seemed to make were whether to fetch two cream no sugar, one black, or the other way around. For the time being, Staff left the post vacant. That turned out to be unwise. With Billy Reay coaching, nobody general-managing and Staff hovering, the Leafs finished last.

At that point, after the 1957–58 season, Staff made the most successful appointment of his hockey life, one that resulted in four more Stanley Cups for the Maple Leafs. The hiring wasn't cleancut, not without a certain amount of equivocation on both sides, but in the end, Staff reached down to the Springfield club in the American Hockey League and picked up the man who, though Staff couldn't know it at the time, would become both general manager and coach of the Leafs. Staff hired Punch Imlach. That livened up things at the Gardens. That put an end to the lousy hockey of the 1950s.

10

Punch

THE "PUNCH" IN PUNCH IMLACH—HIS REAL given name was George—started out as "Punchy." He got it in the years before the Second World War, when he was playing senior hockey for a team called the Toronto Goodyears. In a game in Windsor, Ontario, Imlach took a fierce check that knocked him gaga. A Toronto *Telegram* sportswriter named Bunny Morgenstern wrote that Imlach looked "punch drunk." Those were the days when sportswriters cared neither about players' sensibilities nor about the possibility of libel suits. Morgenstern continued to refer to Imlach in print as "Punchy." At some point, an editor or typesetter shortened it to "Punch." This is the one that stuck, which was unfortunate because there was never a man in hockey who was less addle-headed, as the nickname implies, than Imlach. He was controlled, holding the whip hand in every personal dealing, so imperious on occasion that he could be extraordinarily insensitive in his treatment of the men who played hockey for him.

Imlach grew up quintessentially lower-middle class in the modest district of Toronto just east of the Don River long before it got yuppified into trendy Riverdale. Both parents were Scottish immigrants. His father served with the 48th Highlanders in the First World War, then worked for the Toronto Transit Commission. Imlach was an only child, which may account for his lifelong desire to be the centre of attention. He played junior hockey and, at eighteen, went to work in a branch of the Dominion Bank near his home. He joined the army in the Second World War, didn't get overseas, but discovered to his mild surprise that, as a second lieutenant, he had a knack for leading men.

After the war, he combined his new leadership talents with his love of hockey and went into business assembling, managing and coaching hockey teams. For ten years, he ran the Quebec Aces in the Quebec senior league and had steady success. It helped that, for two of the years, the Aces included one of the great players of the time, Jean Béliveau. But, as a coach and manager, Imlach developed into a master manipulator.

"One thing I learned in Quebec City," he later said, "was how much the human body can take as long as the mind in the body won't give up."

Here was Imlach's approach in a nutshell. No matter what players he worked with, regardless of the level of skill, regardless of age (though he preferred them seasoned), Imlach specialized in motivating the players' minds to take them where their bodies might hesitate to venture. It worked in Quebec and in Springfield, where Imlach ran the AHL team for one season, and it was no doubt this style, and the good results it brought, that prompted Staff Smythe to hire Imlach in the summer of 1958 as the Leafs' assistant general manager.

Note the title: assistant general manager. Imlach noted it and didn't care for it. There was already one assistant general manager, Clancy, and there was no general manager. That seemed to be the way Staff Smythe wanted it. Though Staff appreciated Imlach's hockey abilities, he wasn't yet prepared to let the new man encroach on the clout that Staff himself had only recently acquired around the Gardens. The Leafs' management might have remained in this amorphous state if the team hadn't stumbled into the 1958–59 season with a dreadful string of games, winning only five times in the first sixteen outings and plunging to the basement. That record prompted Imlach to lobby the Silver Seven for more authority. Staff elected to retreat, and the Silver Seven gave Imlach the title, general manager, plus the accompanying power, that would allow him to wheel and deal.

In his first major move as GM, Imlach awarded himself another title: coach. He decided that the incumbent, Billy Reay, hadn't a winning touch with these particular Leafs. To be fair to Reay's contribution, he was astute enough to make two judgments that benefited the Leafs mightily down the road: he recommended the acquisition of goalie Johnny Bower from the Cleveland Barons of the AHL and of the ferociously competitive forward Bert Olmstead from the Montreal Canadiens. Imlach had a couple of guys in mind to replace Reay as Leaf coach. One of them wasn't himself. He took the job only until the new man, whoever he was, arrived. But as various candidates dropped out, as Imlach became caught up in coaching, in coaxing the Leafs out of last place, he got stuck behind the bench. He was still there ten years and four Stanley Cups later.

THE LEAF TEAM THAT IMLACH TOOK OVER SHOOK DOWN this way: Bower and Ed Chadwick split the goaltending. On defence, it was Tim Horton, rookie Carl Brewer, third-year man Bob Baun, and two or three others, including Allan Stanley, whom Imlach had picked up from Boston at the beginning of the season in exchange for Jim Morrison and $7,500 in cash (a slick deal if there ever was one). Among the forwards, the Leafs had such older veterans as Olmstead and George Armstrong; some younger veterans just coming into their prime, Ron Stewart and two new guys who arrived in other brainy Imlach deals, Gerry Ehman (who played for Imlach in Springfield) and Larry Regan (likewise a former Imlach hand, at Quebec City); and a generous sprinkling of youngsters who grew up in the Leafs' junior system—Frank Mahovlich, Dick Duff, Billy Harris, Bob Pulford.

Give or take two or three more key players, add some chemistry, allow time for Imlach's coaching style to sink in, and this lineup was the basis of the team that proceeded to win Stanley Cups. But the first hint that glory lay ahead surfaced only in the very last weeks of the 1958–59 season. Until then, the Leafs stayed inconsistent. Win a couple, drop a couple, poke out of last place, sink back into it. With five games left in the schedule, Toronto was nine points away from the final playoff spot, which the New York Rangers occupied. This perilous situation didn't faze Imlach. Maybe, as a brand-new GM and coach, he couldn't afford to let it faze him. At any rate, he went around saying out loud that the Leafs—nine points out, five games to play—would reach fourth place and meet Boston in the first round of the playoffs.

"What did you get?" Conn Smythe asked one of the Silver Seven. "Did you get a coach or did you get a madman?"

The Leafs opened the five-game stretch with a weekend home-and-home series against their competition for the fourth spot, New York. In Toronto on Saturday, Duff and the Big M got two goals apiece, Bower stopped the Rangers cold, Leafs won 5–0. It was tougher in New York on Sunday, all tied at 5–5 in the third before Pulford got the winner at 17:45. Armstrong scored a hat trick in the game. Was everybody on the team contributing? That seemed to be the ticket to success.

In Montreal for the next game, the Leafs got lucky when the tremendous Canadiens goalie, Jacques Plante, came down with a bad case of boils and didn't play. Duff scored a pair, and the Leafs won 6–3. Since the Rangers lost to Boston, Toronto went into the weekend a single point out of fourth place. Toronto had a Saturday home game against Chicago, then would finish the season on the road in Detroit. Imlach, radiating chutzpah, told the Leafs on Friday to pack extra clothes for the trip because, he said, after the Sunday game against the Red Wings, they'd fly to Boston for the first two games of the playoffs. Oh, really?

On Saturday afternoon, the Rangers beat Detroit, putting them three points up on the Leafs. That night at the Gardens, Mahovlich scored two, and Toronto defeated Chicago 5–1. The margin was back to one point.

It was Sunday night. At seven o'clock, New York played Montreal at Madison Square Garden. At eight, Toronto met the Red Wings in the Olympia. The Leafs began their game haltingly, down 2–0 in the first period. But Larry Regan got a hot hand. He would end the game with two goals and two assists. The Leafs went ahead 4–3 in the second. Detroit tied it. And at just that moment, tie game, 4–4, the public address announcer at the Olympia intoned the final score from New York: Montreal 4, Rangers 2.

Regan was Toronto's big man on the night. Early in the third period, he won a face-off in the Leaf end, stickhandled the puck down the ice, circled the boards behind Detroit's net, laid a pass in front to Dick Duff.

Bang, Duff scored his twenty-ninth goal of the season. A couple of minutes later, Billy Harris sailed into the Detroit zone on a breakaway. He missed. Never mind, at 14:40, Bob Baun sent a looping shot from the point towards the Red Wing net. Harris tipped the puck in the air and redirected it behind the Detroit goalie. That made it 6–4 Toronto. The score stayed that way. And the Leafs, from oblivion to the playoffs in one week, flew to Boston.

They needed seven games to beat back the Bruins. That took them into the finals against the Canadiens, who were looking for their fourth-straight Stanley Cup. They got it. The series went just five games. But each game was tough, two decided by one goal, the other three by two goals. In the fourth game, a Leaf loss, a shot by George Armstrong zipped right through the Montreal net and out the other side. The TV cameras saw it as a goal. The referee didn't. No goal. No win. No Stanley Cup for Toronto.

Ten years later, after he'd been fired from the Leafs, Imlach looked back on 1958–59 and said, "That season is still the greatest thrill of my life."

IN JANUARY 1960, RED KELLY GOT MAD. HERE HE WAS, thirteen loyal years playing defence for the Detroit Red Wings, instrumental in winning four Stanley Cups, six times a First Team All-Star, winner of the Norris Trophy for best NHL defenceman in the first year the Norris was awarded, winner of three Lady Byngs, and Detroit said they were trading him to the Rangers? What was this? Kelly told Detroit management politely—Red never uttered anything more profane than "dang"—to stuff it. He wouldn't report to New York. The league president, Clarence Campbell, warned Kelly on the phone that he'd be banned from hockey if he didn't go along with the trade. Kelly told him to stuff it too. Red took a job with a tool company in Detroit that sold to the auto industry.

Punch Imlach got into the picture. He smuggled Kelly into Toronto disguised as either a diplomat or a mafia don in a Homburg and box overcoat and carrying a furled umbrella. In secret negotiations, Imlach took Kelly out to dinner and persuaded him to join the Leafs. Imlach said he'd work a trade with Detroit, smooth things out with the Red Wings, put a calming word in with Clarence Campbell. All of which he did. The eventual trade was Kelly even up for a young defenceman named Marc Réaume. At the dinner with Kelly, in Winston's, the tony Toronto restaurant of the period, Imlach told Kelly he'd start right away, in a game coming up at the Gardens against Montreal.

"Well, listen, Punch," Kelly said, his Homburg and umbrella on the banquette beside him, "I haven't been on skates for a couple of weeks. It might be dangerous to play defence until I get my skating legs back."

Imlach gave his conspirator's grin. "You're not playing defence, Red."

"I'm not?"

"I'm moving you to centre," Imlach said. "Red, you're the last piece we need to finish the Stanley Cup puzzle."

Maybe Imlach didn't say it in exactly those words, but that's the way Kelly remembers the discussion. The main point is that Imlach's audacious conversion of Kelly to a centre really was a piece in the Stanley Cup puzzle. Not quite the last. Probably the second-last.

The last piece was the arrival on the Leafs at the beginning of the 1960–61 season of the perfect little centre Dave Keon. Keon, from Noranda, Quebec, seemed to have been born with his remarkable offensive skills. He acquired the defensive tools in lessons from Father David Bauer, his Juniors coach at St. Michael's College. He came to the Leafs, twenty years old, a complete player. He won the Calder Trophy as best rookie. Later he won the Lady Byng twice. Each game he played, he was assigned to check the other team's toughest centre—Henri Richard one night, Stan Mikita the next. In his Leaf career, he scored 365 goals and got 493 assists. That's complete.

Now all the pieces were in place for the Leafs. Bower was the regular goalie, backed up by Don Simmons. On defence, Horton paired with Stanley, Baun with Brewer, while Al Arbour and Larry Hillman waited in the wings, usually with the minor-league team in Rochester. Up front, Keon centred Duff and Armstrong. Pulford played between Stewart and Olmstead. And Kelly had the Big M on one wing, and on the other, it was Bob Nevin, another Marlboro graduate who moved up to the Leafs in 1960–61, scoring twenty-one goals as a rookie, which might have been good enough to win him the Calder if Keon hadn't also chosen that year to break in. The reserve forwards were Billy Harris and Eddie Shack. Harris supplied the finesse. Shack, acquired from the Rangers in a trade, was in charge of trouble and strife—for the other team.

In 1959–60, Toronto finished second in the league standings and once again lost to Montreal in the Stanley Cup final. For those keeping score, that meant five straight Cups for the Canadiens. The following year, 1960–61, the Leafs had all manner of individual triumphs, forty-eight goals for Mahovlich, a Vezina Trophy for Bower, First Team All-Star selections for both, the Calder for Keon, the Lady Byng for Kelly. But as a team, they ran out of steam in a contest with Montreal for first place—the Canadiens won by two points on the last night of the season—and went down in the Stanley Cup semi-finals to Detroit in five games.

The next year was different. No player racked up big individual numbers, only thirty-three goals for the Big M (only?), Bower fell fourteen goals short of winning the Vezina, and the All-Star selectors forgot both of their names. The Leafs again finished second to the Canadiens, but this time there was no exhausting fight for top spot. Montreal breezed in, thirteen points ahead of Toronto. All of this relatively low-key activity seemed to work to the Leafs' advantage. As Imlach later wrote of 1961–62, "That year, we really were ready for the playoffs."

The Leafs met the Rangers in the semi-finals, a series that turned on a Red Kelly goal in the fifth game. The teams split the first four, and the fifth had gone into a second overtime period tied at one goal apiece. Mahovlich fired a shot at the New York net. Gump Worsley in goal made the save, but lost sight of the puck. He flopped on his back. The puck, though Worsley couldn't see it, lay under his head. Worsley raised up. That left the puck unprotected. Kelly spotted it first. He nudged it into the net. Worsley says today it was the most heartbreaking goal anyone ever scored on him in his twenty-one NHL seasons. Leafs popped seven past him in game six.

In the final, it was the Leafs versus the Black Hawks, who had upset

Montreal in the other semi-final. Chicago had plenty of tough, hard-hitting characters—Pierre Pilote, Moose Vasko, Dollard St. Laurent—but on offence it was essentially a two-man operation. The two were Stan Mikita and Bobby Hull. Between them, they had a hand in scoring or setting up 159 of the 217 goals Chicago got during the season. Imlach's scheme to muffle the big guns was to match Keon's line against Mikita's, and to make Ron Stewart Hull's personal escort. Stewart was one of hockey's great skaters, effortless and relentless, even if he was playing the series with ribs cracked in a car accident. This scheme, so Imlach's reasoning went, would leave Toronto's Kelly–Nevin–Mahovlich line on the ice with Chicago's dregs and therefore free to frolic.

The Leafs won the first two games in Toronto, 4–1 and 3–2. In Chicago for game three, the Hawks prevailed on muscle, 3–0, which brought up game four and an incident that everybody interpreted as curtains for the Leafs. Halfway through the first period, Hull whapped one of his faster-than-a-speeding-bullet-and-twice-as-fatal slapshots. Bower made like Rubber Man to stop the puck, legs spread in the splits, stick hand flapping far to one side, glove hand reaching, reaching to the far side. The save was successful, but, sorry, we lost the left leg. Bower pulled the hamstring muscle in that limb and was gone for the rest of the series. Don Simmons came in to play goal. This was Don Simmons who had been down in Rochester most of the season and had played in only nine Leaf games. This was Don Simmons who proceeded to look a trifle rattled in relief of Bower against the Black Hawks. Chicago won 4–1 and tied the series.

Simmons' real moment of truth still lay ahead. It came in the second period of game five in Toronto. Hawks were ahead 3–2, and Pierre Pilote broke in alone on Simmons on his way to a goal that would surely crush the Leafs. But Simmons looked Pilote in the eye—looked truth, fate and destiny in the eye too—and produced a brilliant save. The rest of the Leafs, buoyed and exhilarated, raced away to an 8–4 win.

Back to Chicago for game six. The hockey was tense and tight, but Toronto had a huge advantage in goal opportunities, with twenty-seven shots in the first two periods to Chicago's twelve. The trouble was that the marvellous Black Hawk goalie, Glenn Hall, let nothing past him.

Fortunately, neither did Simmons. The score stayed nil-nil until close to the mid-way mark of the third period. That's when Dick Duff fumbled the puck in the Leaf end. Murray Balfour jumped on it for Chicago. He passed to Bobby Hull. Ron Stewart was nowhere in sight, and Hull whipped his shot past Simmons.

The crowd in the Chicago Stadium went bananas. The crowd in the Chicago Stadium was always going bananas. This time they managed to stretch it out for almost fifteen minutes, tossing stuff on the ice — programs, paper cups, other people's hats, anything that came to hand, eggs, beer cartons, hotdogs, enough for a small banquet. In the time it took the attendants to clean the ice, the Hawks cooled out, the Leafs cranked up. Ninety-five seconds after play started again, it was a goal for Kelly's line, the line that was free to frolic. Bob Nevin got it on a pass from the Big M. Tie game. There was no delay for people going bananas and tossing small banquets on the ice.

It took four more minutes of play. It took a terrific ice-long rush by Tim Horton, stickhandling, passing off, receiving the puck back, another stickhandle, another pass. Horton's last pass was to Dick Duff, still aching over his earlier goof, looking to redeem himself. Duff took the Horton pass, shot at the Hawk net — and scored.

The goal stood up as the winner, and Toronto had its first Stanley Cup since 1951.

IN THE OFF-SEASON AFTER THE STANLEY CUP, IMLACH unloaded Bert Olmstead by leaving him unprotected in the annual draft. "One of the toughest things I had to do," Imlach said. Olmstead was getting long in the tooth, thirty-six, but he'd been perhaps the most effective forward in the playoff series against Chicago, a thrashing player, all elbows and guts, dominant in the offensive corners, a creative disturbance in front of the other team's net. Still, Imlach decided Olmstead had to go.

This was to become a pattern with Imlach, trading or selling or releasing a diligent player, then shaking his head over the sorrow of it all. Nevin and Duff were traded in the 1963–64 season — "very tough," Imlach said — and Stewart and Mahovlich a little later. Did these cuts among the core group make sense? Were they necessary? Billy Harris, for one, didn't think so. Of course Harris was another who got the Imlach chop. We'll come shortly to Harris' view of Imlach's moves and to the consequences of those moves

In the meantime, the Leafs cleaned up in the 1962–63 season. Mahovlich scored thirty-six goals and was a First Team All-Star. Carl Brewer made the First All-Stars too. Kent Douglas, a twenty-six-year-old rookie defenceman whom Imlach picked up from his old Springfield club, won the Calder. Keon got his second-straight Lady Byng. And the Leafs, as a team, on the wings of a superb ten-game unbeaten streak (seven wins, three ties) in the last month of the season, finished in first place, a point ahead of the Black Hawks.

The great Leaf team of 1947–48 lost only one game in that season's playoffs. The 1962–63 team was almost up to this standard. It lost two playoff games, one in the semi-final to Montreal, the other in the final to Detroit. Against the Canadiens, the Leafs scored fourteen goals in the five games, and allowed Montreal just six, shutting them out in two games including the 5–0 finale.

That's fairly dominating hockey, and Dick Duff made sure things continued in the same vein against Detroit when he scored two goals in the first sixty-eight seconds of the first period of the first game. Mahovlich got hurt in the second game, but his replacement, Eddie Litzenberger, a rangy guy with a swell scoring touch whom Imlach had bought from the Red Wings a year earlier, played like a star, which is what he was named at the end of the night, one of the game's three stars. Detroit won the third game. Dave Keon scored the winning goal in the fourth. And in the fifth, it was again Keon. The score ended 3–1 for Toronto, and Keon got the first and third goals. Both came with the Leafs short-handed.

The middle goal in the game, number two, the winner, the one that brought the Leafs their second consecutive Stanley Cup, was an Eddie Shack production. But he wasn't bragging about it. The play started when Kent Douglas drilled a shot on the Red Wing net from the point. The puck hit Detroit defenceman Doug Barkley and bounced in Shack's direction.

"I was trying to get the hell out of the way," Shack said later. "But it hit my stick and went in."

It was that kind of wonderfully serendipitous season.

ON JANUARY 18 OF THE FOLLOWING SEASON, 1963–64, A Saturday night at the Gardens, the Boston Bruins shot nine pucks past Don Simmons in two and a half periods. Simmons was playing goal in place of Bower, who had an injured catching hand. "We want ten," the Gardens crowd chanted. Keon, Armstrong and Harris went over the boards for the Leafs. Boston scored again. "We want eleven," the crowd chanted. The mood in the building wasn't ugly. Giddy was more like it, bemused. Boston scored again. Before the crowd could chant for a dozen, the game ended, 11–0 in favour of the Bruins.

The next afternoon in Chicago, Imlach summoned the players to his hotel suite, where he announced that a goalie named Al Millar was flying in from the Leaf farm team in Victoria to replace Simmons in the game against the Black Hawks that night. The phone rang in the hotel suite. Imlach answered and learned that bad weather wouldn't let Millar's plane land in Chicago. It was headed for Des Moines. Imlach cursed. Simmons faced the Black Hawks and shut them out. Leafs won 2–0.

Talk about a season fading in and out of sync, that was 1963–64 for Toronto. Mahovlich had a relative downer of a year, twenty-six goals. Red Kelly looked tired, eleven goals. Kelly had a reason for his fatigue; the previous year, he'd been elected to Parliament (Lib., York West) and he commuted between the Gardens and Ottawa. Kent Douglas and Eddie Litzenberger slumped sufficiently that Imlach sent them to the minors. And so it went.

But the two guys whom Imlach hit on for the blame in this disappointing season were Bob Nevin and Dick Duff. By February, each had a crummy seven goals. Imlach didn't wait for them to come around to their proven form. He traded Nevin, Duff and three minor-leaguers to the Rangers for Andy Bathgate and Don McKenney. Bathgate was the marquee player in the trade, a high scorer, a sometime All-Star right-winger. He played sound hockey in the fifteen games left on the Leaf schedule (three goals, fifteen assists). McKenney did too (nine goals).

But for the other Leafs, the regulars, it was the shock of seeing two front-line players shuffled out of town, two friends, that had the most impact. So, operating on fear (of also being traded) and loathing (of Imlach), the players raised their games, and Toronto finished in third place, behind Chicago and Montreal.

It was more of the same in the playoffs, more up and down, more playing out of desperation. In the semi-final against Montreal, the Leafs were never ahead in the series until the seventh game. That's when Keon took personal charge and scored all three goals in a 3–1 win. In the final, with Detroit as the opposition, Toronto was again in a constant catch-up position, down two games to one, down three games to two.

Game six at the Olympia turned into a stunner of a contest. The Red Wings were ahead 3–2 in the second period. Billy Harris got on to the ice for the first time all night. He was replacing Don McKenney on the Keon line. McKenney had torn his knee ligaments in the fifth game and was gone for the rest of the series. Harris streaked alone and unchecked towards Terry Sawchuk in the Detroit goal. He hollered at Keon for a pass. Keon delivered and Harris scored. Tie game.

The Red Wings launched a period-long attack on the Toronto net in the third. Bower kept robbing them of apparently certain goals. Bob Baun took a shot from Alex Delvecchio in the right ankle. He limped off the ice. In the dressing room, the Leaf doctor, Jim Murray, suspected a hairline fracture of the fibula. Baun begged the doc to freeze the foot. A doctor from Chicago named Bill Stromberg, a visiting Leaf pal, administered the needle. The game went into overtime. Early in the period, Baun, after a pass from George Armstrong, fired at the Detroit net from the point. The puck hit Red Wing defenceman Bill Gadsby and bounced past Sawchuk.

The series was all even.

For the seventh game at the Gardens, Baun's ankle, which was indeed fractured, was given the freezing treatment. So were Carl Brewer's ribs (they were separated), George Armstrong's shoulder (also separated) and Red Kelly's knee (twisted ligaments). The Toronto players who weren't anaesthetized were plain exhausted. But at 3:04 of the first period, Andy Bathgate tore in from centre and scored on Sawchuk. Bathgate had 349 goals in his NHL career. That one, on April 25, 1964, was the goal he'd most care to keep. It was the one that won the Stanley Cup. The game stayed 1–0 until mid-way through the third period, when Toronto scored three more times. Detroit was shut out. It was Toronto 4, Red Wings 0.

Kelly got one of the three late goals. After the game, Red, in agony with the twisted ligaments in his knee, went from the shower to an ambulance to the hospital. The Leafs had won a third consecutive Stanley Cup, a magnificent achievement, but there was a feeling that this team might be seriously fraying around the edges.

11

Billy Harris

ERE WAS LITTLE BILLY HARRIS IN THE WINTER of 1947, eleven years old and hugging to himself this secret and terrible fear. School was going great, in grade six at Withrow Public School in Billy's Broadview–Danforth neighbourhood. Hockey was going great too, playing till the frigid dusk on the outdoor rink in Riverdale Park, tuning into Foster Hewitt every Saturday night, living and dying on the wins and losses of the Maple Leafs. But there was this worry in Billy's life over the letters. Billy had written a lot of letters that winter, one to each Leaf player. He crafted the letters in his careful, erect, grade-six handwriting, respectfully asking each Leaf to send him a signed hockey card, telling each that he alone was eleven-year-old Billy's most favourite player. That was the part Billy came to agonize over, the little white lies about the identity of his favourite player.

"I kept imagining there'd be a day when all the players would open their mail in the dressing room at the same time," Harris explained one late-summer afternoon in 1993. "I could just picture them looking over one another's shoulders. 'Well, wait, this boy Harris says I'm his favourite player. How could you be his favourite?' Funny the irrational things you think of as a kid, but I thought the players'd catch on to what I was up to, and I'd be in disgrace."

The players didn't catch on, not as far as Harris knows anyway. Some of them sent him cards, Max Bentley, Bill Ezinicki, Howie Meeker. Harris still has the cards. Where the Leafs are concerned, he's a packrat. Hockey cards, autographs, photographs (hundreds of which he snapped himself during his ten seasons on the team)—he saves everything. Memories, he saves them too, filed and indexed.

Syl Apps' speech is one. It came in the spring of 1948 at the banquet that celebrated the end of the season for Harris' first team in organized hockey, the Riverdale Garage Pee Wees of the Toronto Hockey League. There they were, fifteen whooping twelve-year-olds in their best shirts and only ties, four men from the car dealership that sponsored the team, Riverdale Garage, all gathered for a humble dinner in the small, musty dining room of an ancient hotel on the Danforth, and the speaker on this night was nobody less than the captain of the greatest team in the world! Such a thing seems so amazing today, so dated and old-fashioned. Would Wayne Gretzky come down from Beverly Hills to pass an evening with a bunch of prepubescent twerps in Hotel Fleabag? Don't even think about it. But Syl Apps turned out on a night in the spring of 1948 and forever fixed a set of values in Billy Harris' mind.

"Syl talked about dedication, loyalty, hard work, pride," Harris remembered almost a half-century later. "Coming from him, what he said really sunk in. He was such an impressive man. Tall and good-looking, you know, and he'd served in the Second War like my dad did. He made a tremendous impression on me. I wanted to be just like Syl Apps."

Harris was talking over a large Molson's draft in Shakey's Bar & Grill in the west end of Toronto. Shakey's is the kind of place that isn't supposed to exist outside of TV sitcoms, unpretentious, service with a wise-crack thrown in for free, where everybody knows Billy Harris' name. The proprietor was another old Leaf forward, Mike Walton. He took his nickname from his father, Shakey, Sr., and he scored 201 goals in a dozen NHL seasons.

Harris has silver hair. He has a long face marked by interesting lines, and he has a manner that suggests he's a thoughtful guy, adept at evaluating life's jolts and vicissitudes. He has endured more than his own share of sobering events. His dad went overseas as the rear gunner in a Lancaster bomber and got shot out of the sky over Germany on August 13, 1944. And a few years ago, Harris lost his wife to cancer. Such heartbreaks appear to have laid a steadying hand on him. Steady but not solemn. Billy Harris laughs a lot.

And it was clear at Shakey's that Maple Leaf blue still runs thick in Harris' veins.

Small wonder. Harris was streamed into the Leaf organization when he was thirteen years old. Staff Smythe was putting together a system of feeder teams for the Marlboro Junior As, and he converted the Riverdale Garage Pee Wees, a championship club in its age group, into the Marlie Minor Bantams. Curious how life works. Harris got taken up and moved along Staff Smythe's chain, Marlie Bantams, Weston Dukes Junior Bs, the Marlie Junior A team that won the 1955 Memorial Cup, and ultimately, in 1955–56, the show itself, the Maple Leafs. Harris, the kid player, and Smythe, the burgeoning executive, locked together.

"I know I was kind of special to Stafford," Harris explained. "Seventeen years I played under him. That meant something to both of us, and Stafford knew I didn't have a father. Maybe for that reason he was extra good to me."

Whatever specialness Staff felt for Harris entered crucially into Harris' career two weeks after Punch Imlach took over the Leaf coaching job in late November 1958.

"I gotta do something about this team," Imlach said to Staff. "Gotta move some people. One trade for sure is Billy Harris to the Rangers. I got it all lined up."

"Trade Billy Harris!?" Staff went ballistic. "You don't trade Billy Harris! Every team he's played on for me, we've won championships. Harris stays."

"It was difficult playing seven years for Imlach," Harris said at Shakey's, "knowing he didn't want me on the team."

What was it in Harris that turned Imlach off?

Maybe Harris' hockey style. "Imlach didn't think I shot enough,"

Harris said. "I never had much confidence in my shot. Used it as a last resort if I couldn't find a teammate in a better scoring position. The thing was I got as big a thrill out of setting up a goal as scoring one." (Harris led the Leafs in assists with 28 the season before Imlach arrived, and in his entire Leaf career, he had 181 assists and 106 goals.)

Or maybe Imlach wasn't hot on Harris' personal style. Harris was working on a B.A. at the University of Toronto, mainly through correspondence courses (he got the B.A.), and later he was an early wearer of a hockey helmet. An intellectual and a sissy? For all Imlach knew, Harris might be a quiche eater.

"On the other hand, Imlach could have been one step ahead of me and everybody else," Harris said, thinking back. "He didn't play me often, so I felt motivated to play better whenever I got on the ice. Maybe that's what Imlach was counting on. Once when Keon was hurt, I played five games and scored seven goals. Three were game winners. And in the Stanley Cup final against Detroit in 1964, I played on a line with Keon, and we scored two goals in the sixth game, two more in the seventh."

Harris shrugged. "Maybe Imlach knew what he was doing with me."

THE MOST FAMOUS OPINION ON IMLACH'S COACHING tenure with the Leafs is Bob Baun's.

"The surprise isn't that we won four Stanley Cups in ten years," Baun has said in a zillion after-dinner speeches. "The surprise is that we didn't win ten."

"Bobby could be right," Billy Harris said at Shakey's. "Of course, if Imlach hadn't been coach, we might not have won four."

That's Harris. Mr. Balance. On the one hand, this, on the other hand, that. But don't mistake him as being wishy-washy. He's worked out his bottom line on Punch Imlach, and it's this:

"I don't think Imlach was the hockey genius he considered himself to be. Imlach was lucky. He gambled. He gambled on older players, gambled that Red Kelly could play centre, gambled on a lot of things. He was a gambler in hockey, and he won. But that doesn't make him a genius."

In Harris' mind, where Imlach blew his chances at the genius category—this was more in general-managing than in coaching—lay in having too much of an itchy finger for trades. Harris can cite many Imlach deals, made to shake up the team or to replace a kid with a veteran, that didn't stand the test of history. Jim Pappin for Pierre Pilote in 1968, for example. Pilote played one year in Toronto and retired. Pappin lasted another ten NHL seasons and finished his career with 278 goals.

"I think the chance for the Leafs to establish a dynasty," Harris said, "ended in February 1964. That's when Imlach moved Dick Duff and Bob Nevin to the Rangers for Andy Bathgate and Don McKenney. Sure, we won a Stanley Cup that year, but who's to say we wouldn't have won that one and many more with Duff and Nevin? You could debate that forever, but the fact is Bathgate and McKenney were gone from the Leafs within two years."

Duff and Nevin, meanwhile, younger guys, rolled on. Duff played on four Stanley Cup teams for the Canadiens, and Nevin became a Ranger foundation stone, ten years with the team, its captain, a scorer of 307 goals in eighteen NHL seasons.

"Imlach was strange," Harris said. "He acted like one of the guys when he took over the team, one of us. But as success came, he got abrasive with the players. After we won the first Stanley Cup, he got really abrasive. He didn't know how to communicate with certain players. He used to make Carl Brewer terribly upset. And Frank, well, Imlach got it all wrong with Frank."

ON AND OFF THE ICE, FRANK MAHOVLICH LOOKED LIKE the male lead in a European movie about doomed love. His face was tragic and beautiful and innocent. He had the dark eyes, shy smile, the dimples. How deceiving appearances can be. Mahovlich was in fact a nice, simple, straightforward guy from the mining country around Timmins. Well, not so straightforward. He was a world-class worrier, and that brought him genuine grief. Twice during his Leaf years, acute depression put Mahovlich in the hospital.

Many Toronto fans didn't understand the Big M, the ones who jeered him almost as meanly as an earlier generation had jeered Gordie Drillon. It was Mahovlich's skating style that bugged these people. They mistook his grace for lack of hustle. Mahovlich may have looked lazy out there, but he got places faster than most Leafs, swept into the other team's zone, did wonderful things with the puck. The fans thought he should appear to be sweating more. But Mahovlich was sweating plenty, physically and psychologically.

"Frank used to think all 15,000 people in the Gardens had come out just to see him play," Billy Harris said at Shakey's. "He put terrible pressure on himself. He couldn't understand why they'd boo him for two periods and give him a standing ovation in the third. A sensitive, caring coach would have helped him deal with that."

"Sensitive" and "caring" weren't adjectives that ever turned up on Punch Imlach's résumé.

"Imlach had the military attitude that the team was a regiment," Harris went on. "All twenty of us should be treated alike. If we lost games on Saturday and Sunday nights, then everybody practised two hours on Monday. It didn't matter whether Frank had been the first star both nights. He had to practise hard too. Everybody got the same treatment, everybody got yelled at. That was a big mistake on Imlach's part. There have to be different rules for different athletes, shout at the ones who need a push to play well, be considerate of the ones who live in more of a shell, the way Frank did."

Imlach's word for the Big M, especially near the end of Mahovlich's time with Toronto, was "inconsistent." On paper, there may be a small case for this view. Mahovlich's goal totals during his eleven Leaf seasons are 20, 22, 18, 48, 33, 36, 26, 23, 32, 18, 19. A numerical roller-coaster all right, but doesn't hockey history tell us that a coach with a prolific scorer on his hands (as Mahovlich established with the monster 48 in 1960–61) is wise to nurture and coddle the prodigy? That was what Glen Sather was to do years later with Wayne Gretzky.

"Not Punch," Billy Harris said. "The way he handled Frank, he only got about 50 percent of Frank's talent out of him."

A supplementary question: isn't it indicative of something lacking in the Imlach approach that in the season after Punch unloaded Mahovlich in March 1968—Mahovlich, Garry Unger and Pete Stemkowski to Detroit for Paul Henderson, Norm Ullman and Floyd Smith—the Big M whacked in forty-nine goals for the Red Wings? Even better, how about Mahovlich's record when he moved to the Montreal Canadiens? Forty-six goals in one season and a large role in winning two Stanley Cups for the Canadiens.

"In Montreal," Harris explained over his beer, "Sam Pollock used to have Frank in for a talk every couple of weeks. Pollock was the general manager, the head man. He collected art. So did Frank. Pollock talked to Frank about their collections. Frank got the idea Pollock cared about him, that he wanted Frank to be part of the organization. That made all the difference."

HERE WAS A LUNCHEON OF MINI-HISTORIC PROPORTIONS. The time was a noonhour in the winter of 1960. The place was the dining room of the Board of Trade Club in downtown Toronto. The lunchers were four young Leafs and two marginally older lawyers. Harris sat around the table that noonhour, Bob Pulford, Carl Brewer and Bob Baun. The lawyers—they picked up the tab—were a pair of juniors from the firm of Blaney, Pasternak, Luck and Smela. Their names were Bob Watson and—an ambitious young man, sharp dresser, the loudest guy in the room—Alan Eagleson. Out of the luncheon meeting, the six men became involved in an investment club called the Blue and White Investment Group. Everybody kicked in a thousand bucks to start, plus fifty more per month, and, principally under Eagleson's guidance, the money went into first and second mortgages.

"We made money," Harris said at Shakey's. "I have to hand it to Eagleson, he did very well by all of us."

Eagleson had been hanging out with the younger Leafs for a few years, barbecues in one another's backyards, a few laughs, turn a little profit on the side. Pulford served as Eagleson's entrée into the hockey circles. The two had lived near each other as teenagers in the west end of Toronto and had played lacrosse in the same leagues.

"Pulford grew up believing in God and Eagleson," Harris said. "I'm not sure in which order."

When Eagleson got to law school—University of Toronto, Class of '57—he began checking over Pulford's Maple Leaf contracts, pointing out which clauses Eagleson regarded as dodgy, corresponding with NHL president Clarence Campbell. That was the modest but nervy start from which Eagleson founded the National Hockey League Players' Association (R. Alan Eagleson, Executive Director), made himself the personal agent for a huge percentage of NHLPA members, became Hockey Canada's chief negotiator for international tournaments, and emerged as the single most powerful force in all of hockey from the late 1960s to the late 1980s. He also emerged as a very rich man.

On a smaller, more local front, in Toronto in the early 1960s, Eagleson's original association with the handful of younger Leafs, as pal and as agent (though never as Billy Harris' rep), brought him on a collision course with Punch Imlach. Imlach disliked Eagleson. He accused Eagleson of carrying on a "vendetta" against him. Vendetta? Eagleson thought it was called "negotiations." He was trying to earn a few extra bucks and better working conditions for Brewer, Mike Walton and the others. The haggling, which frequently descended to mean-spirited and public bickering, had an upsetting impact in the Leaf dressing room. Indeed, it tended to disrupt and flatten out the team, costing the Leafs the services of at least one star player, Carl Brewer, who, just twenty-eight years old, quit the NHL in 1967 to play for the National Team. This wasn't the stuff of civilized labour–management relations.

At the core of the trouble was the fact that Imlach regarded Eagleson as a "rebel." What an incredibly dim reading of Eagleson that was. Eagleson was as much a rebel as Margaret Thatcher, about whom he once said, "She's my kind of operator." Marvin Miller, the man who gave leadership to the Major League Baseball Players' Association, came out of the United Steelworkers of America. Eagleson came out of the Progressive Conservative Party of Canada; he sat as the Tory MPP for the Ontario riding of Lakeshore from 1963 to 1967, the very years when he was forging the basis of the players' union. Later, he bought a house in expensive Rosedale, joined the exclusive Toronto Lawn Tennis Club, took his winters in Palm Beach. This was a "rebel"? No, this was an astute lawyer–businessman who spotted a vacuum—the lack of representation for players in their hockey dealings—and rushed to fill it. Punch Imlach didn't recognize that his adversary was a man with politics and beliefs not unlike his own.

Even in personality, background and style, Eagleson and Imlach were two of a kind. Both grew up in lower-middle-class Toronto. Both fed off a driving ambition. "Both were egotistical," Billy Harris added. "And both had the same vocabulary." (This last refers to the heavy reliance Eagleson and Imlach put on variations of the f-word in routine conversation.) Almost two peas in a pod, and yet their dealings through the 1960s, and again in the early 1980s when Imlach had another brief go-round as Leaf general manager, were marked by *Sturm und Drang*. Maybe that was because they shared one other quality—an apparently irresistible urge to confront.

As for Harris, he split from Eagleson long before it became fashionable to condemn Eagleson, long before the early 1990s when a Massachusetts grand jury, the FBI, the RCMP, Hockey Canada, and the Law Society of Upper Canada began investigating Eagleson's two decades of hockey dealings, before the Massachusetts grand jury laid thirty-two charges of racketeering against Eagleson in March 1994.

"We had a falling out in 1967," Harris explained, keeping forever mum on the details of the dispute. "Eagleson is brilliant, he's a borderline genius, but I had trouble with some of his business practices. And with Al, you're either on his side or you aren't. I opted to be not on his side."

AT THE END OF THE 1964–65 SEASON, IMLACH PERSUADED Staff Smythe there was no need to be permanently ridiculous about this protective thing Staff had for Billy Harris. Imlach got Smythe's okay on a trade: Harris and Andy Bathgate (who'd served Imlach's brief purpose) and a couple of others to Detroit for Marcel Pronovost and some odds and ends.

Harris played four more years of hockey, in Detroit, Oakland and Pittsburgh. He turned to coaching and kept his family (wife, daughter, twin sons, another daughter) on the move to far-flung outposts. Harris coached in Sweden, Ottawa, Toronto (two years with the Toros of the

WHA) and Italy. He took time out to lecture in Sports Administration at Laurentian University in Sudbury, then back to coaching in Edmonton (two years as Glen Sather's assistant with the Gretzky-era Oilers) and Sudbury again, where he coached the Wolves of the senior league.

Sounds hectic? Harris loved it. He's always had an antsy streak, a love of travel, keen to check out wherever his frequent-flyer points will take him. When he was a bachelor Leaf, in the summer of 1960, between hockey seasons, he and three teammates, Pulford, Nevin and Gary Aldcorn, knocked through Europe for fifteen weeks. Billy detoured to the graveyard in the small Belgian village of Hotten. That's where his dad is buried. And in the spring of 1993, single again, a widower, his kids out on their own, Harris kicked around the Middle East. His son Billy, Jr., was teaching school in Bahrain. Harris, Sr., suited up for the Bahrain team in a hockey tournament in Dubai.

"I played on a line with my son," Harris said at Shakey's. "It wasn't exactly like Gordie Howe playing with Mark and Marty. But we had some fun."

Championship game: Dubai 7, Bahrain 5.

HARRIS LIVES ALONE IN AN APARTMENT IN THE WEST end. He belongs to the Richview Public Library. He plays in twenty-five NHL old-timers golf tournaments in the summer, in about the same number of old-timers hockey games in the winter. He's been one of the point men in organizing the lawsuit brought by former NHL players against the league, claiming millions in misappropriation of monies belonging to the players' pension fund. He works from a desk in Maple Leaf Gardens, organizing events for the Maple Leaf old-timers. He likes his life.

"Every day seems like Friday," he says.

Eventually in any conversation with Billy Harris, talk drifts around to a book he wrote in 1989. He's proud of the book. It's about his years with the Leafs. A publisher wanted him to use a ghostwriter—Frank Orr, the publisher said, or Jim Proudfoot. Nothing against Orr or Proudfoot, Harris answered, but he insisted on writing every word himself. It turned out to be a charming, honest, intelligent book—in his own words, illustrated with his own photographs. The book's title says almost everything about the sort of book it is, about how Harris looks back on his Toronto years, about how he has saved his Maple Leaf memories, filed and indexed them and, no matter what Punch had to say about it, cherished them.

The book is called *The Glory Years.*

12

Under New Management

THE FIRST THING TO GO WAS THE PORTRAIT of the Queen at the north end of the Gardens, a huge head-and-shoulders shot. Carpenters pried it off the wall. Then they dismantled the long balcony underneath the portrait. The bands of the 48th Highlanders, the Grenadier Guards and other military regiments used to play martial melodies and show tunes from the balcony before and after games and between periods. Conn Smythe, the monarchist and militarist, had installed the bandstand and the portrait of Elizabeth II— and of George VI before her. Now they were gone. The carpenters built rows and rows of seats in the empty spaces.

This was in late 1961 and 1962, after Conn Smythe sold his controlling interest in the Gardens to the trio of his son Staff, Harold Ballard and John Bassett. With the new owners, the word of the moment was profits. Staff, Ballard and Bassett set out to maximize them in a big way. They raised the price of tickets. Made season-ticket subscribers take seats to exhibition games. Booked in rock concerts and other events to fill the Gardens on nights the place would otherwise remain dark. They sold advertising space on the arena's formerly pristine walls. Ads for

GM and Ford at each end of the rink, Schick Razor promos pasted on the bottom of the seats, Dominion Stores on the Zamboni.

And they installed new seats. There were all kinds of ways to do that. Trim the width of the aisles and add two seats per row. Make the existing seats narrower. Tear down the bandstand, put in fifteen new rows. Tradition? Get outta here. Elizabeth must go.

"What the hell position can a queen play?" Harold Ballard asked.

CONN SMYTHE'S NOTION, WHEN HE BUILT THE GARDENS in 1931, was that if he enticed the elite, the common folk would follow. So he made the seats closest to the ice, the ones he coloured red, into the class of the house. He gave the section svelte usherettes instead of plain ushers, exclusive entrances, cushioned seats, and an atmosphere of instant distinction. Smythe had it figured correctly: Toronto's elite rushed for season's subscriptions to the reds, and the *hoi polloi* tripped after them into the cheaper seats, into the blues, greens and greys.

By definition, given the nature of Toronto's Establishment in the 1930s and '40s, it was essentially a Wasp bunch who took a lock on the choice reds. Their names were familiar around town: Eaton (department stores), Taylor (holding companies, racehorses, beer), Thomson (newspapers), Laidlaw (lumber), Aird (banking and law), Burns (stockbroking), Parsons (bicycles, as in CCM), Duguid (booze, as in Gooderham & Worts). By the 1950s, people with zeds in their names, with names that ended in vowels, were beginning to make it onto the reds' subscription lists, usually for seats in the less-prized rows at either end: Lombardi (*paisano* supermarkets, multicultural communications), Shopsowitz (hotdogs), Ungerman (chickens, boxers), Wayne (laughs, as in Wayne & Shuster). But no matter what the ethnic origin of the reds subscribers, they understood that they had to meet certain lofty standards of decorum and dress, had to set the tone of dignity for the rest of the patrons. Conn Smythe expected it.

Actually, Conn Smythe enforced it. Take, for example, dress. "[Gardens subscribers] are by far the best turned-out of all hockey crowds," the erudite *New Yorker* sports specialist Herbert Warren Wind once wrote. "The man who wears a chesterfield and the lady who wears a mink coat are not overdressed." That measure of style was no accident. Smythe's box-office manager, Jack Hoult (he was married to Conn's daughter Miriam), used to despatch a couple of his men through the reds on any winter Saturday night checking for jackets, ties, frocks (no slacks on the ladies). If somebody's box didn't come up to sartorial scratch, if a subscriber had given his tickets to the family maid whose boyfriend had showed up in a windbreaker, the Gardens fired a letter, often over Conn's signature, to the seat holder of record, pointing out his obligation to the reds. The maid's boyfriend in the windbreaker didn't show up twice.

Which is not to say that the red section of Smythe's reign was a stuffy place to watch hockey. People who qualified as "characters" sat in the reds. Charlie Hemstead was one. Hemstead was in hotels and racehorses. His two reds were at the end of the Leaf bench, and during a lull in a game against Detroit in 1952, the Red Wings leading the Leafs 2–1, Hemstead leaned over to Max Bentley and promised him the gift of a horse if Bentley scored a goal on his next shift. Max scored. "You got the horse!" Hemstead hollered. Later that evening, another reds subscriber, George McCullagh (newspapers—he owned the *Globe and Mail*), heard of Hemstead's generosity. "If Charlie Hemstead can give you a horse," McCullagh said to Bentley, "I can give you a better one." Max ran his two horses on the Western Canada circuit until he lost both in claiming races.

The reds, with their close proximity to the ice and the players, also put their subscribers on more intimate terms with the hockey action. Particularly in the days before Conn Smythe hemmed in the ice with Heraculite glass panels—that happened just after the Second World War—flying pucks arrived in the reds faster, oftener and with more painful results than in other sections of the Gardens. Two lady subscribers on the rails, Mrs. Alan McFee and Mrs. John Stark, used to bring their own plastic faceguards to every game. Still, guards, glass and all, reds regulars saw blood spilled—their own. Probably the most spectacular disaster struck in December 1948 when Rocket Richard, checked ferociously by Vic Lynn and Bill Juzda, cartwheeled into a glass panel at the south end, one skate flying high and shattering the glass into a million pieces. Enough of the million rained on south-end subscribers to send five of them to St. Michael's Hospital for stitches. One of the five was Lloyd Percival, Canada's guru of fitness. We may be confident that Percival and the other four reds persons, waiting in St. Mike's emergency, were immaculately attired.

That thirty-year era of immaculate attire; of an advertisement-free, sleekly maintained Gardens; of a quieter, gentler hockey atmosphere, was doomed to vanish by the early 1960s. "The studiously correct, Ascot-like deportment of Leaf fans," Herbert Warren Wind wrote in the *New Yorker*, "reflects the personality of one man, Conn Smythe." Thus, when Conn sold to Staff, Ballard and Bassett, the change in management meant a drastic alteration in physical style around the Gardens. It meant that seats were installed where the monarch hung. It meant fractious whoops from an electric organ rather than stirring melodies from a full military band. It meant a collapse of the dress code. And it meant an emphasis on turning a bigger buck at the cost of tradition and all the Conn Smythe conventions of old.

CONN CLAIMED IN LATER YEARS THAT HE THOUGHT HE was selling to Staff alone, that he was maintaining a family dynasty, transferring the Gardens from himself to Staff, who would eventually pass it on to Staff's son Tom. That may be hard to swallow. Conn knew that Staff hadn't the money himself, or the collateral to raise the bucks, that would cover the $2-million Gardens price. And he was aware of the long and tight association that Staff had with Harold Ballard, first at the Marlboro Juniors, then in the Leaf offices. Conn had less reason to suspect that Bassett, who wasn't such a Staff pal, would be in on the purchase. Still, Bassett was a guy with fingers in lots of pies — the *Telegram*, the television station CFTO, the Tory party, the Toronto Argo football team — an energetic busybody of a man, a member of the Silver Seven, someone who thrived on the high-profile life. Perhaps Conn should have guessed that Bassett would link with the other two in a Gardens deal.

At the time, in late autumn of 1961, when Conn, finally worn down by Staff's pestering about the state of Maple Leaf hockey, was moved to challenge his son, "If you think you're so smart, why don't you buy my stock?," he owned in the neighbourhood of 50,000 Gardens shares.

There were about 147,000 total shares outstanding. Conn agreed with his son to sell him 45,000 shares at forty dollars per share, which was about six dollars more than market value. Staff hurried to Ballard with the news.

In one very busy day, Ballard arranged a $2-million loan from the Bank of Nova Scotia, putting up as security the Gardens stock that was about to be purchased. Then—still the same day—Ballard and Staff popped around to Bassett's office in the Telegram Building at the corner of Bay and Melinda streets and cut him in on the deal. A third, a third, a third. A key clause in the agreement that the three men worked out among themselves said that if one partner died or wished to sell his shares, the other two got first crack at purchasing them. Ten years later, that clause would come into play in a crucial way.

It's not clear when Staff Smythe told his father that he wasn't alone in the Gardens purchase. In his memoirs, Conn said he negotiated with Staff for three days in mid-November 1961, nailing down particulars, and that a few days later, Staff unveiled the fact and identity of his purchasing partners. If this was the case, Conn probably had time to pull out of the agreement. But he didn't withdraw. Maybe he was tired of the hassle. Maybe he wanted to be alone with his horses and the Crippled Children.

Or there's another scenario. Conn's sale was announced at a press conference late in the morning of November 23, 1961. Before the conference got under way, someone arrived in the room with an early edition of the *Telegram*. It carried a front-page story about the sale. That struck everybody as a bit thick, one newspaper scooping the others before the official announcement was made. But the *Tely* story went even farther. It revealed that John Bassett, publisher of the *Telegram*, was one of the three Gardens purchasers. Rex McLeod, an excellent hockey writer for the *Globe and Mail*, swore he heard Conn, apparently grasping for the first time that Bassett was one of the new Gardens owners, say, "If I'd known that, there would have been no goddamn deal."

Well, too late, Conn.

Among them, Staff, Ballard and Bassett owned 42,000 Gardens shares before the purchase from Conn. Adding in Conn's 45,000 shares, now they held 87,000 shares, or about 60 percent of the Gardens stock, with each partner owning 20 percent. The new generation was in the driver's seat.

STAFF WAS ELECTED GARDENS PRESIDENT.

"We've had a lot of arguments about hockey around our house," Conn said in a mellow moment during the Gardens Christmas party on December 23 that year. "But my wife thoroughly approved of this deal. Stafford has had his hair brushed two times in a row, and that's something that never happened before he became president of Maple Leaf Gardens."

Bassett was named chairman of the board. He looked the part, six-feet-four, silvery-haired, handsome, a man who radiated good breeding, money and Wasp charisma.

Ballard's title was executive vice-president in charge of the Gardens. Staff directed the hockey operations. Ballard looked after everything else. He was the one who booted out the Queen, sold advertising, changed the reds to golds (oh, cheap metaphor), moved the reds up higher in the stands, and raised the price of both colours. And Ballard was the one who shoe-horned in the new seats. In 1961, the Gardens could accommodate 12,737 sitting-down customers. By 1969, the figure was up to 16,115. And many of the seats were two to three inches narrower than they'd once been.

The Hot Stove Lounge was another Ballard brainstorm. He tore out the row of shops along Church Street on the Gardens' east side and replaced them with a bar and restaurant. It was done up in guys' decor—cedar panelling, dim lighting, an ornamentation of 350 hockey sticks bearing in luminous tape the colours of the NHL teams. The menu was likewise hardy fare: Broiled Sirloin Black Hawk, Mixed Grill Canadiens, Chicken Stanley Cup with Face-off Potatoes. People paid good money for Hot Stove privileges, an initiation fee of a hundred dollars and annual dues of fifty, not to mention eight dollars for the Broiled Filet Rangers.

Ballard was especially canny at booking non-hockey events into the Gardens. Under Conn, the building had been a desultory host to ice shows, junior hockey, some boxing, weekly wrestling, an annual circus, the occasional political convention or religious extravaganza. Ballard, aggressively casting around to fill all the Gardens nights, capitalized on the new rage among young people for touring rock bands. Capitalizing was the operative verb. Ballard was so cagey—or was it unscrupulous?—that he outsmarted the Beatles.

This happened in August 1965. The Beatles were booked into the Gardens for one show. Ballard sold tickets for two shows, matinee and evening. The matinee was his little secret from Brian Epstein, the Beatles manager who had never been bested in a commercial deal—until now. When Epstein arrived in Toronto, he exploded at Ballard's duplicity. Ballard pointed out that if the Fab Four failed to play the matinee, 18,000 kids would riot. Epstein capitulated. Ballard wasn't finished. It was a hot and humid summer day. Ballard delayed each of the two shows by almost an hour, turned off the water fountains, jacked up the heat, hid the small cups in the concession booths. Eighteen thousand kids bought a lot of Coke. They could only get it in large cups.

In such ways, profits at the Gardens tripled from $300,000 in 1961 to $900,000 in 1964. In November 1965, when the stock price stood at $144 per share, the shares were split five for one. The price fell by only half.

UNDER THE NEW MANAGEMENT, THE GOLD AND RED SEATS were spared patrons in black leather and tattoos. Beyond that, the dress code among Gardens subscribers vanished. Part of the reason was the general passing of the era when Torontonians dressed up for a night on the town. Now they dressed down. Even scions of wealthy Toronto families were wearing jeans in the 1960s.

But there were two other connected explanations for the scruffier look in the Gardens' best seats. One was that, post–Conn Smythe, no employee policed the subscribers for jackets and ties. And, second, whom exactly would they police? Increasingly, prime season tickets were becoming the property of corporate subscribers, and just as increasingly, particularly after the NHL began to expand in 1967 and the diluted brand of hockey made many games less of a must-see event, tickets got passed on to corporate customers, to out-of-towners who didn't know or care about a Gardens tradition of elegance, and—most heinous of all—to scalpers.

Consider Harry Desmond. He was a tall, white-haired man whose habitual winter attire was a still-smart camel hair coat he had picked up at the Salvation Army. Harry lived hand to mouth as a freelance repairman and as a part-time Saturday-night scalper of hockey tickets. His post on hockey nights was in front of the Toronto Hydro Building on Carlton Street, west of the Gardens. Harry had two steady ticket suppliers. One was an executive at the Sun Life Assurance Company, and the other was Dick Beddoes, the *Globe* sportswriter and later sportscaster at CHCH-TV. Beddoes and the Sun Life guy had access to pairs of corporate season tickets, which they sold to Harry—Beddoes could watch games from the press box—and which Harry dealt at a small profit on the street. It didn't matter to Harry whether his purchasers were dressed like Sonny and Cher. He was in it for the money.

So it was that strange faces and strange costumes showed up in the golds and reds. Conn Smythe wept.

ON SEPTEMBER 5, 1965, HAROLD BALLARD BOUGHT A motorcycle for his older son, Bill. It cost $438.78. Ballard charged the amount to the Marlboro hockey club. He listed it under "hockey sticks." Just a little fiddle on the books. But it was one in a series of events that led, a few years later, to criminal charges, to one man's imprisonment, another man's death. It also led—remember that clause giving the survivor of the three partners first crack at the purchase of Gardens shares?—to Ballard's sole ownership of the Gardens and all the grief that that entailed.

13

1967

IN FEBRUARY 1966, THE WORLD HEAVYWEIGHT boxing champion Cassius Clay issued his famous pacifist manifesto. "I ain't got no quarrel with them Viet Cong," he said. He was speaking to the Illinois Boxing Commission, seeking its sanction for a proposed title defence against a leading challenger named Ernie Terrell. The commission had raised the issue of Clay's refusal to be drafted into the U.S. Army. Clay pointed out that he was a peace-loving devotee of the Black Muslims, an American sect that combined black nationalism with aspects of Islam. Clay said the army might send him into battle in Vietnam against the Viet Cong. He was fighting his induction in the courts. The Illinois Boxing Commission said, in effect, he was an uppity black draft dodger. It refused to approve the fight against Terrell. So did similarly self-righteous bodies in Pittsburgh, Louisville, Las Vegas, Miami, Lewiston (Maine), and Verdon (Quebec). The Ontario Minister of Labour, who controlled boxing in the province, said he didn't care for Clay's views on patriotism either, but he gave the fight his okay. Harold Ballard booked it into the Gardens.

By the time the fight found a home, Ernie Terrell had checked out of the picture. His replacement was the local Toronto favourite, George Chuvalo, a man with the build and finesse of a streetcar. Cassius Clay came to town with Cap'n Sam Saxon, Lana Shabazz and Stepin Fetchit. They were, respectively, the secular head of the Black Muslim mosque in Miami, a specialist in Black Muslim cuisine, and a former straight man for Shirley Temple. Chuvalo's temporary entourage included Greatest Crawford, Bundini Brown and Joe Louis. Greatest was a sparring partner. Brown was an erstwhile pal of Clay's whose field of expertise was the laying of hexes. And the role for Louis, the one-time great heavyweight champ, was to serve as Chuvalo's media consultant.

"Could I have an interview with either you or George?" a radio reporter asked Louis.

"Who's George?" Louis said.

The Toronto sports press went hysterical, and not a little racist, over Clay's appearance in the city. "All the disinfectant in the world will never make the Gardens clean again," Annis Stukus wrote in the *Telegram*. Milt Dunnell wrote in the *Toronto Daily Star*, "Anyone who buys a ticket will be making a contribution to the Black Muslims." And in the *Globe*, it was Dick Beddoes: "Now we are infested with the gladiators and their assorted leeches, avaricious characters looking to make a buck from the pain of two manipulated pugs." Beddoes showed up at ringside on fight night, March 29, 1966. He was the between-rounds radio commentator. It was a paying job.

In addition to Beddoes, 13,918 people filled the Gardens. Clay's brother, Rudolph Valentino Clay, sat in the first row ringside. Between the second and third rounds, Cassius leaned through the ropes to wave at Rudolph Valentino, who shouted, "Take your time and look pretty." Cassius did both. He was twenty-four years old, nearing the zenith of his fighting powers. He moved with the speed and agility of a man much lighter, of a welterweight. He threw punches in artistic flurries. He bobbed, weaved, danced, once held his hands in the air and invited Chuvalo to hammer punches at his body. Chuvalo couldn't touch him. But Chuvalo didn't look the fool. He looked brave and gallant. The fight lasted the distance. Clay won easily, and Chuvalo kept his honour intact. It had been a fascinating struggle. Clay went home to Chicago, changed his name to Muhammad Ali, and eventually became the most popular man in the world.

Conn Smythe was disgusted. He issued his famous denunciation of the staging of the fight at his beloved Gardens. "Cash before class," he said. Conn the patriot was shocked and appalled that the Gardens owners—his son, Ballard, Bassett—would shelter a slacker like Clay. He was so fed up that he resigned his position as a Gardens director and sold his remaining Gardens shares. Thus, a boxing match brought about the severance of the last connection to the Maple Leaf Gardens' founding generation.

GOING INTO THE 1966–67 HOCKEY SEASON, SOME OTHER elderly parties seemed to be nearing the end of their time around the Gardens. The team included many key players who were crowding forty: Red Kelly (39); George Armstrong and Tim Horton (both 36); the tough-as-old-boots defenceman Marcel Pronovost who had come over from Detroit in the Harris–Bathgate trade (also 36); the three-time First All-Star goalie Terry Sawchuk, another acquisition from the Red Wings, by way of the draft in 1964 (38). One player had crossed the forty-year barrier, Allan Stanley (40), and another had obliterated it, Johnny Bower (42 by his account, but rumoured to be 106). By way of small balance, the Leafs had a handful of players in the young-veteran category—Bob Pulford (30), Frank Mahovlich (28), Dave Keon (26)—and a couple who still qualified as kids—the speedy Ron Ellis (21) and the crashing checker Pete Stemkowski (23). But the team depended on its old gaffers.

And they didn't pan out in the two years leading up to the 1966–67 season. In 1964–65, though Toronto got Vezina Trophy–winning goal-tending from the Bower–Sawchuk duo, the team faded to fourth place and was wiped out by Montreal in the Stanley Cup first round. The following year, the Leafs survived a horrendous start to reach third place in the standings, only to have the Canadiens paste them once again in the first round, this time in four straight games.

How humiliating it must have been for players who were venerable but no longer venerated.

IN THE WESTERN MOVIE *RIDE THE HIGH COUNTRY*, JOEL McCrea and Randolph Scott play two aged gunfighters who take on one last job.

Young gunfighter (referring to McCrea): "That old man? He don't look like much to me."

Scott: "Son, don't sell that old man short."

Everyone was selling the old Leafs short in the winter of 1966–67. Small wonder. In mid-January, the team's senior citizens slumped so badly that Toronto went ten games without a victory. The non-winning streak hit Punch Imlach harder than anyone. On February 18, a Saturday, he complained of pain in his left side and of a general all-round malaise. The Leaf doctor, Tate McPhedran, examined Imlach and shooed him off to Toronto General Hospital. The diagnosis: total exhaustion. King Clancy handled the team that night in a game at the Gardens against Boston. The Leafs won 5–3. Imlach wasn't permitted to watch the streak-ending game, not even on television. He stayed two weeks in the TGH and another week at home. While he was out of commission, Clancy continued to coach. And the Leafs continued to win.

Did this make Clancy the saviour?

Not according to the players.

"King's been doing a great job," Tim Horton explained. "But Punch had us straightened out before his health gave out. Instead of criticizing, he went out of his way to build up our confidence and kept impressing us with the fact that we had too much ability to keep skidding."

Imlach's first night back on the coaching job, Saturday, March 11, was for a pivotal game. The opposition at the Gardens came from Chicago, the team that was running away from everybody that season, way out in front, getting the best goaltending in the league (from Glenn Hall), generating the most offence. But with Imlach behind the bench, Toronto blew out the Black Hawks 9–3.

Now nobody was selling those old Leafs short.

TORONTO FINISHED THE SEASON IN THIRD PLACE, NINE-teen points behind the first-place Black Hawks, whom the Leafs met in the first round of the playoffs. As usual, as had been the case all through the 1960s, the Hawks looked to two players for offensive leadership, Bobby Hull and Stan Mikita. Both produced sensational years in 1966–67, fifty-two goals for Hull, thirty-five goals and ninety-seven total points for Mikita, who won the Hart Trophy and the Lady Byng. But this edition of the Hawks probably ran to more depth than those of other seasons, with Kenny Wharram (thirty-one goals), Doug Mohns (twenty-five goals) and Phil Esposito (twenty-one goals) to do some scoring, Pierre Pilote on defence, Hall in goal. Chicago had a superb season—forty-one wins, just seventeen losses—and, on paper, they figured to whip the Leafs in the playoffs.

That was on paper. On the ice, the Leafs played with confidence generated by their 9–3 win over Chicago on March 11. Also on the ice, they had spectacular goaltending from Terry Sawchuk. After the Hawks won the first game of the series, Sawchuk got tough and beat Chicago in the next two. The Hawks took the fourth. In the fifth, with the series tied at two wins apiece, Johnny Bower started for the first time in the playoffs. He looked shakey. He played shakey. He let in two goals in the first period. Imlach replaced Bower with Sawchuk at the beginning of the second. Sawchuk hadn't wanted to play that night. He was tired, beaten, battered and bruised from the first four games. Almost immediately in the fifth game, he acquired a couple of new bruises when a Bobby Hull slapshot caught him, bang, bang, on the facemask and the shoulder. Sawchuk shrugged and shut out Hull and the rest of the Hawks for the next two periods. Leafs won the game 4–2, Pete Stemkowski scoring the winner. The Hawks were now plenty worried.

They had more to worry about than Terry Sawchuk. Dave Keon was checking Stan Mikita to a standstill. A feisty line of Bob Pulford, Stemkowski and a new winger, Jim Pappin—Pappin had scored fifteen goals in the last twenty regular-season games, seven of them game-winners—was giving everyone fits. Another new player, Brian Conacher (nephew of Charlie), a rangy young guy with a good hockey brain, showed marvellous form filling in for the injured George Armstrong. And—this was no small factor—the experience of Toronto's old guys had begun to wear at the Hawks.

"There was a steadfastness to us, a mental toughness," Marcel Pronovost remembered many years later. "Chicago had a lot of finesse, but we had the kind of experience that wins games. We didn't get nervous."

Everything came together for Toronto in the sixth game—Sawchuk's goaltending, Keon's checking, the team's overall maturity—and the Leafs beat the Hawks 3–1. It was Brian Conacher who scored the winning goal. He checked the puck away from Chicago defenceman Ed Van Impe, charged in on Glenn Hall and capped off a resourceful play by putting the puck in the net.

THE STANLEY CUP FINAL, MATCHING THE LEAFS AGAINST the Canadiens, had the makings of the last of a kind. Not just two Canadian teams playing the final, but two quality teams. That potential would disappear the following season when the NHL expanded by taking in six new teams at one stroke—Philadelphia, Los Angeles, St. Louis, Minnesota, Pittsburgh and Oakland. In a piece of stupidity that takes one's breath away, the six expansion clubs, with their necessarily second-class lineups, were grouped in one division and played their own playoffs, with the winner moving straight to the Stanley Cup final against the winner of the division made up of the traditional six teams. It was bound to be a mismatch. And it was. In the next three seasons, the St. Louis Blues emerged as the champs of the expansion bunch, and in three Cup finals, the Blues lost twelve games, won none, allowed forty-three goals and scored seventeen. This was supposed to be a major-league sporting event?

Meantime, in 1966–67, the Leafs and Canadiens met in a final that had everyone riveted.

"What I remember about the series," says Don Chevrier, who broadcast it, "was the sense of vital importance it had to both cities."

It sure did, and the elderly Leafs, again the underdogs, began it by getting bashed in the first game, at the Montreal Forum, 6–2. Sawchuk was less than sharp. He picked up two more wounds—a crinkled nose and a dented ankle. Bower started the second game and shut down the Canadiens 3–0. That meant Bower was again the goalie in the third game back at the Gardens, where he put on a show for the ages—and for the ageless. Montreal gunned fifty-four shots at Bower. He stopped fifty-two of them. The game, tied at two-all, went to the first overtime period. No one scored. It went into the second overtime.

At 8:26, Pulford whipped a shot past Rogie Vachon into the Montreal net. Game over.

The day after that win, Terry Sawchuk took morning practice at the Gardens, showered, dressed, and strolled down Church Street to a bar. He ordered a drink, another drink, a third drink, a couple of dozen drinks. He sat at the bar, bending his elbow, until the place closed at one o'clock in the morning.

The next night, a Saturday, at the Gardens for the fourth game, Sawchuk was so hung over his hair hurt, his vision blurred, his body felt like lead. But, what the heck, he was only along as a spectator that night. Bower would play goal. Except that in the pre-game warmup, Bower reached for a shot and snapped the hamstring in one leg. Sawchuk took over the net. He still couldn't see. Six shots got past him, and the Leafs lost 6–2.

Sawchuk went on the wagon. He had no choice. The only way Bower could play would be on crutches. For the rest of the series, it was Terry Sawchuk for better or for worse.

It turned out to be for better.

In the fifth game, played at the Montreal Forum in front of all those enemy fans, Sawchuk stood tall and steady. It was fortunate for Toronto that he did because, defensively, the rest of the team took a vacation. On the very first rush of the game, the Canadiens' fleet forward Ralph Backstrom broke in alone on Sawchuk. Save! It kept on that way, Montreal pounding at the Toronto goal, Sawchuk throwing up the barrier. One Montreal shot beat him, on a deflection off Tim Horton's body. But that was the limit Sawchuk allowed, and when the other Leafs finally put themselves in order, goals came from Pappin, Conacher, Pronovost and Keon. Toronto 4, Montreal 1.

Sixth game. At the Gardens. A huge thrill of excitement in the air. This was as good as it got for hockey in Toronto. But the first period began, perversely for Toronto fans, with the Leafs playing in a mild daze, the Canadiens pouring it on, Sawchuk coming up with the masterful saves. The period ended in a scoreless tie, a situation that flattered Toronto.

Red Kelly got the Leaf offence in gear in the second period. He took a pass from Allan Stanley at centre, deked two Canadiens, put a shot on

Gump Worsley in the Montreal net. Worsley made the stop, but gave up a rebound. Ron Ellis seized on the puck and whapped it in for a goal. That was at 6:25. Near the end of the period, less than a minute left on the clock, the Leafs drew a big break. Jim Pappin was merely trying to backhand a pass to Pete Stemkowski at the Montreal goal mouth. No large purpose in mind. Just run out the clock. The Canadien defence-man Jacques Laperrière had Stemkowski tied up in an octopus check. Pappin's backhand pass bounced off Laperrière and into the Montreal net. A two-goal lead for the Leafs.

The Canadiens weren't in a mood to quit. At 5:28 of the third, Dick Duff, enjoying a fabulous twilight of his career in the years since Imlach unloaded him from the Leafs, showed Horton and Sawchuk a couple of gorgeous moves and got one goal back for Montreal.

At that point, Sawchuk took over once again. He was all hands and gloves and pads and flashing stops. The Canadiens couldn't shoot the puck past him, not Jean Béliveau, not Bobby Rousseau, not Duff or Backstrom or Henri Richard. With fifty-five seconds left on the clock, Montreal coach Toe Blake pulled his goalie and went with six attacking players. Who did Imlach put on the ice? His old guys: Kelly, Stanley, Horton, Sawchuk, Armstrong, plus one comparative youngster, Pulford.

Face-off in the Leaf end. Stanley won it over Béliveau. Kelly grabbed the puck. Moved it swiftly to Pulford on the left boards. Pulford found Armstrong alone on the right side. Armstrong measured his time—not too rushed, not too nonchalant—and aimed the puck into the empty Montreal net. The goal wrapped it up for the Leafs, the oldest team ever to win a Stanley Cup.

Terry Sawchuk was named the first star for the night's game. Dave Keon got the Conn Smythe Trophy as the most valuable player in the playoffs. The prize meant a thousand bucks to Keon. Sawchuk figured his prize was more valuable—he could treat himself to a few drinks after five days on the wagon.

IN *RIDE THE HIGH COUNTRY*, THE TWO OLD GUNFIGHTERS, Joel McCrea and Randolph Scott, won their last showdown. But at the end, in that final shootout, McCrea took a bullet and died.

In the two seasons after the 1967 Stanley Cup, the Leafs lost, in one way or another, these players: Bob Baun, Frank Mahovlich, Terry Sawchuk, Brian Conacher, Allan Stanley, Red Kelly, Pete Stemkowski, Eddie Shack and Jim Pappin. In 1967–68, the team finished out of the playoffs. The next year, it came in fourth but lost to Boston in four straight games in the first round of the playoffs.

"I want to talk to you," Staff Smythe said to Imlach.

This was in the corridor outside the Leaf dressing room at the Gardens immediately after the Bruins had beaten Toronto in the fourth playoff game.

The two men stepped into a small office off the corridor.

Staff stuck out his hand. "Well, that's it," he said to Imlach.

Imlach, not quite getting it, took Staff's hand. Then he got it.

"You're telling me I'm fired?" Imlach said. "Is that what you're saying?"

Staff took his time over the next words.

"You're through," he said. "I want to run the club now."

14

Staff and Hal

W HEN STAFF SMYTHE WAS A LITTLE KID and suffered from asthma attacks (something that stayed with him all his life), he used to sleep next to a gizmo that burned medication and filled his bedroom with fumes to ease his breathing. Poor little Staff. He grew up, became a man, served in the navy, learned to be a boss at the family gravel pit and at the family hockey team, presided over an organization that won Stanley Cups and made serious profits, but he was never far from the little kid with the gizmo in his bedroom, having a hard time of it just breathing.

Staff was shy. Talking to people, especially strangers, his voice stayed low. Often, he had trouble making eye contact. He liked to sidle up behind friends and acquaintances and murmur remarks as if he were dropping them into the ether. He could be as disputatious as his father, but the impression he left was that it didn't come as easily to Staff as to Conn to be unpleasant and demanding. With Staff, his bark really was worse than his bite. With the old man, the bark could rattle you, but the bite could take a chunk out of your hide. Staff was different. He even seemed uncomfortable with the fame and success that the Leafs brought him. The fellow who said of Staff that he was "a man who enjoyed being unpopular as a defence against an extreme inferiority complex" might have been right.

It couldn't have been easy for Staff growing up in the same businesses as his father. Actually that's an understatement of the worst sort. It must have been hell on Staff. Even in the most personal matters, Conn put Staff through the wringer. Staff fell in love with a woman who happened to be Catholic. He married her, and Conn, the virulent anti-Papist, hit the roof. Later, when Conn realized what a prize Staff had chosen for a wife, he came around, but the sense of exclusion the young couple went through at the beginning of their marriage, as evidenced by a heart-breaking letter written at the time by Staff's bride, Dorothea, must have been horribly debilitating for Staff. He never seemed to get anything exactly right with his father.

SOMETHING ABOUT STAFF THAT CONN MUST HAVE TAKEN pride in was that the younger Smythe turned out to be a sound and sensible assessor and organizer of hockey talent. Maybe he was as good as the old man. He learned the right way by coming up through the ranks. He had the largest role in setting up the Marlboro minor-league organization. He recruited fourteen-year-old kids for the Marlie minor-bantams and guided the best of them—Billy Harris, Bob Baun, Bob Pulford—all the way to the Weston Dukes and beyond. Staff was so astute in marshalling players along the system he established, by way of the Marlboro Juniors or St. Michael's College, that, on the four Stanley Cup–winning Leaf teams of the 1960s, there were seventeen graduates of the Marlie or St. Mike's junior teams. Neither Conn nor Frank Selke could match a number like that.

CONN SMYTHE OBSERVED THIS IN HIS ELDEST SON WHEN Staff was a youngster: "If there were two boys, one straight and good at everything and the other a born troublemaker, Stafford would hang out with the troublemaker every time."

Staff and Harold Ballard first hooked up in 1931 or '32. Staff was the stick boy of the Maple Leafs. Ballard was a *bon vivant*–about-town. Why would a twenty-eight-year-old man, which is what Ballard was, befriend an eleven-year-old kid, which is what Staff was? Drive him to hockey games? Buy him hot chocolates? Maybe because Ballard was looking for a way into the Leaf organization, into big-time hockey. Ballard was a guy who had his nose pressed against the window in the door to the hockey establishment for years. Of course, when he finally got in, he trashed the joint. But through the 1930s and '40s, he was still on the outside looking in.

Ballard had the financial advantage of growing up the only child of a self-made millionaire. His father, Sid, was a wizard with machines. He invented the Ballard Straight-Knife Cloth-Cutting Machine, which was the basis of the family fortune. Sid loved machines both well and too much. In 1936, all the years of tinkering with them in his factory caught up with him. He died of lead poisoning.

Harold Ballard went into the family business early, in 1919, after three years at Upper Canada College and no years at university. He was a natural salesman, heavy on the bluff and blarney, fast to pick up the bill in nightclubs, a tireless teller of dirty jokes, the last one to call it a night (even in his eighties, he got by on three or four hours of sleep). He was athletic in a mild way, a speed skater and a racer of hydroplanes. By the early 1930s, he had begun to involve himself in the organizational end of hockey teams and found early success with a senior club called the National Sea Fleas. It won the Allan Cup in 1932.

Ballard knew Conn Smythe socially—Ballard appears to have known everybody socially—and he made overtures to Smythe about getting into the Gardens in some capacity. "I would not give [Ballard] a job at ten cents a week," Smythe wrote in his autobiography. Ballard tried on Hap Day as a Gardens entrée. The two men, who would appear to be vastly different in temperament and moral standards, hit it off, and Day had some influence in landing Ballard a non-paying position as president and manager of the senior and junior Marlboros in the early 1940s. That, one should note, was the period when Conn Smythe was overseas.

Ballard and Staff Smythe made a nice fit in the Marlie organization. Staff was the hockey man. Ballard, who did an excellent job of maintaining his late dad's machine shop as a constant little money-maker, looked after Marlboro publicity, sales, tickets, press. Ballard knew business. Did Ballard know hockey? Did he want to know hockey? Maybe not at the Marlie level, at the junior level. "You never saw Ballard until the team picture was being taken," Billy Harris says of his time with the Marlboros.

Ballard and Staff stayed thick and fast through the Marlboro years and into the Silver Seven period. "Harold's function was to make Stafford laugh," Staff's brother, Hugh Smythe, has said. "And he was good at that." Whatever it took to be Staff's buddy, it was no problem for Ballard. Sacrifice another friend? Why, sure. That happened in 1957 when Hap Day got squeezed out of the Gardens after Conn Smythe's bombshell about Day's "availability." Day and Ballard had palled around since 1935, went on the road together when Day coached the Leafs, stepped out for dining and dancing with their wives. But in 1957, Ballard gave Day the deep freeze.

"Harold had to make up his mind," Day recalled, speaking in the 1980s. "Either stay close to me or stay close to Stafford. And judging by where he is now, he made the right decision."

AFTER STAFF FIRED PUNCH IMLACH IN THE SPRING OF 1969, he started from scratch to reconstitute the team. That was no easy task. Imlach had traded away many of the Leafs' fine young players, and the cupboard in Toronto's minor-league organization was bare of prospects. In fact, there was no minor-league organization. Staff and Ballard had sold it, sold their farm teams in Victoria and in Rochester in the 1966–67 season. These guys were greedy for money, even when their greed made no sense in terms of the future of the Toronto hockey team. The Leafs lost about twenty players in the various expansion drafts, and management, meaning Staff and Hal, had stripped down to a club that was composed of guys who creaked when they skated (Johnny Bower, Marcel Pronovost), kids who were fresh enough to be the sons of the first group (Rick Ley, Jim Dorey, Jim McKenny), and three authentic stars (Dave Keon, Ron Ellis and Norm Ullman, who came over from Detroit in the Mahovlich deal).

Staff brought in Jim Gregory as the Leafs' new general manager and

John McLellan as coach. Both had spent time in the Leaf organization. Gregory, a serious, soft-spoken man, coached a Memorial Cup winner (Marlies in 1965), managed another (Marlies in '67), and coached briefly with the Vancouver Canucks of the old Western League. McLellan projected an easy-going front, a guy with a nicely self-deprecating sense of humour, but the ulcer he came down with in the 1971–72 season suggested something was seething underneath. He paid his dues as a player, winning a Memorial Cup with St. Mike's in 1947, an Allan Cup with the Marlboro Seniors in '50, a Calder Cup for the American League championship with Pittsburgh in '52 and '55, a world championship with the Belleville McFarlands in '59 (McLellan got a goal and an assist in the key 3–1 win over Russia). He had a cup of coffee with the Leafs — two games in 1951–52, no goals, assists or penalties. As a coach, he won the Central League championship with Tulsa in 1968. Not bad credentials, and it was hardly McLellan's fault, or Gregory's, that the Leafs sputtered through McLellan–Gregory's first couple of seasons, finishing out of the playoffs in 1970 and getting clipped in the first playoff round in 1971. The coach and general manager didn't have a whole lot to work with in those years, and as for the president, well, Staff had more terrible matters on his mind. Staying out of jail, for example. Staying alive.

IT'S IMPOSSIBLE TO SAY WHO LED WHOM INTO WHAT, whether, as Ballard said after Staff's death, "I went along, but Staff started it," or whether the two men joined hands down the road to disgrace. Maybe they brought out the worst in each other. Maybe, running the Gardens alone for ten years, with only a benign and trusting board of directors to answer to, they came to treat what was a public company as their own fiefdom. Gardens money, in their minds, equalled personal money. It's as good an explanation as any for the criminal mischief that Staff and Ballard got up to.

Ballard seems to have been the first to spot the possibilities for a little scamming when he bought the motorcycle from Brown Sporting Goods for his son Bill in the late summer of 1965 and charged it, $438.78, to the Toronto Marlboro account under "hockey sticks." That was the beginning of a long line of penny-ante Ballard cheats. When his daughter got married in March 1967, he stuck the Gardens for the limousine service. Just crossed "wedding" off the limo company's invoice, wrote in "airport services," and put the invoice through the Gardens accounting office. Gawd, this was fun! Installing an underground lawn sprinkler at the Ballard house? Just tell the landscape architect to list the work and the price, $468, under "Gardens sprinkler system." The Gardens paid.

It was so easy, these pieces of deception, that Ballard and Staff decided to go at it big time in the autumn of 1965. A company called Cloke Construction was doing extensive work at the Gardens, installing more seats. Simultaneously, Smythe and Ballard hired Cloke to carry out renovations on their homes. Staff ordered up marble floors, the whole luxury treatment for his house, $206,166 of fancy mansion. Ballard stayed more modest, asking for $74,395 in reno work. For both amounts, Staff and Ballard obtained blank invoices from Cloke, filled them in to make the house renovations look like they were construction performed at the Gardens, and slipped them into the Gardens books. Staff and Ballard were shameless. And they grew even more obvious when they diverted money that the Ontario Hockey Association sent to the Gardens as league payments due to the Marlboros. Staff and Ballard set up a bank account which only they had access to, an acccount under the name "Marlboro Athletic Club," and directed $123,000 into it for their own spending pleasure. The two guys must have thought they were bullet-proof.

But the Gardens was a small village. Many employees knew what the bosses were up to, and one of them blew the whistle. A good bet is that it was a man named Len Heath. He possessed rectitude, a soldier who had served in Conn Smythe's Sportsmen's Battery, the Gardens' treasurer, an employee for twenty-one years until the day in April 1968 when Staff instructed him to doctor a Cloke invoice. Heath told Staff to get lost. Heath resigned his job, and three months later, the RCMP, acting on behalf of the federal income tax people, descended on the Gardens and seized hundreds of pieces of paper, including those damning Cloke Construction invoices.

There were other whistle-blowers around the Gardens. Maple Leaf players, for example. Some of them buddied with a sharp young prosecutor in the Ontario Attorney General's Office named Clay Powell.

"What my hockey friends were telling me," says Powell, who declines to name the players, "was, never mind the tax thing, you should see the fraud these guys are getting away with."

That put Powell on the case in the winter of 1969–70. In timing, he was far behind the feds, who laid income tax-evasion charges against Staff ($278,919 for undeclared income realized from the house construction and the Marlboro money) and against Ballard ($134,685) on July 9, 1969. But Powell came along two years later, in July 1971, with another rocket for Staff and Ballard. He brought fraud and theft charges, $146,000 in theft of money and securities against both men, $249,000 in fraud against Staff (ah, the expense of those marble floors) and $83,000 against Ballard.

"It wasn't a tough case," Powell says. "We had the documents. We had the witnesses. I knew we had Smythe and Ballard cold."

CONN SMYTHE FORMED A THEORY ABOUT HIS SON'S PROBLEMS with the law. More than a theory, a fixation. Conn thought the Liberal government in Ottawa was punishing Staff for Conn's transgressions. During the Second World War, Conn had stirred a colossal uproar over Prime Minister Mackenzie King's pusillanimous position on compulsory military service. King didn't push for compulsory service out of fear he'd alienate voters in Quebec, where military service in the Second World War was considered much less than a holy crusade. Conn argued publicly that the lack of fresh troops in combat, troops that universal service would provide, was costing the lives of Canadian soldiers. Conn was undoubtedly right, but King didn't like to be reminded of it, and he couldn't get Conn to shut up.

That was one black mark against the Smythe family. Conn recorded a second when another Liberal prime minister, Lester Pearson, introduced the red maple leaf as Canada's new flag. Conn fumed and raged to reporters. He'd fought under the Union Jack! It was the flag of the Queen! And now, thanks to the Liberals, what must Canadians run up the pole? "Pearson's diaper!" Conn said in contempt.

So, according to Conn's conspiracy theory, the Liberal government set out to get even with the Smythe family by nailing Staff (and nailing

Ballard since he happened to be in the same neighbourhood). This notion suggests that the Liberals had exceptionally long memories for slights, that there were government officials in Ottawa who carried a twenty-year-old grudge on behalf of a dead prime minister. Still, Conn produced a couple of pieces of evidence that seemed to support his theory. For one, he was himself subjected to a nonsensical income tax investigation in the 1960s that appeared to owe more to spite than to law. And for another, he said he had it on reliable authority, from a guy with a pipeline into the Liberal cabinet, that the cabinet itself directed that Staff and Ballard be proceeded against by indictment rather than by summary conviction on the income tax charges. The difference was significant: a conviction under summary proceedings allowed for a fine, while a conviction by indictment guaranteed a prison term.

The Liberals, Conn said, wanted to put a Smythe in jail.

IF THAT WAS TRUE, STAFF CHEATED THE LIBERALS OUT OF their revenge. He showed them. He died.

From the time the charges were laid, Staff gave signs of caving in. He drank. He withdrew. He got sick. On October 6, 1971, nineteen days before the scheduled start of the tax-evasion trial, he threw up blood. At Wellesley Hospital, doctors told him he had a bleeding ulcer. They took out most of his stomach. Staff didn't fight particularly hard against his ailments. He died on October 13. Someone in the family wrote on Staff's gravestone—in a stunning instance of paranoia carried to the afterlife— "He was persecuted to death by his enemies."

IN THE MONTHS BEFORE STAFF'S DEATH, JOHN BASSETT made a run at gaining control of the Gardens. Instead, after quarrelsome negotiations, Staff and Ballard bought Bassett out. They borrowed $6 million, mostly from the Toronto-Dominion Bank, partly from a businessman and Gardens director named Don Giffin, to finance the purchase of the Bassett shares.

After Staff's death, Ballard brought into play the ticking time bomb of a clause in the original agreement among himself, Staff and Bassett, the clause that permitted the survivor to exercise first call on the

Gardens shares belonging to a deceased member of the trio (actually a duo now that Bassett was out of the picture). Ballard wanted Staff's stock.

Staff's survivors—wife, Dorothea; son, Tom; brother, Hugh—were shocked at the speed and nastiness of Ballard's move. Talk about two-faced. The night before Staff's funeral, Ballard spent hours weeping beside the coffin, "frequently opening the casket," sportswriter Earl McRae reported in a later magazine profile of Ballard, "to see if Smythe was truly dead." As soon as Staff was in the ground, Ballard turned remote. No kind words for Staff's grieving family. No words at all. In the familiar Ballard pattern, he gave the Smythes, who were no longer useful to him, the silent treatment.

It was no problem for Ballard to acquire the Smythe shares in the Gardens. Ballard was Staff's executor. All it took was a stroke of his own pen to make the transfer. Ballard went back to the T-D Bank and to Don Giffin, borrowed $7.5 million, and paid the Smythes market value for Staff's stock. That was in February 1972, and Harold Ballard was now a 71 percent owner of the Gardens. He enjoyed more absolute control than any other owner, than any Smythe, including Conn, had ever exercised over the arena and the team. Ballard was sixty-eight years old and in charge. Just one problem—this sixty-eight-year-old in-charge guy was on his way to jail.

AFTER BALLARD PAID THE INCOME TAXES THAT THE government said he owed, and after he reimbursed the Gardens for the money he conned, the feds dropped the tax case against him. But Clay Powell pressed forward with the fraud and theft charges. The trial started on May 23, 1972, before County Court Judge Harry Deyman. Ballard had arguably the most accomplished courtroom lawyer in Canadian legal history acting for him, John Robinette. That didn't matter. Ballard could have been represented by Socrates, Clarence Darrow and Rumpole of the Bailey and he still would have been convicted.

"It was like a show trial," Powell says. "Day after day, witnesses came to the stand with their signed invoices. I had everything on my side, and Robinette had absolutely nothing to work with. It was agony in the courtroom."

The only witnesses Robinette called were those who testified to Ballard's good character. They were a revealing mix: the radio news reader at CFRB, Jack Dennett; sportswriters Milt Dunnell and Jim Coleman; the head of an advertising agency, Harry "Red" Foster; *Toronto Sun* publisher Doug Creighton; and two lawyers, Richard Meech and Terry Kelly (the same Terry Kelly who became a director of the Gardens under Steve Stavro in 1992). They testified that Ballard was a generous donor to charities, a swell all-round companion, good family man—the usual compliments that character witnesses lavish on a man who looks like he's headed for the Big House. The witnesses seemed to leave a good impression on Judge Harry Deyman (they left a great impression on Ballard; listening to the catalogue of his virtues, he wept in the prisoner's box). Deyman might even have been persuaded to go easy on Ballard in his sentencing. But another factor came into play. The trial had concluded with Deyman's verdict of guilty on forty-seven counts of fraud and theft on August 15, and sentencing had been put over until September 7. September of that year, 1972, marked the first, historic Canada–Russia hockey series, and some of Ballard's friends begged Deyman to postpone sentencing long enough that Ballard could attend the games in both Canada and Russia. Deyman agreed. He rescheduled sentencing until October 20. But Deyman didn't like it. Not one bit.

"I think the pressure Ballard's friends put on Deyman upset him," Clay Powell says. "I'm sure Deyman was thinking originally in terms of time in reformatory. Under two years. But the phone calls about the Canada–Russia series led him to think in stiffer terms."

"You were in a position of trust," Judge Deyman said sternly to Ballard in court on October 20, "and you violated that trust."

The sentence: three years in the penitentiary.

15

Ballard Unleashed

BALLARD RETURED TO THE GARDENS IN THE autumn of 1973, paroled from prison with time off for good behaviour, and for the next dozen years, he devoted himself to getting rid of things. Exclusively, these were things of long standing around the building, ancient hockey artefacts, the treasures of past Leaf regimes. Ballard couldn't rewrite history, but he could put the boot to much of its physical manifestation.

Conn Smythe's famous sign in the dressing room—"Defeat Does Not Rest Lightly On Their Shoulders"—went. Accompanying it to the incinerator were the dressing-room plaques listing the names and records of each Leaf team down the years. Ballard got rid of them. He got rid of John Bassett's head. Ballard loathed Bassett for not propping up him and Staff when the criminal charges came down against the two men. Bassett, then the Gardens chairman of the board and mindful of the mud flying off the two accused thieves, distanced himself from Ballard and Smythe. And now Ballard, seriously into trashing, snipped Bassett's head out of team photographs that hung on the Gardens walls and replaced it with someone else's likeness. Anyone else's would do; in the 1967 team picture, the last Stanley Cup Leafs, Bill Ballard's head materialized on John Bassett's shoulders.

Ballard got rid of Foster Hewitt's gondola, the perch from which Hewitt broadcast Leaf games beginning in 1931 and ending with his last game in 1978. Hewitt looked on the gondola, though it was no longer in use, as a piece of hockey tradition. Most fans shared his view. Not Ballard. In September 1980, he ordered a Gardens crew to dismantle it.

The dismantling might have passed unpublicized if, a day or two after it took place, Rick Boulton hadn't happened to glance up and notice something missing at the Gardens. Boulton was an enterprising young freelance writer who had been editing the Gardens hockey program for five years. He thought there was a story in the gondola's demolition—not for the hockey program, but for the *Toronto Star* sports pages. The *Star* bought the idea, and Boulton wrote the piece, quoting from interviews he'd done with Hewitt, with the curator of the Hockey Hall of Fame, with the Gardens man who'd supervised the removal, with everybody except Harold Ballard.

"We'll run the story tomorrow," a *Star* editor told Boulton. "One thing, though, you need a Ballard quote. Phone him, but make sure you phone at 10:30 tonight, right on deadline."

"Why on deadline?"

"Because," the *Star* editor explained, "that won't give Ballard time to call his pal at the *Sun*, George Gross. Whenever Ballard sniffs a guy from one paper with a story, he phones his buddies at the other papers and tells them what's going on. If somebody at the *Sun* gets something, Ballard'll call Milt Dunnell at our place. It's just the way he operates. Create trouble, stir a little confusion."

Boulton rang Ballard at 10:30, got a handful of sentences ("Hell, we're not in the historical business, and that gondola wasn't so old anyway"), and stitched them into his piece. Late the following morning, Ballard read the day's *Star* and decided he didn't care for the image of himself that emerged from the gondola story. He sent word to the Leafs general manager, Jim Gregory: get rid of Rick Boulton. Boulton wasn't exactly a part of Maple Leaf tradition, but, like the gondola, he was gone from the Gardens.

Ballard got rid of the words "Toronto Maple Leafs" on the front of the Leaf players' sweaters. This wasn't a blanket removal. It applied to a single set of players, the ones in the nine floor-to-ceiling panels that artist Charlie Pachter created on a platform in the subway station at College and Yonge in Toronto.

The Toronto Transit Commission had ordered a series of artworks through the 1970s and early '80s to spruce up its subway stations. An enormous Joyce Wieland quilt featuring prancing deer was mounted behind glass at the Spadina Station's north end. In the same station, Louis de Niverville did a lovely rendition of a sedate rush for a train, and Gordon Rayner enlivened the St. Clair West Station with an arrangement of bands of eloquent colour. By 1984, the TTC's art fund was down to $65,000, and for that sum, it wanted to do something with the College Street Station. Charlie Pachter—celebrated for his paintings of the Queen mounted on a moose, of floating streetcars, of other works of whimsy, symbolism and social comment—accepted the assignment, and this is when the episode, thanks to Harold Ballard, took on a quirky comedy that Stephen Leacock would have appreciated.

"I'm not a big sports person," Pachter says. "But I certainly knew about the great rivalry between the Leafs and the Canadiens, English and French, the blue and the red, the clash of two cultures. What better thing was there to depict in a subway station that was a block from Maple Leaf Gardens?"

Pachter came up with baked porcelain-enamel panels of Leaf and Canadien players in action—players skating, passing, diving, shooting—nine panels of Montreal players on the northbound platform, nine panels of Toronto players on the southbound platform. It seemed the ideal solution—colour, competition, hockey, art that was accessible to the most unsophisticated subway rider.

"Well, Ballard went crazy," Pachter says. "He didn't personally come to see what I was doing. He just read about it and heard about it, and what he announced basically was, 'no way those fuckin' frogs are gonna be in the subway with our guys.'"

Julian Porter counselled caution to Pachter. Porter was the TTC chairman at the time, and perhaps more to the point, he was an intelligent lawyer who specialized in libel law.

"Just in case Ballard thinks about suing us," Porter said to Pachter, "you'd be wise to make the Leafs a generic kind of hockey team. Not like the real team."

Pachter went back to his panels. He narrowed the stripes on the Leaf uniforms, and he altered the faces of the players, removing the nose from the player he'd modelled on a photograph of Rick Vaive and switching it with one taken from a Borje Salming photo. He changed the Leafs into figures of hockey anonymity. The Canadiens, since Montreal had raised no objections, continued to look more like the genuine article. But the Leafs were just a bunch of guys in weird blue-and-white gear. Even the magic words were gone. No "Toronto Maple Leafs" in the crest on the front of the sweaters.

"You can look at the silly side of it," Charlie Pachter says. "The players didn't end up the way I intended them, not like the Leafs, and when it was all over, I only made about $2,000 on the job. But it's still my one work that people who don't know art recognize as mine. And, another thing, whatever Ballard objected to, he couldn't do anything about the title I put on the work. It stayed—'Hockey Knights in Canada.'"

BALLARD GOT RID OF PEOPLE AS WELL AS THINGS, PEOPLE whose names had a resonance in Leaf history.

Bob Davidson, as we've seen, learned he was no longer wanted around the Gardens on the day just before Christmas of 1978 when, after forty-four years as player, coach, and finally scout in the Leaf organization, his salary was cut by two-thirds. Davidson quit.

George Armstrong was on the receiving end of the same sort of treatment at the pay window in the same year. Armstrong had coached the Marlboros for seven years, winning two Memorial Cups. He resigned the job in November of 1978, but assumed he was keeping his other job as the Marlie general manager. Uh-uh, sorry, George. Armstrong got the news when he stopped by the Gardens to pick up his GM's cheque and found there was none. He took a job scouting for the Quebec Nordiques.

At least Ace Bailey received a letter. He had been assistant to the penalty timekeeper at the Gardens since 1937, just a couple of years after he'd recovered from the Eddie Shore slam that came close to killing him. Assistant to the penalty timekeeper? Not a high-skill job, more a recognition of a player who'd given almost his all for the team. Then in 1984, Ace received the letter from Ballard. "He didn't say why," Bailey reported, sounding as plaintive as an eighty-one-year-old was entitled to. "He just said my services were no longer required."

And Ballard got rid of other, less historically steeped people. General managers and coaches, for example. All hockey owners sack general managers and coaches. Ballard just did it with more frequency and turmoil than the others. Among general managers, he fired four within a decade, 1979 to 1989: Jim Gregory, Punch Imlach (back again), Gerry McNamara and Gord Stellick. During the same ten years, just to give the inconsistency in the Leaf offices a bit of context, three of the period's dominant NHL teams, the New York Islanders, Edmonton Oilers and Calgary Flames, stuck with one GM each—Bill Torrey, Glen Sather and Cliff Fletcher, respectively.

Ballard dismissed coaches at an even swifter rate. From the time he took over in 1972 until he died in 1990, he went through nine coaches: John McLellan (it was actually an ulcer—Ballard-induced?—that took him out), Red Kelly, Roger Neilson, Floyd Smith (a car accident on the Queen Elizabeth Highway put him on sabbatical from coaching, then Ballard made it permanent), Joe Crozier, Mike Nykoluk, Dan Maloney, John Brophy, and George Armstrong (yes, the same legendary Leaf who was banished in 1978 was re-embraced ten years later by a Ballard who appeared to have forgotten the earlier banishing).

If the above lists indicate that Ballard had little respect for general managers and coaches, both the people and the posts, that seems to have been the case. In the view of one of the fired GMs, Gord Stellick, Ballard "was never convinced that a good coach or general manager could have a significant effect on the team." Whom would Ballard have preferred to handle the scouting, trades, contract negotiations; to run the practices; choose the players; make the line changes? Apparently a couple of low-paid, invisible, media-proof bureaucrats. How contemptuous was Ballard of his GMs and coaches? So contemptuous that when he fired Gerry McNamara in the winter of 1988, Ballard converted McNamara's former

The man in the fedora, Punch Imlach, was abrasive, smart and a winner —
four Stanley Cups as Toronto's GM and coach.

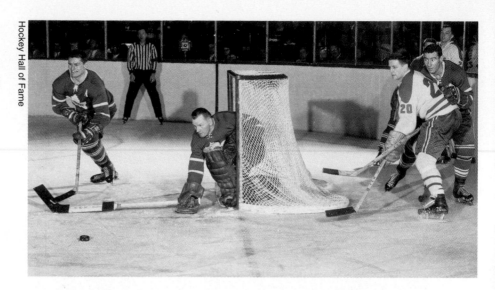

Johnny Bower — rumoured to be somewhere in age between forty-three and 106 — anchored Toronto's Stanley Cup teams of the 1960s.

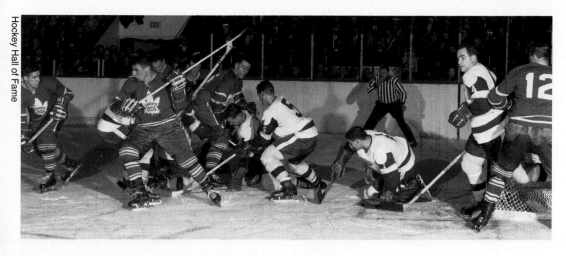

Ferocious Leaf action (note the extra skater) in a 1950s game against the Red Wings. One of the Wings, Red Kelly (second from right), was soon a Leaf himself.

Imlach lines up a row of champs: the 1961-62 Stanley Cup winners.

Stafford Smythe and Harold Ballard check out the menu at the Hot Stove Lounge in happier times before death (Smythe's) and unpaid taxes (both men's) broke them up.

A record-breaking occasion for Captain Darryl Sittler — April 22, 1976, the playoff game when he scored five goals against Philadelphia's Bernie Parent.

Only two seasons as coach, but Roger Neilson's intensive planning and clever tactics helped bring Toronto respectability in the late 1970s.

One of Toronto's all-time popular guys, the man with the shrub on his upper lip, Lanny McDonald.

Here's one reason for Lanny's popularity: he popped the winning goal on Glenn Resch in the seventh game against the Islanders in the 1978 quarter-finals.

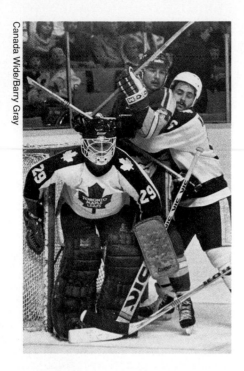

Nothing much fazed the plucky little Leaf netminder of the late 1970s and early 1980s, the ever-confident Mike Palmateer.

The man with the boarding house reach on the left played 1,099 stellar games for the Leafs, Borje Salming.

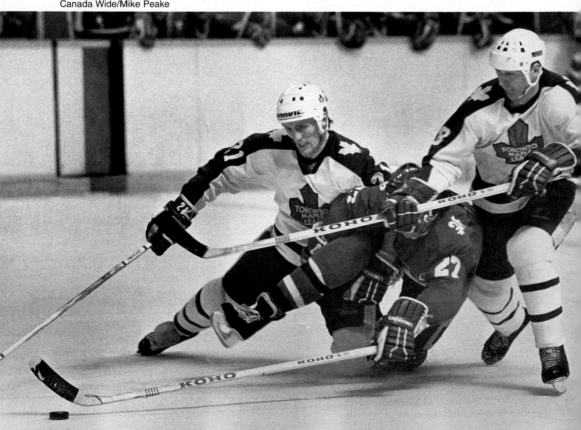

office into a walk-in closet for the wardrobes of himself and his companion, Yolanda.

Parenthetically, it's worth recording that, in the matter of showing the door to employees, Ballard came from the school of Richard Nixon: a reluctance to do it face to face. Sometimes Ballard delegated the chore to another employee. More often, the poor fellow who was about to be handed his hat learned of it by reading Milt Dunnell's column, where Ballard liked to leak the news. More often than that, Ballard spread the word of his intentions to fire someone so widely and indiscriminately that it filtered back to the victim himself. It was firing by attrition, as Jim Gregory, for one, experienced.

"Jim," NHL vice-president Brian O'Neill said on the phone to Gregory on a summer day in 1979, "I've got a job for you in the league offices, right up your alley."

"I've already got a job with the Leafs."

"No, you don't," O'Neill said. "Ballard just told me he isn't keeping you on."

As of 1994, Gregory was in his fifteenth year with the NHL, vice-president of hockey operations.

THE REASONS BEHIND BALLARD'S SCORCHED-EARTH POLICY lay in control and ego. Ballard was a control freak. Not only did he insist on running the whole show, he insisted on being perceived as running all of it. He probably figured he'd earned the right after years of operating in the shade of the two Smythes. "Mine, all mine" became Ballard's mantra, and damned if he was going to share any of it, any of the Gardens or the Leafs, with anyone. He wouldn't let other people's memories intrude on his Gardens either. Better to burn the gondola, dismiss Bob Davidson, keep the past at bay.

As for ego, Ballard had a tremendous lust for gratification of his. Don't we all, but Ballard had worked himself into a position where his ego, which was larger than the norm to start with, could be stroked on a scale usually reserved for people who are identified by one name — Madonna, Magic, Saddam. Ballard owned the most famous sports team and probably the most famous building in Canada, and those ownerships translated into fame for him. It was his opinions in the papers, his face that people on the street reacted to, his name that commanded attention. Ballard lived in egomania heaven.

But he learned that fame could be flighty when he hired Punch Imlach as the Leaf general manager in 1979. Suddenly media people were quoting Imlach, seeking his opinions, shooting his photograph. Ballard sulked. Jesus, he had to get rid of this goddamned Imlach. Punch was too colourful, too quotable.

Fate played into Ballard's hands. When Imlach suffered a heart attack in late August 1980, Ballard seized on Punch's absence to sign Borje Salming to the biggest contract ever given a Leaf player, and he restored Darryl Sittler to the captaincy he'd dramatically resigned a year earlier. Those were a couple of headline grabbers. That'd show Punch. Several months later, in the fall of 1981, Ballard used Imlach's history of heart weakness (though doctors declared Punch fit as a fiddle) to turf him out of the GM's office. "I'm not going to be the one who puts him in a pine box," Ballard said. And he never again made the mistake of appointing a general manager who might get his name in the newspapers. Indeed, the next fellow in the job, Gerry McNamara, became known for running from reporters, physically running from them, for banning reporters from the Leaf dressing room, from Leaf practices, even from the Gardens press box. This was Ballard's kind of guy, a GM who knew there was room for only one celebrity around the place.

IF BALLARD WERE PORTRAYED IN A MOVIE, IT MIGHT BE by an actor who combined the talents of John Goodman and John Malkovich: jolly on the outside, a borderline wacko on the inside. And it must have exacerbated Ballard's tendencies to the eccentric that he led a curiously cloistered existence over the last two decades of his life.

It all began when his wife, Dorothy, died in December 1969. Not that Ballard was a model husband. On the contrary, he stayed out most nights with the boys (and sometimes the girls), went off on Leaf road games, and was often a remote presence on the occasions he arrived home for a meal. Dorothy, strikingly attractive and popular with all who met her, evidently possessed the saintliness of Mother Teresa. Instead of taking a club or a divorce lawyer to Harold, she devoted herself to family and good works. She did most of the raising of the three kids, Mary Elizabeth, Bill and Harold, Jr.; she volunteered at the Cancer Society and the United Church; and she waited for Harold to show up.

Cancer changed everything, the diagnosis of Dorothy's breast cancer in the late 1960s.

"Once Dorothy got sick," Dr. Hugh Smythe has said, "Ballard decided she was pretty nice, but before that, he ignored her most of the time."

Ballard did his best to cram a lifetime of attention into the couple of years left to Dorothy, and after she died, a part of him withdrew. He moved out of the family home and into a tiny apartment on the second floor of the Gardens. This became his home for almost twenty years. On game nights, after play finished and the hockey crowds filed out, after the lights were switched off, one man stayed behind, padding around the building in his underwear, Harold Ballard, alone with his Gardens. Why does the image of Quasimodo haunting the upper reaches of Notre Dame creep to mind?

For companionship, Ballard entertained a series of women friends. But his constant sidekick was a man, King Clancy. For some reason, that comes as no surprise. It didn't surprise Hap Day. "King was the biggest apple-polisher in the world," Day said in the mid-1980s. "And why not? He was paid to do nothing by Staff Smythe, and then by Ballard." Ballard and Clancy shared the same compulsions—cussing, women with big knockers, and sports. It made for a narrow frame of reference, particularly in a man, Ballard, who was supposed to be running a major organization. Many sports moguls aren't renowned for their breadth of culture, but Ballard, with his cramped lifestyle through the 1970s and '80s, seemed especially unaware of the world beyond hockey and the Gardens.

BALLARD WAS A CHEAPSKATE, AT LEAST IN HIS OPERATION of the Leafs. It's not certain whether this parsimony was inbred or was forced on him. In support of the latter view, it's true that interest payments on the large sums he had borrowed from the Toronto-Dominion

Bank to finance the buyouts of John Bassett in 1971 and of Staff Smythe's family a few months later kept Ballard squeezed (though he continued to pay himself a hefty salary and to collect plenty more in dividends). The financial pressure eased in the 1980s, first because Ballard cut a deal with Molson Breweries (more about that later) and second because Gardens shares shot up in value on the stock market. Nevertheless, in both flush financial times and in more strapped periods, Ballard ran a ridiculously tight ship at the Gardens.

He skimped on scouting, employing only three full-time scouts in the early 1980s (Floyd Smith, John Bower, Dick Duff) while wiser, more successful teams were bulking up to scouting staffs of three and four times that number. He refused to finance recruiting trips to Europe, which was odd since the Leafs, by signing Borje Salming and Inge Hammarstrom of Sweden in 1973, blazed the trail for Europeans in the NHL; no European players followed Salming and Hammarstrom to the Leafs until the mid-1980s, a time when the Islanders and Oilers had already won Stanley Cups with Finns and Swedes. And he set a salary scale at the Gardens that made maintenance workers the lowest-paid throughout the entire NHL and that compelled many of them to work at wages near the poverty line.

The pathetic tale of Stan Obodiac illustrated Ballard's niggardliness. Obodiac started work as the Gardens' publicist in 1958. He added the chores of the team publicity man in 1976 at no raise in salary. The salary, by the early 1980s, for a man sixty years old, for an employee approaching a quarter-century of service, was a stunningly inadequate $23,000. For this, Obodiac, a decent, simple man who loved his job despite everything, wrote press releases that were effulgent in Ballard's praises. Obodiac was sincere about the encomiums. He considered Ballard a great Canadian. There seems to be a moral here: Ballard expected employees to kiss the hem of his garment, but he rewarded those who embraced him most fervently with the back of his hand.

The Obodiac story gets sadder. In 1983, Obodiac was found to have cancer. Ballard gave him a holiday ticket to Hawaii. One ticket. Obodiac, who had been living on advances against his salary for years, couldn't afford to take his wife, Emma. He went by himself, and, alone, with cancer, he was probably the only visitor in the history of Hawaiian tourism who had a miserable time on the islands.

But Ballard didn't forget Emma. On an early morning in December 1984, a knock on the Obodiac door awakened Emma. It was the day after Stan's funeral.

"Yes?" Emma said to the man standing at the door.

"I'm from the Gardens," the man said. "Mr. Ballard wants Stan's company car back. Now."

BALLARD'S STINGINESS MADE HIM PARTICULARLY VULNERable to the World Hockey Association. The WHA started in 1972 as a rival league to the NHL. It endured for seven seasons, put franchises in twenty-eight cities (two of which, in San Francisco and Dayton, didn't last long enough to acquire team names), employed 803 players at one time or another, paying them about $120 million in salaries, and became a recurring pain in the pocketbook to the NHL. It stole away some of the older league's stars, notably Bobby Hull and the Howes *en famille*, and it signed underage whiz-kid juniors like Wayne Gretzky. The WHA made times tough for all NHL teams, driving up player salaries and upsetting team rosters, but probably no team suffered from the WHA's seven years of existence quite so much as the Toronto Maple Leafs.

A typical incident: the Miami Screaming Eagles of the WHA offered the young Leaf goalie, Bernie Parent, a contract for $150,000. Toronto was paying him $25,000. Parent's agent, Howard Casper, invited Ballard to enter into counter-negotiations, a chance to hang on to the kid who would blossom into one of the top two pro goalies of the decade. "If Parent can get that kind of money," Ballard said, "I won't stop him." End of negotiations, beginning of Toronto's long struggle to find an adequate goaltender.

Other Leafs followed to the WHA, the promising young defencemen Rick Ley and Brad Selwood to the Hartford Whalers, captain Dave Keon to the Minnesota Fighting Saints. In all, as a result of Ballard's tight-fisted approach, the Leafs lost eighteen players, counting minor-leaguers, to the World Hockey Association, departures that left serious holes in the organization's roster.

(Perversely, when peace between the NHL and the WHA was at hand in the late 1970s, when a merger was proposed to bring four WHA teams into the NHL—Hartford, which was partly owned by a New England Yankee named Howard Baldwin; Quebec City; Edmonton; and Winnipeg, principally owned by Jewish businessmen—Ballard was among the small handful of NHL owners who held out against the merger until the last moment. Why? His reason might be partly explained in a remark he made to Susan Bassett, the wife of John Bassett, Jr., a WHA owner. This came on an early morning in 1977 when Ms. Bassett ran into Ballard and King Clancy at the Atlanta Airport. "Merger?!" Ballard exploded. "No way. You think I'm gonna vote for something that'll bring in those Hebes from Winnipeg and that mackerel-snapper from Hartford?")

LOOKED AT FROM ONE ANGLE, ALL OF THIS LUNACY MIGHT seem comic. *Wayne's World* meets Abbott and Costello. But Leaf fans soon stopped laughing. It was no joke when the team began to lose far more often than it won. Who saw the humour in an organization too cheap to bid against the WHA, to hire the scouts needed for first-hand reports on the best junior and European prospects, to sign free agents, to buy the time for young players to mature rather than to be rushed into NHL service?

Harold Ballard's attitude, policies and ego, his resentment of past triumphs, were stripping the Maple Leafs of success, tradition and pride. For years, the larger part of two decades, it was no fun to be a Leaf fan. It was harder to be a Leaf player.

16

Brian's Song

BRIAN GLENNIE CAME ON AFTER A BARBERSHOP quartet of seventy-somethings sang "Zippity-Doo-Dah." Before that, a man with a mournful expression stood at the microphone and read a list of Leaf players who had died since last year's dinner. "Larry Cahan, poor Larry's left us. And this'll come as a shock to a lot of you fellas, Bunny Larocque, still a young man, Bunny's gone..." Finally, Brian Glennie had his turn. He was the evening's featured speaker.

This was on a Friday night in early May 1993 in a banquet room at the Fire Fighters' Hall in the exurbs north of Toronto. There were about 150 men sitting at tables for eight. They'd had dinner, iceberg lettuce slathered in deep-red Kraft dressing, roast beef cooked grey, plenty of Blue Light. The event was billed as the NHL Old-Timers Annual Dinner, and while there was a handful of ex–Boston Bruins in the room, Leo Labine, Jerry Toppazzini, some ex–Rangers, ex-Red Wings, ex-Canadiens, others, the large majority of these Old-Timers had worn the blue and white of the Maple Leafs.

Bob Davidson sat at one table, Gus Bodnar at another, Sid Smith and Mike "Shakey" Walton and Bob Baun. George Parsons was there, seventy-nine years old, erect and dignified in the Stanley Knowles manner. Parsons had been a real comer on the Leaf team of the late 1930s, a natural goal scorer, until the night in Chicago in March 1939 when a Black Hawk player, Earl Robinson, flicked his stick across Parsons' right eyeball. Parsons said he never carried a grudge against Robinson—what happened was an accident—but the flick cost George his eye and his hockey career. Johnny McCormack was present too, nick-named "Goose" in the old days for his rangy physique, a utility centre on the Stanley Cup Leafs of '51. Goose—he loved telling this story—was the guy Conn Smythe sent down to the minors for having the nerve to get married in the middle of the hockey season.

And, speaking of storytellers, Doc Murray was on hand. Dr. James Murray, a distinguished surgeon and, from 1948 to 1964, the Leafs' res-ident physician. At Doc's table, he told the one about the time at the Gardens he set Tim Horton's badly broken leg. "I got to Tim inside of three or four minutes of the break," Murray explained. "It simplifies things when you get them that quick. 'Okay, Tim,' I said, 'take a deep breath.' I yanked his broken leg, and all the bones fell into place as perfect as you could ask. Must've hurt like the devil, but Tim was the strongest player I ever saw."

And then at last it was another former Leaf, a defenceman who came to the team in 1969 and played ten years in the NHL, Brian Glennie, stepping to the microphone on the low stage at the front of the banquet room. Glennie looked like Kenny Rogers, the same waves of flowing hair, same beard going to grey, same air of the romantic toughing it out. His stomach rolled over the top of his tan slacks. He told overweight jokes. "Fat," Glennie said, "means always being on the bottom when you have sex." Then he got down to the serious hockey stuff. He told the one about Stan Mikita throwing up on the ice in Moscow.

It seems that Glennie and Mikita, a couple of spares on Team Canada in the 1972 series against Russia, were taking part in a one-on-one drill between games. Mikita, looking grey and drawn, had been on the town the night before, getting seriously into the Stolichnaya, and just at the moment in the drill when he made his deke to skate past Glennie, he vomited. Glennie jumped back. Mikita gathered himself and scored. Six weeks later, as Glennie told the story, in a regular-season game at the

Gardens, Chicago versus the Leafs, Mikita broke loose on a rush. Glennie was the only Leaf back. He was giving Mikita plenty of room. He knew Mikita had a nifty little cross-over move he liked to pull on defencemen who played him too close. Glennie laid back. To his astonishment, Mikita jammed on the brakes and rocketed a slapshot into the net.

"What's the matter, Brian?" Mikita said to Glennie. "You think I was gonna throw up on you again?"

The story drew a huge laugh from the audience of Old-Timers. This was real Canadian hockey culture, vulgar and good-natured, beer and laughs and reminiscences of nights on the ice. Glennie told more stories and got more guffaws. He had a rough, wingy, ingratiating style, a low-rent David Letterman. But towards the end of his routine, he changed manner. He turned sentimental, more Jack Paar than David Letterman. His eyes went misty.

"After I quit playing hockey, I kind of stayed away from the game," Glennie said, his voice raspy. "I didn't see much of the guys I knew in hockey. But I look out here tonight and see old buddies, Bob Nevin sitting over there, and the Boomer, Bobby Baun, and I realize it's a great fellowship we have in hockey. It was a privilege to play hockey. It was a privilege to be able to play for the Toronto Maple Leafs."

Glennie paused. "It was hard for a few years there to say you were a Maple Leaf. But now, today, the way things have changed in the last couple of years, it's a hell of a great thing to say you're a Toronto Maple Leaf."

Brian Glennie got a standing ovation.

SIX MONTHS LATER, GLENNIE TALKED MORE SPECIFICALLY about his years in hockey. It was a crisp November morning. A hint of frost was already in the air, but frost came early to Glennie's part of the world, in cottage country, Muskoka, 102 miles north of Toronto. The view from Glennie's handsomely renovated house, standing alone at the edge of a hundred acres of brush land, was past a huge, majestic old pine to a corner of Lake Muskoka. In late autumn, it was still and quiet, no summer crowds, no traffic, nothing moving out there. Glennie seemed to like it that way.

He grew up in Toronto, graduated from Don Mills Collegiate, played his hockey as a kid on teams that were coached by one of his future Leaf coaches, Roger Neilson. "Bick's Pickles Midgets," Glennie said. "That was one of Roger's teams. We won the city midget championship. Roger knew how to put a team together."

The Leafs had their eye on Glennie, and he was captain of the Marlboro Junior team of 1967 that won the Memorial Cup. But Glennie resisted moving up to the big team immediately, to the Leafs. He enrolled at the University of Toronto, eventually getting his degree, and he played a year of hockey with the 1968 Olympic Team. Glennie did things a little differently from other young hockey players. He wasn't sure why. That year, 1968, Canada won a bronze at the Games in Grenoble. After the Olympics, Glennie signed with the Leafs.

"They paired me with Tim Horton the first year," Glennie said, drinking coffee, smoking a cigarette. "I was always partners with someone like Timmie, guys who could move the puck. I played a lot with Jim McKenny, a lot with Borje Salming. I was the standup guy who would take the man out, and the other guy, Timmie or Jim or Borje, would get the puck and start something happening."

Glennie blew out a jittery stream of smoke. "I was the defenceman people seemed not to notice."

JOHN MCLELLAN COACHED THE LEAFS IN GLENNIE'S first four years.

"John was a gentleman," Glennie said. "A player's coach. He made me want to play my heart out for him. But there was too much pressure on John to get a good team on the ice after the Leafs had gone downhill in the late 1960s. And, another thing, I got the impression John didn't always have control over which players dressed. Ballard or Clancy or Jim Gregory might tell him to dress somebody John didn't want on the ice. The ulcer that John finally got, I guess you could say he earned it."

In 1973, Red Kelly was hired to replace McLellan, who took his ulcer to the office of assistant general manager. Kelly, after his playing career ended with the Leafs in 1967, had coached the NHL expansion teams in Los Angeles and Pittsburgh. His coaching style was low-key, distant even. "Red was a quiet guy," Glennie said. "He always looked like someone who was thinking deep thoughts."

Another characteristic of Kelly's, unique in a hockey player, he never swore. "Dang" was as close as he came to profanity. A guy whom most players might refer to as a son of a bitch was to Kelly "a sea cook and bottle washer."

But there came a night when the Leafs played such a terrible first period of hockey that Kelly's tongue got away from him.

"Dang," he said in the dressing room, "you guys aren't playing worth hell."

A hush covered the room, the players stunned at the word that had passed Kelly's lips.

"Hey, look, Red," Jim McKenny said into the silence, "I know we're playing bad, but you don't have to swear."

GLENNIE SAID, "BY THE TIME RED ARRIVED, WE WERE starting to see good guys come out of the draft, come up from the farm teams. We had the basis of a real team. We had Borje and Lannie, Sit, Ian Turnbull, Tiger, and Palmy in goal."

DARRYL SITTLER CAME TO THE LEAFS, A SOUTHWESTERN Ontario boy, the team's first draft choice in 1970, eighth draft pick overall, with all the equipment—size, strength, the big shot, guts, a mean streak, great looks, a certain presence which earned respect. So he lacked sophistication? That came with time, and after he was named team captain in 1975, he had the loyalty of every player in the locker room.

Sittler's abiding characteristic was consistency, but when he had big games, they were giants. On February 7, 1976, at the Gardens, against a very good Boston team, he got six goals and four assists. The ten points for one game is an all-time NHL record. That same year, in the Canada Cup, it was Sittler who scored the winning goal in a 2–1 game against Czechoslovakia that gave Canada the championship. And again in 1976, on April 22, Sittler scored five goals in a playoff game against Philadelphia. That tied an all-time NHL record.

Also giant-sized, and growing larger as the years passed, were Sittler's emotions. He was an extravagant guy in that department, big tears, big laughs, grand gestures. Talk about hubris—immense pride carried Sittler to mighty feats on the ice in the 1970s, and it was this almost insupportable pride that would crash his hockey career in the early 1980s. The turnaround probably began when he became the Leaf captain. At that point, 1975, the dramatic events lay far ahead—the ripping of the C from his sweater, the tears over the trading away of his best pal, Lanny McDonald, the rages at Punch Imlach. But as early as '75, he seemed to sense that the Gardens wasn't the best place for a man of such *hauteur* as he. In the meantime, while he sorted it out, Sittler scored almost 400 goals for the Leafs.

BY THE END OF BORJE SALMING'S SEVENTEEN-YEAR CAREER in the NHL (sixteen years with the Leafs), he didn't have a bolt through his neck, but otherwise his head looked like the one on Frankenstein's monster. He had his forehead stitched nine times, his eyebrows an even twenty times, left earlobe once, chin a dozen times. He broke his nose five times and took one wound to the right eye, cheek and nose that needed 300 stitches to close. Salming started out whole and handsome and ended up resembling a creature from the imagination of Mary Wollstonecraft Shelley.

He was a hard and fearless defenceman. Those qualities wouldn't be altogether foreign to a kid growing up in Kiruna, far to the north in Sweden, beyond the Arctic Circle, stuck in a valley between two mountains of iron ore, where the only jobs in town were mining the ore. Salming's father, Erlund, died in one of Kiruna's mines when a conveyor belt crushed his head. Hockey got Borje out of town. Eventually it got him all the way to Toronto. A Leaf scout, Gerry McNamara, spotted Salming in a Christmas 1972 game between Sweden's Brynas team and the touring Barrie Flyers. Salming impressed McNamara with his tough NHL-style play, and a year later, Borje was on the Leaf blueline.

He had hockey smarts as well as hockey courage. He was a fine puck carrier, an even finer passer of the puck; he had three seasons of more than 60 assists, and a total of 620 assists in his Leaf career. At his best, a period that stretched through most of the 1970s and into the '80s,

Salming was one of those rare players who seemed to make the game his own, controlling the play, arranging the tempo, engineering the strategy.

What he was not, curiously, was a leader. He did many unleaderly things during his Toronto years: sniff cocaine, establish the pace as the team's party animal, knuckle under to management when a little frank talking from a senior player was called for. "If I was looking for someone for the young guys to look up to, someone who set an example away from the rink," Darryl Sittler wrote in his autobiography, "it wouldn't be Borje." That was away from the rink. At the rink, Salming was the best Leaf defenceman of his time.

WHEN LANNY MCDONALD HIT TORONTO IN THE FALL OF 1973, somebody could have sold him the T-D Centre. He looked like a hick, the big goofy smile, the black-and-white-checked suit, the black velvet bow tie. He really was a hick, twenty years old and just out of Craigmyle, Alberta (pop.: 103). And somebody did take him to the cleaners. The sharpie was his agent, a fast-talking former Manahattan journalist named Richard Sorkin. He negotiated a fair contract for McDonald with the Leafs, who had made Lanny their number-one pick in the '73 draft, the fourth junior player chosen overall. The contract — $500,000 over five years — wasn't the problem. The problem was that Sorkin embezzled from his hockey clients, about a million dollars. Some of it was Lanny's money. Worse, Revenue Canada nicked McDonald for $38,000 in taxes on income that had disappeared in Sorkin's fast shuffle. Welcome to the big city, kid.

On the ice, McDonald took a couple of years to find his feet. That was literally finding his feet; McDonald had early difficulties just standing up on his skates. But in his third year, he got it going: thirty-seven goals and ninety points. If Guy Lafleur hadn't been around, McDonald might have been the premier right-winger of the 1970s. He made a close second, averaging forty-four goals over seven seasons after his breakthrough year.

Off the ice, McDonald never lost the touch of naïvety he brought from Craigmyle. He had a sweetness that attracted fans. And he had the trademark moustache. He grew it in the summer after his rookie year.

He experimented with a full beard, a goatee, a Fu Manchu. Then he spotted a photograph of Sparky Lyle, the baseball relief pitcher. Lyle wore something on his upper lip that resembled an alien shrub. McDonald grew a moustache just like it. It came in red, the colour of a ripe tomato. It looked ludicrous, but every hockey fan for the next fifteen seasons could pick Lanny out of the lineup.

IAN TURNBULL, FROM MONTREAL, TORONTO'S SECOND draft pick in 1973, after McDonald, was as cosmopolitan as Lanny was rural. In his time with the Leafs, Turnbull drove a Rolls-Royce, he was co-owner of a chic restaurant called Grapes on College Street west of the Gardens, and he put the hustle on Punch Imlach. The latter came in the summer of 1979 when Imlach had returned for his second go-round as the Leaf general manager. Turnbull took to dropping in on Imlach each afternoon when the lunch-hour ended at Grapes. Imlach thought Turnbull was showing friendship, chewing the fat with the new boss. Turnbull had a different strategy in mind. His contract was up. He wanted a new one. When he'd chewed enough fat to win a long-term deal at around $200,000 per year, Turnbull found other things to do with his afternoons. Imlach realized he'd been suckered.

Turnbull had a less concerted approach to playing the game than he did to negotiating a contract. His skills were enormous — fast skater, deft puck carrier, consistent scorer (123 goals in ten NHL seasons). But staying in top condition, working industriously at practice, keeping his head in the game — those were concepts that Turnbull didn't entirely embrace. His natural talents carried him far in hockey. His concentration, which was often wavery, didn't get him much farther.

TIGER WILLIAMS, TAKEN BY THE LEAFS AS THEIR SECOND draft choice in 1974, arrrived in Toronto from Weyburn, Saskatchewan, only twenty years old but with the sensibilities of a middle-aged right-wing Prairie populist. He was principled, rigid and conservative. He collected guns and drove a Jeep. He worked hard, drank little, got on the case of any teammate who took what Williams judged a lackadaisical approach to hockey. In his first scrimmage on his first day in training camp as a rookie winger, Williams started a punchup with—no surprise here—Ian Turnbull.

Williams advocated honesty as the best policy, no matter what the fallout. Years after he retired, he wrote a warts-and-all autobiography which contained, among other revelations, descriptions of his teammate Jim McKenny's adventures with hockey groupies, no details spared.

"Thanks a lot, Tiger," McKenny said when, in his capacity as a sportscaster for CITY-TV in Toronto, he interviewed Williams on air about the book. "I've always wanted to tell my kids those stories, but I never had the guts. Thanks for doing the job."

Williams played tough. He also played dirty. He had 338 minutes in penalties in 1976–77. That led the league. Eventually Williams learned to score goals—he ended his fourteen-year NHL career with 241 goals (and sixty-six hours in penalties)—but it was his toughness that prevailed during his early seasons with the Leafs. He generated the atmosphere, mostly of fear, that helped Leafs like Sittler and McDonald score goals.

NOBODY QUESTIONED MIKE PALMATEER'S CONFIDENCE. Mike didn't. When he made the Leaf team in the autumn of 1976, he announced, "Relax, guys. I'm here to save the franchise." This was from a goaltender who didn't get picked until the fifth round of the 1974 draft, who spent three seasons playing for Saginaw in the International League and Oklahoma City in the Central League. But he was almost right; if he didn't precisely save the franchise, he gave the team, which had gone through seven goalies after Harold Ballard allowed Bernie Parent to escape in 1972, stability in the nets.

It was, at times, a scarey sort of stability. Palmateer, a little guy with the face of an altar boy, invested every stop, even of a shot that came without force or guile or surprise, with a sensational fillip. Routine shot, spectacular save. Difficult shot, spectacular save. Palmateer knew only one kind of save. He was a showboat, but a nice showboat, a sincere showboat, our showboat.

ALONG WITH THIS SIX-PLAYER NUCLEUS, THE LEAFS HAD some solid role players. Errol Thompson could skate like the wind and score goals (forty-three of them in 1975–76). Inge Hammarstrom—the stylish winger who accompanied Salming from Sweden—knew a thing or two about speed and goals too, though he wasn't hard-nosed enough for Harold Ballard and found himself on the receiving end of Ballard's famously cruel crack: "He could skate into a corner with six eggs in his pocket and not break any of them." Others provided toughness on the wings, Pat Boutette for one, and Brian Glennie and Bob Neeley did the same on defence.

Still, the Leaf team was essentially middle-of-the-pack. And it happened to come along when other organizations were putting together dynasties of different sorts. Philadelphia had the "Broad Street Bullies," a club built on guys named "The Hammer" and "Hound Dog," on organized aggression and plain old intimidation, and on two stars, the centre Bobby Clarke and the goalie—ah, yes, Harold—Bernie Parent. At the same time, Montreal's squad of great defencemen (Larry Robinson, Guy Lapointe, Serge Savard) and wizard forwards (Guy Lafleur, Yvan Cournoyer, Steve Shutt) was setting itself for domination, and the young New York Islanders (Mike Bossy, Bryan Trottier, Denis Potvin, et al.) were on the verge of something marvellous.

Did the Leafs belong in such swift company? Hardly. In 1974–75, Toronto finished twelfth overall out of eighteen NHL teams and got flattened by Philadelphia in four straight playoff games. But the following season, 1975–76, the same Leafs gave off whiffs of promise. This time they finished seventh in the final standings, and when they again encountered the Flyers in the playoff quarter-finals, they brought some snap to the battle.

The Flyers won the first two games in Philly. But they weren't shoving the Leafs around. In the third game, at the Gardens, the Flyers tried to shove harder. Major fights erupted. Tiger Williams versus Jack McIlhargey. Kurt Walker versus Dave "The Hammer" Schultz. Borje Salming versus Mel Bridgman. The fans got into it: they hurled eggs and golf balls at the Flyers. The cops got into it: one of them took a high stick from the Flyers' Joe Watson. Roy McMurtry got into it: he was Ontario's attorney general, and he laid charges of assault and of possession of a dangerous weapon (a hockey stick) against four Flyers (two of them, including Watson, eventually pleaded guilty to reduced charges and paid fines). Meanwhile, back on the ice, the Leafs won the raucous third game and, for good measure, the fourth game too.

Series all tied.

BRIAN GLENNIE SAID, "YEAH, THAT WAS THE SERIES WHERE Red brought in the pyramids. Hell of a lot of good they did me."

Kelly had learned from his two sons, who had recently visited Egypt, of a property in pyramids that centred the energies of those who submitted to them. He consulted a pyramid man at the University of Toronto and had six of them constructed. One large pyramid was hung from the ceiling in the Leaf dressing room and five smaller ones found places under the players' bench. Kelly encouraged the players to open themselves and/or pieces of their equipment to whatever force radiated from the pyramids. The total cost of the pyramids was $25,000. Kelly went first class on the project.

Did he also go a little berserk on it?

Not really. Maybe Kelly saw mysterious powers in his pyramids. More likely, he saw a diversion in them. Kelly, who is nobody's fool, recognized that the Leafs were under terrific pressure to beat the Flyers, to restore a touch of prestige to the Maple Leafs. Harold Ballard had predicted at the beginning of the series that Toronto would win in five games. Oh, sure, whip the team that had won the last two Stanley Cups. No problem, Harold. To deflect such thinking, to give the media and fans another subject to dwell on, Kelly came up with the pyramids. That ought to take some heat off the players.

The pyramids came in for major play in the minutes before the sixth game. The Leafs had been blown out in the fifth game in Philadelphia, leaving them down three games to two. Now, back in the Gardens, they were on the brink of elimination.

"So Darryl put his stick under the big pyramid in the centre of the room," Brian Glennie remembered. "Just his stick. That was the night he scored five goals. Put his stick under the pyramid, got five goals, and we won the game, 8–5. Me, I sat under the damn pyramid, and out on the ice, on one of my shifts, I was standing in front of our goal. Bill

Barber for the Flyers wound up and let go a slapshot. The puck hit me in the jaw and rebounded all the way out to centre ice. The shot broke hell out of my jaw. I was four and a half hours on the operating table. That's what pyramid power did for me."

The Leafs lost the seventh game of the series to the Flyers in Philadelphia. Kelly never used the pyramids again.

THE FOLLOWING SEASON, 1976–77, ALMOST EVERYTHING went sour for Kelly. The Leafs slumped off slightly during league play, and once again met the Flyers in the playoff quarter-finals. Toronto won the first two games in Philadelphia, then lost four straight. For Kelly, that wasn't the only painful event of the year. He'd had a bad back from his playing days, and when Lanny McDonald accidentally bumped into him during a practice, the pain turned to agony. Ballard, looking for an excuse to rid himself of Kelly, on whom he'd now turned, saw Red's aching back as the ideal out.

"I don't think it's fair to Red to take the chance of aggravating his injury," Ballard announced. "So the Leafs won't be renewing his contract."

FOR THE 1977–78 SEASON, TORONTO BROUGHT UP THE MAN who had coached its Dallas farm team.

"He was a new coach to the other guys," Brian Glennie said. "But he was an old coach to me, all the way back to Bick's Pickles Midgets."

The new Leaf coach was Roger Neilson.

17

Roger

WHEN JACQUES DIED IN 1976, ROGER Neilson buried him at his cottage on Buckhorn Lake, north of Peterborough. A wheelbarrow tray marked the grave: "Here Lies Jacques. The Greatest Dog Ever. 1958–1975." Jacques was part collie, part German shepherd. Dogs seem to have been Roger Neilson's best friends through his adult life. Years after Jacques died, Neilson was coaching the New York Rangers. His companion was Mike, a husky, smart, good-natured Labrador retriever. On the day the Rangers fired Neilson, January 4, 1993, Mike died of cancer. Neilson wasn't sure which hurt most, the loss of his job or of his dog.

Neilson never married. He put in long, almost brutal hours at hockey, and he had his dogs for company. Harold Ballard, when he became disenchanted with Neilson, something that seemed to happen in record time, told people that Neilson was gay. Ballard meant it as the worst, most humiliating insult. Ballard called plenty of men he disliked gay. Frank Orr was one, the *Toronto Star* hockey writer who'd been critical in print of the Leafs' failings. Ballard was wrong about these men's sexual orientation, wrong about Orr, wrong about Neilson. One day, he saw Neilson embracing a beautiful woman at an airport. He stopped calling Neilson gay.

Neilson's parents were members of the evangelical Christian Missionary Alliance in Toronto. The religion rubbed off on young Roger. In his early years as a hockey and baseball coach, he refused to handle Sunday games, and after a trip to parts of Africa in the late spring of 1977, after exposure to African poverty and hunger, he said he might return one day as a missionary. Neilson worked his way through McMaster University delivering newspapers. Earlier than that, in his mid-teens, he started coaching. He moved up, he coached Bick's Pickles, he became coach of the Peterborough Petes Junior A team. At one convergence of careers, he delivered papers in the early morning, taught high school history and phys ed by day, coached the Petes at night. His reputation spread, principally as an original strategist and, in a phrase that doesn't really come within a hundred miles of characterizing Neilson's devotion to hockey duty, as one hell of a hard worker.

NEILSON WROTE A LETTER TO DARRYL SITTLER. THIS WAS in the summer of 1978 after Neilson had coached the Leafs for one season. "Try to be less sensitive about ice time," Neilson wrote. "Next year we intend to use you penalty killing. However, it is disastrous to our team when sensitivity toward ice time affects your play." The piece of advice was one of thirteen that Neilson passed on to Sittler in the letter. Another was, "Be concerned with positioning in our defensive zone on 4 on 4s." Neilson wrote letters with varying advice to every player on the team. The man was incredibly thorough.

A year earlier, in the summer of 1977 after Neilson was appointed Leaf coach, he analysed videos of twenty-five Toronto games from the 1976–77 season. He decided that the team was weak in positional play, that its style was too wide open and allowed the opponents too many goals, that several players came up short in conditioning. He set out to remedy all the defects. The conditioning problem was easiest. Neilson ordered a summer program of running and calisthenics, effective immediately. Be in shape to run five miles a day in thirty-five minutes or fewer by the time training camp opened. No excuses accepted.

In the matter of strategy and practice, Neilson put all sorts of novel ideas in place. At practice, players went through competitive drills rather than the usual and unvarying scrimmages. After games, Mike Palmateer and his backup, Gord McRae, were required to write a report on each goal that beat them. Strategy? Neilson was probably the first coach to switch wingers on the power play, putting the right-hand shooter on the left side, and vice versa, thereby giving each a better angle on the opposing net. That's old hat today, but it wasn't when Neilson brought it to the Leafs. The same went for the matter of setting picks on power plays, something Neilson introduced: one offensive Leaf would be designated to take a defensive man out of the play, meaning that the Leafs would go five-on-four rather than six-on-five, thus providing the offence more room to move around. So it went with Neilson the innovator. In one game in Pittsburgh, the Leafs down by three goals in the second period, Toronto got a two-man advantage, and Neilson pulled the goalie. Unorthodox? For sure, but Neilson was a guy with a mind for the edge. Too bad the Leafs lost the game in Pittsburgh.

Or consider Neilson's in-and-out-the-doors stratagem. At Maple Leaf Gardens, the Leaf bench had two doors, one at the south blueline and the other near the centre redline. On a Toronto power play, in the first and third periods, when the Leafs played out of the south end, Borje Salming would set up behind the Toronto net. The Leaf right-winger hovered at the blueline close to the door to the bench. The checking forward on the opposing team would invariably stay right there in the Leaf right-winger's vicinity. Salming, behind the net, would toss the puck forward to his centre—say, Sittler. At the same moment, the two Leaf doors flew open. The right-winger stepped off the ice, through the door at the blueline. Another right-winger, Lanny McDonald usually, leaped onto the ice through the door close to the centre redline. Swish, swish, slam, slam, and McDonald was headed down ice, on the fly, a solid few strides ahead of the opposing checker, who'd been fooled into loitering at the blueline. McDonald had the jump, ready to take a pass from Sittler, set for a possible break past the other guys' defence. Well, okay, it sounds like something Curley, Moe and Larry might cook up, but who knew when it might produce a goal? That's what Roger figured.

ON THE MATTER OF THE LARGER PICTURE, THE OVERALL
plan, the problem of the drawbacks that Neilson perceived in Toronto's
positional play and its overly wide-open style, he retinkered the team
from the essentially offensive-minded outfit it had been to something
more defensively minded. In a sense, it was less a defensive system that
Neilson installed than a defensive philosophy. "Not giving up the defensive zone," Brian Glennie remembered. "That's what Roger taught. He
taught us to be determined about it, to think about keeping the other
guys off the puck, think it constantly."

Slight changes in personnel went with the change in style. Inge
Hammarstrom for Jerry Butler—that was one trade, made in November
1977, Inge, the speedy goal-scorer, to St. Louis for Butler, the hard-as-
nails checker. Then, in March 1978 came the trade which, as we'll see
later, may have cost both Neilson and Jim Gregory their jobs in the long
run: Errol Thompson to Detroit for Dan Maloney, the Leafs giving up a
scorer in exchange for a winger with impressive tough-guy credentials.

Part of the notion behind the extra muscle was to provide protection
for Toronto's primarily offensive players—Sittler, McDonald, Turnbull.
Butler and Maloney supplied help in that area, and Sittler and McDonald ended up with sensational numbers on the season: 45 goals and 117
points for Darryl, 47 and 87 for Lannie. In total, the Leaf scoring was
down from the previous year by thirty goals, but—here's a measure of
Neilson's defensive success—the team allowed forty-eight fewer goals.
The Leafs accumulated ninety-two points, eleven more than in 1976–77,
and they finished sixth best among the league's eighteen teams.

ALL OF THIS SET THE STAGE IN THE PLAYOFFS FOR A
thriller of a Stanley Cup quarter-final round, the series that wasn't to be
matched for Toronto fans in excitement, skill and hope (illusory as the
latter turned out to be) until the Kings–Leafs semi-final of 1993.
Toronto's opponent was the New York Islanders, the touted team of the
future, the team of Bossy, Trottier and friends, the team that finished
nineteen points ahead of the Leafs in the NHL standings that year and
was expected to brush away Toronto on the way to a showdown with the
reigning champs, the Montreal Canadiens.

The series started out according to expectations, the Islanders winning game one at the Nassau Coliseum. Game two turned out the same way, an Islander victory, but a couple of things happened in the game that stirred in the Leafs an emotion rather like optimism. For one thing, the Islanders needed an overtime goal to take the win, and for another, late in the game, medium-sized Jerry Butler rocked extra-large-sized Clark Gillies with such a flattening check that other Leafs began thinking, hey, maybe we can out-smack these guys.

Back in Toronto for the third game, Mike Palmateer did everything except stand on his head—and maybe there was a little of that—in shutting out the Islanders (remember, this was a team, the Islanders, that scored 334 goals, second-best in the league that season). Toronto won the fourth game too, 3–1. But the news on the night was otherwise discouraging.

Borje Salming was cutting around the Islanders' Lorne Henning. Henning's stick, as he tried to hook Salming, stabbed Borje's eye. Blood emitted from practically every Salming orifice. His sinuses bled. He vomited blood. The sight was wholly gross. Poor Borje had to rest in hospital for the next seven days, both eyes bandaged shut.

Ian Turnbull stepped forward in Salming's absence. The guy who was long on talent, short on concentration played the hockey of his career. He took extra shifts, shut down the Islanders on defence, and led the charge on offence. That wasn't good enough to win game five in Nassau—the Leafs again lost in overtime—but at the Gardens for game six, Turnbull was once more all over the ice. So was Jerry Butler. He hit Mike Bossy such a check that Bossy left the building via stretcher. Leafs won the game 6–2.

On Long Island for the deciding game, the Islanders took a large edge in play—more rushes, more shots, but not more goals. Palmateer was hot, and the rest of the Leafs were beginning to get the idea that maybe Kismet was on their side. The damned Nassau Coliseum sound system kept playing the Islanders' new theme song, "We Are the Champions." Screw that, the Leafs said, and the game, tied at one-all, went into overtime.

It was Lanny McDonald, Lanny with a broken bone in one wrist and a busted nose, who made the difference. At a little past the four-minute mark of overtime, Turnbull carried the puck up the left side, fired a waist-high pass to McDonald. Lanny brought the puck down with his glove. Three Islanders—Clark Gillies, Dave Lewis, Denis Potvin—were in position to check McDonald. It turned into an Alphonse–Gaston routine. You check him, Clark. No, I insist, you check him, Dave. While all the Islander bowing and scraping was going on, McDonald got off a fluttering wrist shot that dipped past Chico Resch in the New York net. Game over.

It was the most significant win for a Maple Leaf team in eleven years—and would remain the most significant for another fifteen years.

BRIAN GLENNIE SAID IN NOVEMBER 1993: "AFTER WE beat the Islanders in that series, we didn't have enough for the Canadiens in the semi-finals. Montreal took us four straight. But what I remember from our good games against the Islanders was the electricity at the Gardens. The crowd would be in their seats forty-five minutes before the games started, and they'd be going crazy. So were we, the players. Something fantastic was in the air."

Brian Glennie also said in November 1993: "All through 1977–78, we were a very good hockey club. We were tough. We could score. We had Roger. Every night, we knew all twenty players would show up and play hard. There was a chemistry among us. Sure as hell the New York Islanders would never have beaten us in a playoff series after that year. And yet the same Islander team, without any player changes, went on to win four Stanley Cups in the early 1980s. And the Leafs, well, the Leafs faded right out of contention for anything. Most of us felt we were probably one draft choice away from a Stanley Cup. If we drafted one more goal scorer, or if we traded for a scorer, that might have pushed us over the top. But what happened was that management fooled around with the makeup of the team. It was like a jigsaw puzzle. It was like moving around too many pieces, looking for the one that would complete the puzzle. Instead, they ended up taking the whole damned puzzle apart."

THE GOAL SCORERS, TWO OF THEM, WHOM THE LEAFS might have acquired in the summer of 1979, were Anders Hedberg and Ulf Nilsson. They were tremendously gifted offensive players who'd formed a dynamite line with Bobby Hull on the Winnipeg Jets of the WHA through most of the 1970s. Now they were looking for contracts with an NHL club. They—and their wives—favoured Toronto. But when they visited the city, expecting to be wooed by the Leafs, the largest impression they took away was of Harold Ballard. Such a boor, Hedberg and Nilsson thought, a loud guy who told racist jokes. In New York, by contrast, the Rangers wheeled out everything from a tour of the city's Swedish-American neighbourhoods to a seminar on tax structure. Hedberg and Nilsson signed with the Rangers, and a year later, in 1978–79, the team went to the Stanley Cup final.

THE LEAFS, PUSHING AROUND THE PIECES OF THE JIGSAW puzzle, made two trades that summer of '78. Both were for large and rugged defencemen. In one trade, they got Dave Burrows from Pittsburgh in exchange for the veteran forward George Ferguson and the rookie defenceman Randy Carlyle (who went on to a sixteen-year NHL career, winning the Norris Trophy as the league's best defenceman in 1980–81). The other trade brought Dave Hutchison from the Los Angeles Kings to the Leafs, who gave up Kurt Walker, Scott Garland... and Brian Glennie.

"How I found out about the trade," Glennie remembered, "was when a reporter from the *Toronto Sun* phoned me at 1:30 in the morning. I told him the equivalent of, don't bullshit me, how could it be true, what he was telling me? I was traded? I'd just played the best year of hockey in my life for the best team I'd ever been on. Trade me? No way. But it happened to be true."

Life in La-La Land wasn't bad for Glennie as long as he was away from the rink. "I lived right on the Pacific in a place called Manhattan Beach, wore shorts and T-shirts, and never had to push a car out of a snow drift." But at the rink, things went on the bum for Glennie. He injured his back. Surgery didn't fix the problem, and Glennie's career ended. He returned to Toronto. He opened a restaurant called Wheels on Church Street, near the Gardens. It lost money. He took a salesman's job at York Litho, a company he was still with in 1994. The retreat to Muskoka came earlier, in the late 1980s.

"I thought I'd handle retirement from hockey better than I have," Glennie said, lighting another cigarette, looking edgy, then waving his hand in a dismissive gesture. "But never mind that. I had my time. Great bunch of guys on a team that was almost great."

AT THE GARDENS IN THE WINTER OF 1978–79, HAROLD Ballard grew profoundly unhappy. This was the season the Leafs would break through, go all the way, a Stanley Cup. The fans expected it. Ballard predicted it. The team had finished on a high the previous season, beating the Islanders. Now it was supposed to take the next step, the next couple of steps. But things refused to happen that way.

Statistics don't explain what went wrong. The team scored almost as many goals as in 1977–78, just four fewer, and it allowed only fifteen more. There were even stretches when the Leafs played very classy hockey. But, count on it, the good streaks would be followed by flat patches. Somehow, maybe in the trades, maybe partly in giving up a guy like Glennie, who'd been a presence in the Toronto dressing room for almost a decade, the team chemistry was dissipated. It wasn't the fault of the new players; Burrows and Hutchison played hard and honest hockey. But the outcome—the result of the hot–cold play, the difference in team balance—was a season of barely better than .500 hockey, thirty-four wins, thirty-three losses. In the first preliminary round of the playoffs, the Leafs beat Atlanta, then, as in the previous year, got hammered in four straight by the Canadiens, who, as in the previous year, won the Stanley Cup.

Footnote: The Leafs didn't achieve another season of .500 hockey for exactly a decade.

BALLARD PLANNED TO FIRE ROGER NEILSON AS EARLY AS March 1979. Ballard never could figure out why he'd allowed Jim Gregory to talk him into hiring Neilson in the first place. Neilson wasn't Ballard's kind of hockey guy, not a familiar face in the hockey circles Ballard moved in, not a coach on whom somebody else's organization had put a stamp of approval (Ballard counted heavily on other people's opinion). And Ballard didn't go for Neilson's cerebral style, all that damned studying of videotape, all the charts and notes and graphs. Neilson was too reclusive, too private, practically invisible, for gawd's sake. Ballard liked a coach who'd sit around with him, with Ballard, and talk some hockey, tell old war stories. Hell, Neilson probably didn't know any old war stories.

Partway through March '79, on a Wednesday night, in the minutes after the Leafs lost a heartbreaker to Montreal 2–1 at the Forum, Ballard dropped the word to his pal Dick Beddoes: Neilson was history. Beddoes had a post-game TV show on the Hamilton station CHCH at the time, and he rushed to air with the scoop. Harold Ballard, Beddoes told his viewers, has just fired Roger Neilson. Except that Beddoes, a man given to the baroque, phrased it more like this: "The panjandrum of the Cashbox on Carlton Street has whispered in the ear of your obedient servant that he is tying the can to the Einstein of the hockey bench, the immanently departing Roger Neilson."

One problem: Ballard didn't have a replacement coach lined up. He offered the job to Eddie Johnston, who was coaching the Moncton team in the American League. No thanks, Johnston said, I'm expecting to be named the Black Hawk coach (Johnston was right about that; he coached Chicago for the 1979–80 season). Ballard turned to the Leaf assistant general manager, John McLellan. No thanks, said McLellan, my health wouldn't stand the pressure (McLellan was probably right about that; he died in October '79 of a heart attack).

One other problem: the Leaf players wanted Neilson to remain as their coach. On the Friday after the Wednesday of Neilson's firing, and a day before a Saturday-night game at the Gardens, the players took a vote. It was close to unanimous in Neilson's favour, Ian Turnbull registering the notable anti-Neilson ballot. Darryl Sittler, as captain, conveyed the wishes of the players to Ballard, who, according to Sittler's later report, did some growling and door slamming. But he gave in. He rescinded the firing of Neilson. After all, somebody had to coach the Leafs on Saturday night.

Ballard tried to turn the situation, already embarrassing, into his concept of a public-relations coup. He asked Neilson to make his entrance on to the floor of the Gardens on Saturday night, a few seconds before game time, wearing a bag over his head. Off would come the bag—this was Ballard's idea of great PR—and the crowd would go nuts with surprise and relief and joy. Neilson refused. When he took his bare-headed place behind the Leaf bench on Saturday night, the crowd went nuts anyway.

AT THE END OF THE SEASON, AFTER THE CANADIENS eliminated the Leafs from the playoffs, Ballard fired Neilson for keeps. He fired Jim Gregory too, the idiot general manager who'd brought Neilson to the Leafs.

A couple of weeks after Neilson left Toronto, the Buffalo Sabres took him on as associate coach to Scotty Bowman. For the last twenty-six games of Neilson's first Buffalo season, 1979–80, and for all of the next, he was Buffalo's head coach. The following year, he moved to Vancouver as the Canucks' associate coach. With five games left in the regular schedule, he moved up to head coach. Vancouver finished in twenty-second place that year, but Neilson guided the team all the way to the Stanley Cup final, where it finally lost to the Islanders. Neilson had another year and a half as Canucks coach, twenty-eight games in 1983–84 as the Los Angeles Kings coach, then three seasons as Chicago Black Hawks co-coach (with Bob Pulford) and two more as a Chicago special scout. In 1989, he began a term of three and a half years in the head-coaching job with the New York Rangers. The Rangers won fifty games in Neilson's third New York season, the most in franchise history; the team finished first overall in the league that year, but was eliminated in the second round of the playoffs. The following year, 1992–93, the Rangers' captain and star player, Mark Messier, crabbed publicly about Neilson's coaching tactics. Neilson, for his part, felt Messier had slipped from his prime and cut Messier's ice time. New York management took Messier's side in the dispute—they were paying the guy $3 million a year, much more than Neilson was getting—and fired Neilson in January '93. A few months later, the Florida Panthers, new to the league, named Neilson as its first coach.

Through all of these remarkable travels, from Toronto to Miami, as Neilson became the eighteenth coach in NHL history to win 300 games, Mike kept him company on all except the last stop in Florida. This was Mike the Labrador retriever, Mike the successor to Jacques, Mike the wonder dog. Mike was genuinely a wonder dog. During Neilson's two years of coaching in Buffalo, when he left his apartment each day to head for team practice at the Buffalo Auditorium, Mike stayed home alone. But Mike didn't care for the solitary life. One day, he trotted out to the busstop by himself and rode a bus to the Auditorium. Mike knew which stop he wanted. He got off the bus and joined Neilson at the practice. Neilson swears it's a true story. Smart dog, smart master.

18

Punched Again

IN EARLY MARCH 1978, IT SEEMED THAT PRACTICALLY everyone in the Leaf organization wanted Dan Maloney on the team. Maybe somebody who played in the Maloney manner would be okay — a tough guy — but preferably Maloney himself. Darryl Sittler and Maloney had been buddies from the time they played junior hockey together in London. Sittler loved Maloney's style. Roger Neilson felt the Leafs needed a hard-checking Maloney type to ride shotgun for some of Toronto's offensive players. General manager Jim Gregory was anxious to accommodate his coach, to acquire a power winger before the trading deadline for the season passed. Harold Ballard wanted a tough guy, and he was specific about the man he had in mind. A season earlier, he told *Globe and Mail* writer Don Ramsey that he'd swap Lanny McDonald to the Detroit Red Wings for Maloney any day. That struck most people as a dumb trade, but it didn't lessen Ballard's yearning for Maloney and his aggressive play. "The Carlton Street chickens," Ballard said of the Leafs in the winter of 1978, "need someone like Dan Maloney." When Ballard said "someone like Dan Maloney," he meant exactly Dan Maloney.

WHO WAS THIS DAN MALONEY?

He was promising enough as a junior with the London Knights that in the 1970 draft, the same year his Knights teammate Sittler went to the Leafs as the number-eight pick, he was named as the fourteenth choice by the Chicago Black Hawks. In the juniors, Maloney balanced toughness with a degree of finesse. In the NHL, the judgment was made that he didn't have quite the quickness, quite the touch to qualify as a finesse player. And so Maloney was slotted: tough guy.

The statistics he compiled over his 11 NHL seasons, 737 league games, reflect the role he was handed: 192 goals (not bad) and 1,489 minutes in penalties (a solid tough-guy number). Maloney also earned a reputation as what hockey calls a "character" player, someone who asks no favours, plays while in pain, sticks up for his teammates. But apparently he wasn't enough of a character player to be declared indispensable by any one team—not by the team that drafted him, the Black Hawks, who traded him to Los Angeles; nor by the Kings, who traded him to Detroit; nor by the Red Wings, who, on March 13, 1978, traded him to Toronto.

WAS THERE EVER A GENERAL MANAGER IN A MORE VULnerable deal-making position than Jim Gregory? Everybody knew he was shopping for Dan Maloney, everybody who read the newspapers, who could hear Harold Ballard's heavy-breathing lust after Maloney. For Ted Lindsay, negotiating with Gregory, it was like plucking a loose wallet out of an unbuttoned pants pocket. Lindsay was the Detroit general manager, a newspaper reader, and when Gregory came asking about Maloney, Lindsay said, right, I'll just help myself to Errol Thompson plus your first-round draft picks in 1978 and 1980. That was a steep price, about what was usually paid for a front-line player, one who was almost guaranteed to make an immediate and positive impact on his new team. Maloney didn't fit that description, but Gregory, with all the pressures on him and zilch room to wheel and deal, had no choice except to ante up.

Maloney played his part in the marvellous Leaf playoff win over the New York Islanders that spring. The victory turned largely on cuffing the Islanders around, and that was right up Maloney's alley. But against the Canadiens in the semi-final, he disappeared along with the rest of the Leafs. Indeed, Maloney was approaching the spent-force category. He was closing in on thirty, the age when players assigned to his sort of duties—knocking people down, handling the fighting for others, bumping and banging—often begin to feel the muscles resisting the instructions of the spirit. Maloney gave Roger Neilson an honest sixty minutes of work in each game, but all that got the Leafs the next season was another four-and-out playoff series against Montreal.

ONE OF THE PEOPLE WHO WAS FAST OFF THE MARK IN criticizing the trade for Maloney was Punch Imlach, former Leaf general manager, now Buffalo Sabres general manager.

"What are you assholes doing over there?" he said to King Clancy the day the trade was announced in 1978.

"Huh? What're you talking about, Punch?"

"Tell me this," Imlach said, "who wins Stanley Cups?"

"Montreal fuckin' Canadiens," Clancy answered.

"Right," Imlach said. "So the only way to beat them is if you get yourself a team that can skate with them. Dan Maloney? Are you fuckin' kidding? You guys gave up a skater, which the Thompson kid is, and you gave up a couple of first picks where you could draft kids who're skaters too. Jesus, you're out of your fuckin' minds over there."

About here, things get tricky. It appears that it was Clancy, a long-time convert to the Conn Smythe dictum about not being able to beat them on the ice if you can't beat them in the alley, who hipped Ballard on the idea of acquiring Maloney. Ballard didn't think it up himself. Clancy did the thinking. But, as time passed, as the Maloney deal was made, as no Stanley Cups immediately came Toronto's way, as Ballard got fed up with Neilson and Gregory and fired both of them, Clancy did some more thinking. Actually, some double-thinking. Wasn't his old pal Punch, Clancy thought, a smart fella? Putting his finger on what was wrong with the Maloney trade the way he did? And wouldn't it be great to get him back in Toronto? A guy from the old school, a guy who didn't go in for all this shit with the videos, a guy who's already won Stanley Cups for the Leafs? That's the proposition Clancy kicked around with Ballard, and after Ballard had gone through the motions of unsuccessfully pitching for Scotty Bowman and Don Cherry to come to the Leafs, he told King to make the call. Clancy telephoned Imlach on Friday, June 8, 1979.

"You wanna be the fuckin' general manager, Punch?" Clancy asked.

IMLACH HAD PULLED A FEW RABBITS OUT OF HATS IN Buffalo. Starting from square one as the GM of an expansion team in 1970, he got the Sabres into the playoffs in three years. In the fifth year, 1974–75, he took them all the way to a first-place finish overall in the NHL and to the Stanley Cup final, where Buffalo lost to Philadelphia. It was a team of one superstar, Gilbert Perreault, and two or three others who came close to that level, Richard Martin, Danny Gare, René Robert. Alas, Buffalo slumped off the quick peak, out of Stanley Cup contention by the quarter-finals in each of the next three seasons. Many of the players blamed the tumble on Imlach and his tactics, which the players considered harsh and old-fashioned. Buffalo's owners agreed with the players. In December 1978, they fired Imlach. That meant he was available when King Clancy made the phone call six months later.

IMLACH FIGURED HIS MANDATE WAS TO MAKE CHANGE IN Toronto. Even if it wasn't his mandate—who was mandating things at the Gardens anyway?—change was the only way he saw of turning the Leafs into his kind of club. Imlach said the team had only "five or six good hockey players." Change was needed there. There was "something like a country-club atmosphere around the Leafs." More change necessary. And Sittler, where did this guy think he was getting off? All the influence he had in the dressing room? Telling Ballard he couldn't fire Roger Neilson? Definitely a major change to come here, something to trim Sittler's sails.

Imlach started small. Tossed the ping-pong table out of the dressing room. No more beer on team-plane flights. Barring Sittler from doing an interview on *Hockey Night in Canada*. Those moves were just for warmup. Then Imlach got serious. He made trades, many trades, big trades, trades that, within a year, practically performed a vanishing act on the team of 1977–78, the one that beat the Islanders.

Over the course of six months, beginning on December 24, 1979, Imlach unloaded the following players: Pat Boutette (a pal of Sittler's from London Knights junior days), Lanny McDonald (Sittler's best friend on the team), Joel Quenneville, Dave Hutchison (yet another London Knights alumnus), Tiger Williams and Jerry Butler (this was the one Imlach trade, bringing Rick Vaive and Bill Derlago to the Leafs from Vancouver in exchange for Williams and Butler, that could be rated a plus in Toronto's favour), Walt McKechnie (whose junior hockey was — guess where? — with the London Knights) and Mike Palmateer.

The trades generated a large amount of disorder in the Leaf ranks. More than that, it pushed the captain, Sittler, over the emotional edge. Two days after Imlach got rid of Lanny McDonald, and minutes before a Saturday-night game at the Gardens, Sittler ripped the C off his sweater. More accurately, the team trainer, Guy Kinnear, unstitched the C while the two men crouched out of sight in a washroom cubicle off the Leaf dressing room. The act wasn't as spontaneous as it might have seemed; in anticipation of it, Sittler had spent the Saturday afternoon writing and copying a statement for the press ("...I have had little or no contact with Mr. Imlach and it is clear to me that he and I have different ideas about player and management communication..."). But the resignation from the prized captain's position created tremendous drama. Sittler, though he seemed to have a streak of self-righteousness, won most of the press and fan support. Imlach came off looking like a hard-hearted goof. That didn't appear to bother Punch. He was too busy making changes.

FLOYD SMITH GOT THE JOB AS THE FIRST LEAF COACH under Imlach. He was an Imlach man of long standing. When Smith played hockey, a right-winger of the grinder school (129 goals in thirteen NHL seasons), Imlach brought him to the Leafs in the March 1968 Mahovlich trade. Later, Imlach dealt to get Smith for Buffalo. He made Smith the team captain, and then the Sabres coach. Smith was behind the bench in the year when Buffalo went to the Stanley Cup final. His coaching approach tended to be low-key. He was, personally, a relaxed gent, and he asked nothing more complicated of his players than hard work and aggression. The Leaf players, for their part, thought Smith was none too bright and that, anyway, he just fronted for Imlach, who called the shots.

Player opinion of Smith became moot on March 14, 1980. That was the day when Smith apparently had a few drinks at Archie Katzman's Parkway Hotel in St. Catharines, somehow got his car into the wrong lane on the highway leaving the hotel, and smacked another car head-on. Two people died in car number two. Smith came out of the accident with a shattered leg and a couple of criminal charges. He was acquitted on the more serious count, convicted of a lesser offence. His coaching job disappeared with the accident, but it's a measure of some talent in Smith—native smarts, an ability to roll with the punches—that he lasted in the Leaf organization through the 1980s and into the '90s. For two of the years, during the virtual interregnum when Ballard was fading and the next ownership waited in the wings, Smith held the top job, general manager. But most of his time has gone into scouting. Has he produced in that job? One answer: Smith's work played a large part in giving the Leafs Felix Potvin, who is shaping up as a Vezina Trophy sort of goaltender.

AFTER THE CAR ACCIDENT, JOE CROZIER SUCCEEDED Smith as Leaf coach. Crozier went even farther back than Smith in association with Imlach. He played for Punch in Quebec City, played for him briefly in Toronto, coached for him in Buffalo, went partners with him in business deals. Crozier, a stubborn, abrasive sort, gave the Leaf players a shock after the relatively laid-back Smith. He gave them a shock, yes; he drew respect from them, no. Maybe it was the case with Crozier, as with Smith, that the players trusted no one who was tight with Imlach. Poor Punch had traded away a third of the team, and he still couldn't put together a core of guys who would play hockey for him. The Leafs finished the 1979–80 season with thirty-five wins and forty losses, good for seventy-five points and fourth place in their division, eleventh overall in the league. In the first round of the playoffs, they went out in three straight to Minnesota.

HAROLD BALLARD REALIZED TOO LATE THAT HE REALLY liked the players Imlach was trading away. McDonald, Williams and Palmateer—they were at the heart of the best team Ballard had owned. Take a guy like Tiger Williams. He gave Ballard a bearskin rug. It was one of Ballard's favourite possessions. It decorated the floor of his office at the Gardens. Everybody who arrived to do business with Ballard commented on the rug. Tiger drilled the bear himself. Drilled it with a bow and arrow, skinned it, and presented it to the boss. How could Ballard not love Tiger Williams?

Sittler and Borje Salming were Ballard's pride too, and Imlach talked of moving them from the team. Imlach thought both players had lost something off their game, that Sittler got caught out of the play too often, that Salming was prone to giveaways. Dealing Sittler was complicated because he had a clause in his contract giving him the right to approve or nix all deals affecting his future. Nevertheless, in late August 1980, Imlach designed a trade with Calgary, Sittler in exchange for two solid forwards, Bob MacMillan and Guy Chouinard. But before the deal got down to the fine print, Ballard leaked the news to the press, and Calgary pulled out of the agreement. Maybe, unconsciously, Ballard wanted the deal to fail. Or maybe he scuttled it with deliberate intent.

For the first months of Imlach's employment, Ballard had backed his general manager, taking Punch's side against Sittler and the other complainers in the dressing room. But after it dawned on Ballard that Imlach was breaking up the old gang and that the breakup wasn't bringing Toronto closer to a Stanley Cup, after Ballard became fed up with all the publicity Imlach seemed to attract to himself, taking away the press and TV coverage that Ballard used to get, well, all of that was too much for Harold. He turned against Imlach.

Then, in what Ballard might have interpreted as a felicitous stroke of fate, on the very day in August 1980 when the Sittler trade to Calgary blew up, a heart attack hit Imlach. It was his second. The first had occurred in 1972 during Imlach's Buffalo days. When the second attack isolated Punch in hospital, Ballard seized the moment to get active on the player front. He signed Salming to a five-year contract calling for $300,000 per year. That was at least fifty grand a year more than Imlach thought Salming was worth. And Ballard gave Sittler back his captaincy. In Imlach's view, that was like pinning a medal on a traitor.

Ballard relished the renewed feeling of hands-on power. He kept wielding it after Imlach returned to work. Ballard focused on Joe Crozier. He had it in for Crozier on two counts: one, Crozier was an Imlach man, and, two, he wasn't getting the players to put out. By early Janauary 1981, Toronto was on a free-fall of nine losses in ten games. The ninth loss, at the Gardens, was the killer, 8–2 to the Winnipeg Jets, who were not only the worst team in the league but, until that night, hadn't won a single road game. The next day, Crozier got the axe.

Imlach's first choice for the new Leaf coach was Doug Carpenter. He was the bright young guy who was handling the Toronto farm team in Moncton. Imlach liked Carpenter's hockey brain, though he wondered whether Carpenter, young as he was, could keep the edge on Sittler, who had grown so accustomed to asserting authority in the Leaf dressing room. Imlach's ponderings over Carpenter became strictly academic when Ballard announced that his own choice for coach was somebody else. He wanted Mike Nykoluk, a guy who'd had coaching experience in the Flyers and Rangers systems. Nykoluk got the job.

The Leaf players responded to Nykoluk's presence—or maybe to Crozier's absence—by improving to .500 hockey for the remainder of the season. That gave them a total record of twenty-six wins and thirty-seven losses, sixteenth overall in the league, at the bottom of their own division but in the playoffs. Just barely in the playoffs, squeezing in on the last day of the schedule. Then, a familiar story, they got swept in three straight by the Islanders, who went on to win the Stanley Cup.

THE FOLLOWING SEPTEMBER, DURING THE LEAFS TRAINING camp in St. Catharines, Imlach felt pains in his chest and arm. The heart again. This time he needed a bypass operation. The procedure and his recovery took him away from the Leaf offices until mid-November. During the weeks in hospital, in therapy, at home, Imlach heard nothing from Ballard. No get-well card from the boss, no phone call of reassurance. Harold was applying the old Ballard freeze, and when Imlach finally returned to the Gardens on November 17, feeling snappier than he had in a couple of years, Ballard told him that he wasn't wanted in the general manager's job any longer, but that he could stick around the organization as an, um, "adviser."

To a man of Imlach's age, accomplishments and pride, "advising" didn't cut it. Still, he couldn't believe that Ballard would actually let him go. He didn't believe it until the day a week or so later when he drove down to the Gardens and found something missing. It was his personal parking space. And his Gardens phone had been disconnected. In that foolish moment, Imlach knew that his second term as the Leaf general manager—a short, unhappy, unproductive, loony term—was over.

19

En Route to the Nadir

IKE NYKOLUK LIKED THE SIMPLE THINGS IN life. Smoking a cigar. Laying a bet at the racetrack. Watching a hockey game. He was a large, affable man. He had no neck and usually wore a guileless expression. James Christie, writing in the *Globe and Mail*, once compared Nykoluk's looks to Fred Flintstone's. That was after the Leafs under Nykoluk's coaching had confirmed themselves as a team headed no place particularly wonderful. Nykoluk was starting to lose his affability. He didn't like the Flintstone comparison. Another *Globe* writer, Al Strachan, wrote that, as a coach, Nykoluk lacked "intensity." Now Nykoluk was really getting mad. He shoved Strachan out of the Leaf dressing room. A *Globe* photographer, anticipating just such a reaction from Nykoluk, snapped a picture of him in mid-shove. Nykoluk, in the paper the next day, looked crazed. There was nothing like a spell as Leaf coach in the 1980s to convert a formerly affable man into a mini-monster.

As a kid, Nykoluk had come up through the Marlboros system. He was a fair journeyman player, but, unwittingly, he contributed mightily to the Marlies, and later the Leafs. It happened that Nykoluk lived in the east end of Toronto, a student at Scarborough Collegiate, and when the

Marlies asked him to play for the Junior B Dukes, which were stationed in Weston on the far western edges of Toronto, Nykoluk declined to make the long daily hike across town for practices and games unless he had the company of his pal from school, Bob the defenceman. Okay, the Marlies said, bring Bob along. In the space of a few days, Bob leaped from the Marlie minor-midgets to the Junior Bs, to the Junior A team. A couple of years later, he was on the Leaf blueline. Nykoluk's pal from Scarborough Collegiate was Bob Baun.

Nykoluk was captain of the Marlboros' 1955 Memorial Cup team. He played thirty-two games for the Leafs in 1956–57 and spent the rest of his career, fourteen years, in Hershey. Fred Shero hired Nykoluk as assistant coach in Philadelphia, which meant he was part of the Broad Street Bullies organization that won two Stanley Cups in the mid-1970s. He followed Shero to the New York Rangers, again as assistant coach, expecting to succeed Shero as head coach. When that didn't pan out, he switched to radio, doing the colour comments in Toronto for the Leaf games. One of his comments was, "If Joe Crozier has a system, I don't know what it is."

Nykoluk's own coaching approach, vastly different from Crozier's, leaned to the laissez-faire. He took it easy on the players. No tough talk from Nykoluk, no rants or temper tantrums in the dressing room.

"I just hate that word, 'motivation,'" he said not long after he became the Leaf coach. "I don't get my wife to give me a pep talk to get me to come to the rink every day. These guys are paid well to do a job, and I don't think any athlete, after they've won something, remembers what the coach said."

Maybe Al Strachan was right. Maybe Nykoluk lacked intensity.

NYKOLUK WANTED AN ASSISTANT COACH, SOMEONE TO concentrate on the younger Leafs. He suggested Gary Aldcorn, a teammate from his own Marlboro days. Aldcorn had played five years in the NHL. But Harold Ballard carried a grudge against him from a disagreement the two had had almost thirty years earlier. Ballard vetoed Aldcorn. Well, Nykoluk said, how about Jim Morrison? Morrison had played twelve years of NHL defence, six of them with the Leafs. Ballard rejected Morrison too. No reason specified.

One day, out at the track, King Clancy met a guy named Doug McKay, twenty-eight years old, had played some minor pro hockey, coached for a year in Cortina, Italy. Clancy liked the kid. Hey, you wanna be a coach with the Maple Leafs? Sure, McKay said, why not? Clancy talked up McKay down at the Gardens. He's a nice young guy, Clancy said, and he'll work cheap. Ballard didn't have any grudges against McKay. He'd never met McKay. Neither had Nykoluk until the day McKay was introduced as his new assistant coach.

Things were getting crazier at the Gardens.

THINGS WERE ALSO GETTING MORE MEAN-SPIRITED.

Laurie Boschman was a young Leaf centre who found religion. His manner of playing wasn't notably Christian—he earned far more penalties than goals—but his beliefs were born-again and fundamentalist. When he got off to a sluggish start in his third season with the Leafs, 1981–82, Ballard made a crack about Boschman's religion sapping his energy. Boschman, offended, wrote a letter to Gerry McNamara, the Leaf general manager in succession to Punch Imlach. The happiest day of his life, Boschman wrote, was the day in 1979 when the Leafs named him their number-one draft selection. But, he went on, he had trouble playing for a team whose owner mocked his religious convictions. If Boschman was expecting gentle understanding from McNamara, he hadn't read his man correctly. McNamara turned the letter over to Nykoluk, who pinned it on the team bulletin board. Now poor Boschman was not just offended; he was humiliated too. Not long after, McNamara traded Boschman to Edmonton. Ten years later, Boschman was still in the NHL, captain of the new Ottawa Senators.

CURIOUSLY, GIVEN THE INCIDENT, GERRY MCNAMARA was also a religious man, a devout Catholic. He prided himself on never using four-letter words. That made him the odd man out in conversations that included Ballard and Clancy. McNamara seemed an odd duck to be the general manager in more than a few ways.

For one thing, he didn't especially want the job. He'd been a scout with the Leafs for ten years. He liked scouting and was pretty good at it.

Before that, in his playing days, he was a goaltender, all in the minors, except for seven games with the Leafs. Ballard asked McNamara to be the general manager mostly because McNamara was available, just down the hall, a familiar face. McNamara couldn't say no to Ballard. He took the job and held on to it for almost seven years. But it couldn't have brought him much pleasure, not with all the losing. In McNamara's time as general manager, the Leafs won 166 games and lost more than four times as many, 671. It's the poorest record for a general manager in Toronto history.

And for another thing, McNamara had no touch at all with the media. He was a looming sort of man, looking rather like a formidable Jesuit priest, though he didn't have anything like a Jesuit's talent for debate and sophistry. In fact, McNamara was regarded as thin-skinned and humourless. Those were hardly qualities that equipped him to explain years of losing hockey to nosy reporters. McNamara got around the problem mostly by keeping on the move whenever anyone with a notebook or microphone showed up in his vicinity.

But in his most famous media exposure, McNamara gave a performance that invitably drew comparisons with Captain Queeg of *The Caine Mutiny*. It happened in a between-periods interview with Ron McLean on *Hockey Night in Canada* in November 1986. The Leafs had started the season impressively, six wins, two losses, three ties, and McNamara took the opportunity to rub it into the media.

"I know quite a bit about these reporters," he said, a nervous smirk playing across his mouth, "more than they think I know about them. And I look at the credibility of these reporters, and I can tell you I don't find too much credibility in a number of them.... When I get wound up some day, we'll, heh, heh, take the gloves off and we'll go at it pretty good.... And I'm going to get pretty nasty, I can tell you, don't think there's anyone who can get as nasty as I can..."

Harold Ballard, practically alone in his view, thought McNamara had done a great job of sticking it to the media. But then Ballard was the boss who compelled McNamara to operate on starvation finances, without the funds to compete against other teams in scouting, in player budget, in support-staff salaries. Whatever McNamara honestly thought of

Ballard—he appeared to do Ballard's bidding willingly—it was McNamara who had the last laugh. When Ballard fired him in March 1988, more than two years remained on his contract. McNamara walked from the Gardens with compensation in the six figures.

AGAINST ALL ODDS, EVEN WITH BUNGLING THAT SEEMED endemic to the Leaf organization of the 1980s, the team managed to put terrifically talented players on the ice. The trouble was that not all the talented players showed up at the same time, and most of them seemed to vanish from the team, by way of trade or free agency, before they reached their peak. Usually they reached their peak with some other, smarter team.

Steve Thomas, for example. He arrived on the Leafs from the Marlboros in 1984–85, a swift young forward who had a swell touch around the other team's net. He scored thirty-five goals for Toronto in 1986–87 and generally comported himself as the sort of winger a team counts on to flourish on its second line. But the year after the thirty-five goals, McNamara decided Thomas' agent wanted too much of Harold Ballard's money. He allowed Thomas to play out his option and traded him to Chicago, where Thomas scored forty goals in 1989–90.

Too many of these good young players weren't being kept by the Leafs. Gary Nylund, a mountain of a kid defenceman, tough and a team player, got away to the Blackhawks too, as a free agent. And another defenceman, Al Iafrate, wasn't handled with the care he might have rated. Well, granted, Iafrate was part flake, part emotional basket case; he loved heavy metal, multicoloured tattoos, and fast Harley Davidsons; got himself in romantic scrapes (one paternity suit, one marriage that went on the rocks, with the wife finding comfort in the arms of another Leaf, Gary Leeman); and had a problem dealing with the mental side of hockey. Nevertheless, just a teenager when he joined the Leafs, Iafrate developed perhaps the hardest shot in the league and skated with glorious bursts of speed. He scored twenty-two goals in one season, twenty-one in another. Then Toronto let him go. The point isn't that the Leafs gave up on Iafrate; it was a later Toronto regime which traded him to Washington on January 16, 1991, for two players, Bob Rouse and Peter

Zezel, who became stalwarts in the Stanley Cup semi-finalist team of 1992–93. The point is that earlier Leaf management, during the bungling period, didn't seem to know how to fold an immensely talented if loopy kid into the environment of an effective, winning organization.

Then there was the fatal attraction that Gerry McNamara developed for Czechoslovakia. McNamara had scored one spectacular coup in European hockey when, as a Leaf scout in the early 1970s, he came up with Borje Salming. Perhaps he hoped to duplicate this wave of his wand and produce one more Salming. Or a Czech equivalent of Salming. Under the McNamara program, at least five refugees from the Czech hockey system were spirited to Canada and into the Leaf uniform. Alas, there were no Salmings. There was, at best, a Peter Ihnacak who played eight Toronto seasons at centre and scored 108 goals. More typically, it was the unfortunate Leafs who ended up with the older, slower of the Stastny brothers, Marian (70 games, 23 goals) rather than the younger, swifter siblings, Peter of Quebec City and New Jersey (477 goals) and Anton of the Nordiques (252 goals). And it was the Leafs who got fooled on Peter Ihnacak's younger brother Miroslov. Word from behind the Czech border was that Miro was large, strong and talented. Something terrible happened when he skated on to the Gardens ice: he turned out to be small, a pushover and not so talented. Altogether—smuggling fees, hockey contract, English lessons—Miro cost the Leafs about $750,000. He played fifty-six games and scored eight goals.

AMONG THE ZIRCONS, RICK VAIVE WAS THE DIAMOND. HE scored goals. He was the first Leaf to break the fifty barrier in a season. He scored more than fifty goals in three successive seasons—fifty-four in 1981–82, fifty-one the next year, fifty-two in the following season. Better still, Vaive brought a flourish to his goal scoring. He was a big, dark, handsome kid. He had a dramatic sweep when he headed for the other team's net, and his shot was heavy, the kind that came hard and hurt the goalie who got in its way. And Vaive didn't back down from a fight. The year he scored fifty-four goals, he got 229 minutes in penalties. The fans loved Vaive. Ballard made him team captain.

The captain part was probably a mistake. Ballard, feeling pleased and expansive, awarded Vaive the captaincy on January 5, 1982, succeeding Darryl Sittler, who had at last been traded (to Philadelphia for a mess of pottage). Vaive was only twenty-two at the time, the youngest Leaf captain ever by three months over Ted Kennedy. But, in personality, Vaive was far from a Kennedy or Sittler, not so mature or assertive or experienced in the ways of pro hockey. Leadership didn't sit naturally on his shoulders.

Within his own line, Vaive had a comfort zone. He played right wing. Bill Derlago, who'd come with Vaive from Vancouver in the February 1980 trade for Tiger Williams and Jerry Butler, was at centre, and John Anderson, a Toronto youngster who proceeded up from the Marlboro ranks, took care of left wing. The three shared an offensive frame of mind. Anderson possessed great wheels and knew how to put the puck in the net. Derlago, though inclined to be a free spirit, had all the offensive skills down pat, skating, passing, puck handling. Anderson, Vaive and Derlago—a unit on the ice, the same off the ice. After the game at the Gardens on March 24, 1982, when Vaive got his fiftieth goal, he and his wife, Joyce, celebrated at Mr. Greenjeans with Derlago, Anderson and companions. Tall drafts, cheeseburgers, good friends together, Vaive picking up the tab.

But this one splendid scoring line didn't get the Leafs close to a Stanley Cup, and it was one of the friendships, Vaive's with Anderson, that eventually brought Vaive down. In the summer of 1985, the season after the line was broken up and Vaive fell off to thirty-five goals, both Anderson and Derlago were traded, Anderson to Quebec for defenceman Brad Maxwell and Derlago to Boston for centre Tom Fergus. Later in the following hockey season, on February 21, the Leafs were in Bloomington for a game against Minnesota. The Nordiques happened to be passing through town. That put Vaive and Anderson, old buddies, together for an evening. They celebrated over a few drinks, and next morning, a little bleary, Vaive missed the Leaf practice. Toronto management overreacted. Or perhaps Ballard was looking for a reason to demote a player he'd soured on. Whatever the reasoning, without a fair hearing, without a moment of compassion, Ballard stripped Vaive of his captaincy. Thus another Leaf, poor Ricky, had been publicly humiliated.

And the mortification wasn't finished. Three nights later, back at the Gardens, the Leafs beat the Rangers, 7–3. Vaive, without the C, no doubt feeling more than sheepish, showed tremendous courage and played a forceful, aggressive game. It was just too bad for him that another Leaf played an even more rambunctious and productive game. This was Wendel Clark.

Clark was a rookie, a farm kid from Kelvington, Saskatchewan, whom the Leafs made the first choice overall in the 1985 draft. He wasn't particularly large, under six feet, under 190 pounds, but he played like a thunderbolt. He had a hurtling manner of skating, a shot that would crack cement, and a compulsion to put his fists to an opponent's head. He was an unpretentious young guy, so unsophisticated in that rookie year that he had a subscription to the *National Inquirer*. But no one, certainly not Toronto fans, could resist his *joie de vivre*—or his toughness.

So in the game against the Rangers when Rick Vaive tried so valiantly to redeem himself, Wendel Clark scored three goals and won one fight. Clark was named the night's first star. The crowd cheered him to the rafters when he made his post-game appearance on the ice. Vaive was named the third star. He appeared on the ice. The crowd dumped boos and abuse on his head. The people had a new choice, and it was Clark. Vaive, the forgotten hero, the once-celebrated goal scorer, now yesterday's man, played one more season for Toronto, then was traded to Chicago, where he scored forty-three goals in his first season with the new team.

MIKE NYKOLUK COACHED THE LEAFS FOR THE LAST PART of the 1980–81 season and for the next three full seasons, losing his affability all the way. The team won only twenty games in 1981–82 and missed the playoffs. It rallied the next season, won twenty-eight games, but went out in the first playoff round. In 1983–84, it was all bad news, for the team and for Nykoluk, twenty-five wins, out of the playoffs again, and Ballard gave Nykoluk the heave-ho in favour of the man who had been appointed assistant coach in the spring of 1982.

This new coach was Dan Maloney, the fellow who had been at the centre of the controversy in the winter of 1979. Traded to the Leafs for Errol Thompson and two first-round draft choices—was it a smart move or was it, as Punch Imlach had insisted, totally stupid? It hadn't produced the hoped-for Stanley Cup challenge, but it had given the Leafs someone who was, in Gord Stellick's description, "a classy, considerate guy." Stellick would know. He worked in the Leaf organization for more than fifteen years, from a kid gofer in the mid-1970s to general manager in the late 1980s. He found Maloney to be tough and inflexible but entirely fair. Maloney played hockey in that style, and when he retired as a player—270 games with the Leafs, 65 goals, 538 minutes in penalties—he brought the urge towards the same qualities to the coaching job.

It took the Leaf players one absolutely lousy season and part of another to adjust to Maloney. His first year as a coach gave the team a rock-bottom record, forty-eight points, dead last in the league. But towards the end of the following season, 1985–86, the players caught on to Maloney's message: play gritty hockey out there, bear down, be brave, work hard. With a push through the last part of the schedule, the team made the playoffs. Its record was hardly glittering, twenty-five wins, fourth in its division, nineteenth in the league overall. But in the playoffs, the Leafs suddenly looked like a bunch of all-stars.

The first round matched them in a best-of-five series against Chicago, a team that had finished twenty-nine points ahead of the Leafs. Nevertheless, thanks to an all-round group effort, to crisis scoring by Steve Thomas and Wendel Clark, and to excellent handling by Maloney, who was judged to have out-coached Chicago, the Leafs swept the Hawks in three straight games. They looked equally sharp and determined in the next round against St. Louis. After four games in a best-of-seven series, the teams were tied at two wins each, and in game five, in St. Louis, the Leafs took an early 3–0 lead. But the Blues cracked back to win in overtime. Toronto tied the series once again with a victory at the Gardens. Game seven took place in St. Louis. It took place without the Leafs' most consistent scorer. Rick Vaive had a wrenched back. He didn't dress, and the Leafs lost again in overtime when a little guy named Kevin LaVallee scored to end the game 2–1.

It had been a gutsy run by the Leafs, maybe promising good things ahead, but not gutsy enough to satisfy Harold Ballard. He remained cheesed off that the Leafs had lost the fifth game in St. Louis, the one where they had been ahead 3–0. And when Dan Maloney asked for a new two-year contract, Ballard decided to make him the goat of the St. Louis loss. A one-year contract, Ballard told Maloney, or you can walk. Maloney walked, and the very next day, the Winnipeg Jets signed him to a multiyear coaching contract.

The Leafs of the 1980s were masters at screwing up good things.

20

Todd Gill

TODD GILL WAS FEELING DOWN. YOUNG, good-looking guy, earning $675,000 a year, lovely wife and two small daughters, home in upscale Clarkson— what did he have to feel down about?

"My groin," Gill said. He grimaced. "All the tests and therapy I've had, they don't know whether it's just an ordinary pulled muscle or if the muscle's come off the bone. So this afternoon"—it was November 25, 1993—"I have to fly to Vancouver and see a specialist out there. If he says I got to be operated on, I won't be playing for two months. Maybe three."

This was rottten irony. The Leafs' record was running at sixteen wins, four losses. They stood first in the entire league. If any Toronto player should have been present and playing and thrilling in the prosperous days for the team, it was Todd Gill. No one—apart perhaps from Wendel Clark—deserved to savour the good times more than Gill. He'd been around the Leafs longer than any player, taken more grief than any player except Clark. The time Gill coughed up the puck in Chicago in 1987? Probably cost Toronto a spot in the playoffs? He heard about that. He wouldn't read the newspapers and tried not to turn on the radio. He knew what people were writing and saying about him. But by this season, by 1993–94, everyone recognized that Gill was the best all-round defenceman the Leafs had. Just turned twenty-eight on November 9, and he was playing at the top of his game, his name on the All-Star ballot for the first time. And now this damned ache in his groin. It wasn't fair.

TODD GILL GREW UP IN SMALL-TOWN ONTARIO, VERY small, Cardinal, population not over 1,000 at the time, a town on the St. Lawrence, downriver from Brockville. He was the third of four boys in the family, and he insists one of the older brothers, Trevor, was really the best player among the Gills, the fastest skater, the slickest on the ice, but just didn't quite have the size. Isn't that part of the story of every NHL player from a small community, always a brother who was actually a better player?

Most things about Todd Gill fit the warm cliché of young Canadian hockey guys, what we like to think is still true. He played in Cardinal's kid hockey system, Red Bird they called it, and his dad was his first coach. Somebody from the big town up the road, Brockville, spotted Todd, and he moved into its hockey system, Tier 2, better teams, better hockey, out-of-town trips all the way to Ottawa. Todd was growing up. He had a girlfriend. She was from Roebuck, a town even smaller than Cardinal. Today she's Todd's wife. Her name is Krista.

Sixteen years old, Todd left home to play for the Windsor Junior A team in the Ontario Hockey League. He loved it, loved the whole experience—on his own; attending school in the day; hockey practice from four o'clock to six; homework; a game two or three nights a week, or, if not a game, then hanging out with his friends, a movie.

"Homesick? Well, a little maybe," Gill says. "But going from Cardinal to Windsor, that was like getting out and seeing the big world."

In ways that Todd couldn't guess, playing for Windsor was perfect preparation for playing in Toronto, preparation not just in hockey but in chaos. The Windsor team, while Gill was there, went through three ownerships and five coaches. So far in Toronto, he's played under three Leaf presidents and five coaches. In Windsor, things settled down with the fifth coach, a man named Wayne Maxner. Gill figures the fifth coach has done it for the Leafs too, Pat Burns.

Wayne Maxner got Gill ready for the pros, made him the team's co-captain, put him on the ice in crucial game situations, gave him a chance to stand out. Everybody told Todd he'd be a first-round pick in the NHL draft, no problem. So on a June Saturday afternoon in 1984, Todd and his mum and dad, along with all the other hot junior players in the country and their parents, came to the Montreal Forum for the draft. TV cameras, official parties from each NHL team, player agents, micro-phones, the press — a very big deal in the life of an eighteen-year-old hockey player. Then the draft began.

"I was devastated," Gill remembers now of what happened over the next couple of hours.

The teams made their choices. Pittsburgh going first, taking Mario Lemieux from the Laval Juniors. Mario Lemieux, well, who else? New Jersey taking Kirk Muller from Guelph second. The whole process stretching through the afternoon, the NHL teams deliberating over choices, the announcements coming over the Forum sound system from NHL president John Ziegler, the kids chosen rushing forward, putting on the sweaters of the teams that had picked them, photographs snapped, interviews on TV, lot of smiles and relief. And still, down to the end of the first round, Edmonton choosing Selmer Odelein of Regina, no team had gone for Todd Gill.

"It was so bad," Gill says, "that when they finally called my name — I had my head down, sort of in shock — I didn't even hear it. The first I realized I'd been chosen was when I noticed my mother jumping up and down."

It was the fourth pick in the second round, the twenty-fifth of the day. The Toronto Maple Leafs took Todd Gill, but what a rough time for a kid.

GILL THINKS THE BEST THING THAT HAPPENED TO HIM was playing most of the 1985–86 season, fifty-eight games in all, for St. Catharines, Toronto's farm team in the American League. He'd been with the Leafs for ten games the year before, spending most of the season back in juniors with Windsor. He played some for the Leafs in 1985–86, fifteen games, the guy they brought up when a regular defenceman was hurt. But for most of the season, he was with St. Catharines.

"The best time I've had in hockey, the most fun," Gill says of that year. "It was a great bunch of guys. We should've gone all the way, won the league, but we got beaten by Hershey. It was a great year for me anyway. It was when I learned how to play hockey."

Todd Gill's coach in St. Catharines, the coach in the year he learned how to play hockey, was John Brophy, and the following season, 1986–87, when Gill moved up to the Leafs for good, his coach in Toronto, successor to Dan Maloney, was again John Brophy.

IN THE FUNNIEST SPORTS MOVIE EVER MADE, AND POSSIBLY the best, *Slap Shot* from 1977, Paul Newman, the player-coach of a minor pro hockey team called the Charlestown Chiefs, delivers a pre-game pep talk that includes these exhortations: "Show them what we got! Let'em know we're there! . . . Put a fuckin' stick in his side! Let'im know you're there! . . . Put some lumber in his teeth! Let'im know you're there!" The Chiefs, which include the mad Hansen brothers, three guys with horn-rimmed glasses on their faces and murder in their hearts, charge on to the ice, and whack and hack and slice and plunder their way to victory.

That's where John Brophy came from, from the real-life version of the Charlestown Chiefs, from the Eastern Hockey League, where blood was spilled by the quart, where a player's fame was measured in stitches, where hardly anyone was headed for the NHL anyway, where guys settled into the league and accumulated small paycheques and large scars. Brophy played and coached in the Eastern League for more than a quarter-century, venturing out from time to time, most notably when Floyd Smith recommended him for the Leaf organization, first as assistant coach to Dan Maloney, then as coach at St. Catharines, then as Leaf head coach.

Brophy was in his early fifties when he got the Toronto job, and, apart from the scars on his cheeks, he didn't look like a killer hockey guy.

He had dramatic white hair, a spiffy wardrobe, and a demeanour that was almost distinguished. But he had been born to toughness. He grew up, a virtual orphan, in poor circumstances in Antigonish, Nova Scotia. He worked in high steel construction. And he developed such an obsessive personality that later he would watch his favourite movie over and over, Oliver Stone's hyperkinetic Vietnam war epic, *Platoon* (come to think of it, Brophy could pass for the older brother of the movie's star, Tom Berenger). Brophy, at the rink and on the job, was intense, noisy and hard as nails. He screamed at his players for a kamikaze effort—"Let'em know you're there!"— and when he decided a player wasn't putting out, the player was forever on Brophy's reject list.

"He raved a lot," Todd Gill says. "But he was the kind of coach who'd go through the wall for the team. He won in the minor leagues doing it his way. I saw that in St. Catharines. I never knew why he couldn't do it in the NHL."

Brad Smith saw Brophy another way. Smith was a career defensive forward, an intelligent, responsible player, nine years with five NHL clubs, including two seasons at Toronto, 1985–86 and 1986–87. And he told *Globe* sportswriter Bill Houston, "[Brophy] had no plan for anything. There wasn't one game where he had an actual plan. And of course he couldn't teach anybody anything."

The interesting little quirk in this clash of views on Brophy, Gill's and Smith's, is that in the 1993–94 Maple Leaf media guide, Gill lists Smith as his "Childhood Hockey Hero." That's Gill's little joke. He had never heard of Smith when he was a child. But the admiration is genuine.

"I met Brad when I played for St. Catharines," Gill explains. "He didn't have much talent, but he worked so hard. He was a good role model for a guy like me. I mean, he worked hard and got to the NHL."

Today, Smith is a scout for the Edmonton Oilers. He and Gill remain good pals.

DOING IT BROPHY'S WAY, THE LEAFS BUMBLED AROUND for most of the 1986–87 season. They began strongly enough, sloped off in mid-season, and nipped into the playoffs only when the Minnesota

North Stars went into such a swoon that they won just two of their last seventeen games. On the minus side, the Leafs had the fifth-worst record in the league; on the plus side, they recorded thirty-two wins, the most for them in seven seasons, and they came to life in the playoffs. With Wendel Clark doing the leading, they upset St. Louis in the first round and gave the impression they were going to do something similar to Detroit in the second round. The Leafs went up three games to one on the Red Wings. Then they ran out of legs, numerically out of legs—injuries cut the playing roster to three forward lines and four defencemen. The series went seven games. The Red Wings won it over the exhausted Leafs.

"Losing to Detroit that year," says Todd Gill, speaking as one of the four remaining defencemen, "it was brutal."

On the basis of the promising playoff showing, the Leafs expected the next year, 1987–88, to be—here's that word again—the breakthrough season. It wasn't. A senseless trade didn't help: Steve Thomas and Rick Vaive to Chicago for Ed Olczyk (a left-winger who eventually delivered the goods) and Al Secord (a one-time big scorer who turned out to be way past his prime). Brophy's tactics—working his best players into the ground—misfired too, and the team won eleven fewer games than the previous year. Lucky for the Leafs, Minnesota was still in the division, still setting records for hopelessness. Toronto squeaked into the playoffs, one point up on the North Stars, by winning their last game of the season.

That win came in Detroit against the Red Wings, the very team the Leafs met in the first playoff round. A happy omen? The Leafs might have thought so after they took the first game in Detroit behind terrific goaltending from Allan Bester. Detroit won the next two games. The situation was dangerous but not permanently hopeless. That was before the fourth game, played at the Gardens. After the fourth game, after Detroit obliterated the Leafs, scored eight goals to the Leafs' none, after the fans got into a rage, after they littered the ice with every object that came to hand, including Leaf sweaters, Toronto was shamed and humbled, rendered meek and lowly. Somehow—maybe Detroit was celebrating too early and vigorously—Toronto won the fifth game. But Detroit wrapped up matters in the sixth.

THE FOLLOWING SEASON, 1988–89, THE LEAFS, FROM A soap-opera point of view, bottomed out. Ballard hired a general manager who was younger than many of the players. He hired a coach who insisted, who shouted—wasn't anybody listening?—"I DON'T WANT THIS JOB." Then there was the defenceman who had a nervous breakdown and vanished from the team. Another player got mononucleosis. Everything around the Gardens seemed shrill and overwrought. The kid general manager learned that Ballard had ticketed him for the position when he read about it in Milt Dunnell's *Toronto Star* column four days before he was actually offered the general-managership. He discovered he was on the way out a year later when Ballard gave Dunnell an interview describing the general manager as "too young and has too much to learn." At about the same time, *Toronto Sun* sportswriter Wayne Parrish spoke of Ballard's actions, in print, as "the stupidity, intemperance and monstrous incomprehension of this demented old coot." Any questions?

Gord Stellick was the beleaguered young general manager. When Ballard fired Gerry McNamara, he found a replacement in his customary fashion—by glancing down the corridor at the Gardens. Hey, you! Yeah, you! What's yer name? You're the new general manager! In truth, Stellick was bright, industrious, a dedicated Leaf fan from his childhood. It was just that his childhood wasn't far in the past. He was only thirty years old. He'd been around the Gardens from his late teens, climbing ever upward through a series of administrative jobs until he emerged as McNamara's assistant. His youth worked for him in the sense that the Leaf players trusted him. It worked against him when he went one-on-one with the older sharks who were the general managers of the other NHL teams.

One of Stellick's early moves was to bring George Armstrong back to the Leafs as a scout. George Armstrong, the legendary Leaf, half-Indian on his mother's side, hence his nickname "The Chief"; possessed of courage and stoicism that came from his dad, who worked forty years in the Falconbridge mines; George himself a Toronto right-winger for twenty years, the captain for eleven years, 296 goals, four Stanley Cups. Ballard had bounced him out of the Leaf organization in 1978, but that was all forgotten, at least by Ballard, in the rejoicing over The Chief's return. Ballard was so taken by what he perceived as Armstrong's wise ways that when Ballard ran out of patience with John Brophy after thirty-three games of the 1988–89 season, he fired Brophy and named Armstrong the new coach. Armstrong was appalled. No, no, no, he told everyone—his wife, the press, Stellick, the players, Ballard. He didn't want to coach. Everybody accepted his protestations except Ballard, and Armstrong reluctantly took the job.

"George in effect quit [coaching] after four games," Stellick later wrote. "His continued presence behind the bench became a joke with the players." Assistant coach Garry Larivière took charge of much of the work—the practices, the teaching, even many of the line changes during games. And the team endured various other traumas, the emotional breakdown of one player (that was Iafrate), another's mononucleosis (Mark Osborne), a clunk on the head that cost the services of one of the few good Leaf goal scorers (Gary Leeman).

Nevertheless, the Leafs went into the last night of the season with a chance to make the playoffs if they won the final game against the Blackhawks in Chicago. They were up on the Hawks 3–1 in the third period. Chicago came back to tie the game. It went into overtime. Todd Gill had the puck in his own end, bringing it up. Chicago's Troy Murray reached out quick as a cobra. He pokechecked the puck away from Gill. Gill turned. Too late. Murray got the puck first. He put a wrist shot past Allan Bester. The Leafs were out of the playoffs, and Todd Gill quit reading the papers for a couple of months.

CONSIDER THE FATE OF THE HOUND LINE. THESE WERE three excellent Leaf players—Gary Leeman, Russ Courtnall and Wendel Clark. All were within a couple of years of one another in age, all spent high school time at Saskatchewan's Notre Dame College (thus, the "Hound" after the name of the school's hockey team), all were high draft picks for the Leafs, all made the big team at a young age. And all— here's where their mutual experience stands as a metaphor for the plight of many Leaf players of the 1980s—endured periods of bafflement and despair in Toronto.

Leeman, a medium-sized right-winger with high-calibre offensive skills, was, in personality, a curious mix of the easy-going and the unremittingly honest. The offensive ability made him a big-number goal scorer, 51 of them in 1989–90, 176 altogether in his 545 Leaf games. The honesty made him a guy who drew trouble from coaches, teammates and fans. Some teammates thought Leeman and Ed Olczyk, who joined Toronto in the Vaive trade, were selfish players, keen only on running up their own statistics. The grumpy teammates complained, anonymously, to the press. Word was out. The fans made Leeman the point of their jeers. Olczyk didn't lighten matters when, on *Hockey Night in Canada*, immediately after his trade to Winnipeg on November 10, 1990, he looked into the camera and said, for Leeman's benefit, "I love you, buddy." Through all of these strange and troubling events for Leeman, did Leaf management step in to ease his burden? Apart from a small and failed try at making him an assistant captain, not that anyone noticed. Leeman's goal scoring dwindled, and on January 2, 1992, he was traded, the former whiz kid, to Calgary.

Russ Courtnall, a centre, could skate, probably faster than any contemporary Leaf player. He had a wonderful shot. He had three straight seasons of twenty-two or more goals. He was handsome and personable and knew his way around a media interview (and he married Paris Vaughan, the gorgeous actress — see *Heathers* and other films — and daughter of the late, great jazz diva, Sarah Vaughan). So why was Courtnall on one end of possibly the dumbest trade Toronto ever made? November 7, 1988, Courtnall to Montreal for a right-winger named John Kordic who played small parts of 105 games for the Leafs, scored 10 goals and got 446 minutes in penalties, and who died on August 8, 1992, in a grungy Quebec City motel room of a heart attack brought on by the ingestion of cocaine, steroids and liquor. The immediate explanation for the trade was that John Brophy, coach at the time, preferred muscle, which he divined in Kordic, over speed, which everybody knew Courtnall had in spades. Courtnall, who continued on a fine career with Montreal and then Minnesota–Dallas, came up with a broader, more philosophical explanation a few years later. "The Leafs were a weak team," he said, "and it was as if they had a few thoroughbreds and had to run hell out of them. When we couldn't do what they expected, they gave up on us."

Wendel Clark was the one who survived. Over the years in Toronto, without losing his unpretentious, kid-from-the-prairies quality, he developed a rough sort of sophistication. He lived in a fourplex in the Annex, a downtown Toronto neighbourhood with a high concentration of lawyers, writers, actors and other trend-setters. And he evolved a personal style, part *Miami Vice*, part Bruce Springsteen, that half of the young men of the city seemed to emulate.

He also came down with horrendous back pains. They owed at least part of their source to a fight Clark had with Montreal's Chris Nilan at the tryouts for the 1987 Team Canada. Clark took treatments and advice from many medical people—from doctors at the Mayo Clinic; from a London, England, osteopath named Nidoo who was recommended by another famous back-pain sufferer, Lord Kenneth Thomson. Some remedies worked temporarily, some did no good at all, and Clark missed 159 games in three seasons, 1987 through 1990.

That's when the calumny started. Harold Ballard led off, evoking the old-time expression to describe a malingerer. "I sometimes think," Ballard said in February 1989, "Wendel's swinging the lead." It got worse. It got bizarre. *Frank* magazine ran with a rumour that Clark might be gay. The Leafs had a trade lined up in 1992 which would have sent Clark to Edmonton. It collapsed at the eleventh hour.

Through it all, Clark played the class act. No complaining. No whining. "You have to laugh," he said at one point. "That's all you can do, laugh." And he weathered everything—the sore back, the insults from the boss, the slump in scoring—and came out the other side in the spring of 1993. He was a major force in the three playoff series of those months and he maintained the same hot pace into the 1993–94 season. Clark, among the Leafs who suffered through the 1980s, was a champion survivor.

GOING INTO THE 1989–90 SEASON, THE LEAFS HAD A NEW general manager, Floyd Smith (Gord Stellick, fed up with Ballard, quit and moved to the New York Rangers), and a new coach, Doug Carpenter

(George Armstrong finally convinced Ballard he wasn't a coaching kind of guy and returned to scouting).

Carpenter was the man whom Punch Imlach wanted to replace Joe Crozier back in 1981. Ballard had another choice at the time, Mike Nykoluk. Ballard notwithstanding, Carpenter was a hockey guy of considerable intelligence. He'd been a high school teacher, had coached the Cornwall Royals to the Memorial Cup in 1980, had coached effectively in the minors for the Leafs. After the 1981 rejection by Ballard, he had put in two and a half years as head coach of the New Jersey Devils. With the Leafs at last in 1989–90, he adopted primarily a defensive system. That got them off to a positive start, and the team finished the year with an even .500 mark — thirty-eight wins, the same number of losses, twelfth overall in the league, a spot in the playoffs. But the Leafs had begun to falter badly late in the schedule, and over their last twenty-nine games, they recorded seven wins, two ties, twenty losses. Those numbers included a fast elmination by St. Louis in the first round of the playoffs.

TODD GILL REMEMBERS THE PERIOD IN THE LATE 1980s as a miserable time for him in hockey: "When we started to get beat so badly, the coaches wanted us to get defensive. That's not my style. I've always been better offensively when I'm allowed to be. I think, in hockey, you can't restrict a guy who can play a good offensive game, even if he is a defenceman. But during the bad period for us, the coaches kept saying to me, get the puck up, get the puck up! I wasn't allowed to make plays. So my point totals came down. It used to be I led the defence in assists, but not any more. Reporters started writing in the papers that I was slipping. The coaches must've read the papers because they started to say I was slipping too. I didn't feel that was true, but with all the talk, I could feel my confidence dropping off. I began forcing passes and making major mistakes. Things didn't turn around for me, I didn't get my confidence back, until we had a new coach, Tom Watt."

TOM WATT CAME TO THE LEAFS WITH CREDENTIALS A yard and a half long. They started with his fourteen seasons coaching the University of Toronto Blues. Under Watt, the Blues won nine national championships. He coached two teams in the NHL, the Winnipeg Jets and the Vancouver Canucks. He got no Stanley Cups with either, but he won one as assistant coach for the Calgary Flames in 1988–89. He was an assistant coach in many other places, at two Olympic Games, two World Championships, two Canada Cups. He arrived in Toronto—his home town, incidentally—as assistant coach to Doug Carpenter in 1989 and moved up to the head coaching job when Floyd Smith fired Carpenter eleven games into the 1990–91 season.

Watt brought obvious experience, brains and sense of hockey strategy to the task. All he lacked, as it turned out, were the horses. Over his time with the Leafs, coaching most of one season and all of the next, Toronto began to acquire solid players, even a star or two—Doug Gilmour, Peter Zezel, Bob Rouse, Jamie Macoun. These were the guys who would take the Leafs back to winning hockey. But that didn't happen during Watt's stewardship. The team had twenty-three wins in 1990–91, thirty in 1991–92. Neither total was enough to get Toronto into the playoffs, and when the major changes came in the Leafs' ownership and management, when the new people came on the scene, Steve Stavro as chairman and Cliff Fletcher as president and general manager, Watt lost his job as head coach. But he didn't vanish from the Leaf picture. Fletcher appointed him director of pro scouting. There was no sense losing a man with credentials as long as Watt's.

UNDER WATT, TODD GILL'S OFFENSIVE STATS PERKED UP, twenty-two assists in 1990–91, fifteen the next season, then all the way to thirty-two, plus eleven goals, under Pat Burns in 1992–93. Gill had a terrific playoffs that season too, one goal and ten assists. There was just one problem—towards the end of the playoffs, particularly against the Los Angeles Kings in the Stanley Cup semi-finals, Gill felt a growing tightness in his groin. It didn't stem from a specific injury, from a hit somebody laid on him. It was simply the result of wear and tear over his years of hockey, an annoying and sometimes painful ache somewhere inside his lower body.

Gill took it easy over the following summer, spent some time in Cardinal, didn't do a whole lot of things more strenuous than playing with his two little daughters. Chloe was a year and a half old. Madeline was still a baby, born just the previous February, and she was a worry, afflicted with bronchitis. Madeline made a wheezing noise just breathing, and she needed an inhalator in her room. "You feel so helpless when you watch her," Gill says. "Just a tiny baby, and one time there, she turned blue." Madeline's difficulties put Todd's sore groin in a different perspective. Compared with a baby's bronchitis, Gill thought, my groin isn't that bad.

But back on the ice, playing hockey again, in the fifth game of the new season, 1993–94, against Detroit at Joe Louis Arena, Gill felt something go in his groin, a pull, a really crippling ache. He played in pain for three more weeks. Then he went out of action. He tried therapy. He tried rest. He tried practising with the Newmarket Royals. "Playing at 75 percent, I was okay," he said after the practice. "But I couldn't push it past that. The kind of game I play, I have to skate and jump, do both of those really hard, 100 percent. I couldn't do that in Newmarket." He flew to Vancouver on November 25. The doctor out there, a specialist named Ross Davidson, told him surgery wasn't necessary, no operation needed to repair any damaged abdominal muscles. Rest was the only answer. Just to be certain, the Leafs sent Gill to Los Angeles nine days later to have another doctor look at him, a soft-tissue specialist. He said the same thing, just a matter of time. Gill, the Leafs' best offensive defenceman, one of the good ones in the NHL, flew home to rest and wait and take therapy. Maybe a month, the doctor had said, and Gill would be back on the ice.

"It's weird going through something like this," Gill said. "The team's doing so great, and I'm not really part of it. One thing, though, I like this situation a whole lot better than the way it was a few years ago when the Leafs were everybody's favourite joke, when I personally was treated like a joke. I'm just so glad to see the end of those days. Of course, that didn't happen until Mr. Ballard was gone and Mr. Stavro finally came in."

Todd Gill smiled.

21

Ballard in Decline

WAS THERE ANYTHING PRAISING TO SAY about Harold Ballard?

Three things for a certainty.

One, he was a gardener. Both at his home in west Toronto, before he holed up in the Maple Leaf Gardens apartment, and at his cottage on Georgian Bay, he grew flowers. Got his hands dirty, planted bulbs, weeded, watered, and rejoiced in the blooms. "He didn't take his nose out of the garden," Ballard's son Bill, remembering his own childhood, told the sportswriter Bill Houston.

Gardeners, according to one view, partake of a certain nobility. They're better people than the rest of us, closer to the earth and to God. Rudyard Kipling shared such a view:

Oh, Adam was a gardener, and God who made him sees
That half a gardener's work is done upon his knees.
So when his work is finished, he can wash his hands and pray
For the glory of the Garden, that it may not pass away!

Two, Ballard gave to charity. By the 1980s, he was said to be donating amounts annually that totalled in the six figures, money that went to the Salvation Army, the Cancer Society, Easter Seals, Crippled Children.

Three, Ballard was perfectly aware that he was outrageous. Is that in his favour? Probably. It would mean that he wasn't an unconscious, undirected eccentric. He calculated his behaviour. He intended the acts that, often at someone else's expense, got him the publicity he adored. Brian Glennie says, "Ballard pulled off his stunts, then sat back and said, 'Do you believe everybody swallowed what I just did, the newspaper guys wrote about it, the TV people put it on air? Can you believe anything so stupid?'" Many other Ballard-monitors go along with this interpretation. Maybe that's in Ballard's favour, that he had the talent to mould such a bizarre and frequently offensive self-creation.

IN THE SUMMER OF 1982, SOMEONE NEW ENTERED Ballard's life, a woman who shared the Ballard talent for mischief. She was Yolanda Babic MacMillan. Born in Port Arthur, Ontario, on January 3, 1933; married to a Windsor, Ontario, lawyer named William MacMillan; mother of two children; divorced from MacMillan in 1967; constant companion of another lawyer, Robert Irwin of Wallaceburg, Ontario, with whom she conspired in the late 1970s to forge a will which would have brought the conspirators, if the plot worked, a million bucks. The plot didn't work. On November 9, 1981, Yolanda pleaded guilty to conspiracy to commit fraud and to perjury. She got three years, reduced to two on appeal, and served four months.

The above recital makes Yolanda sound like the Barbara Stanwyck character in a piece of Billy Wilder *film noir*, a slim, beautiful woman with a slight sense of menace, dark, smoked cigarettes, lied without blinking. That wasn't quite Yolanda, apart possibly from the prevarication. Yolanda was round and soft. She might have been Harold Ballard's twin separated at birth, a pair of endomorphs, hair dyed gold (hers) and orange (his). She swore just like Harold did, she dramatized. She plotted—that made her different from Ballard, who was spontaneous—but otherwise, it was a match, Harold and Yolanda, made in the singles' club from hell.

Yolanda set her cap for Harold. Her first arrival at the Gardens, unannounced, in that summer of 1982, was in a limo and mink. When Harold gave her the slip—the two hadn't, so far as anyone knows, been previously introduced—she stepped up the campaign. Love notes, gifts of flowers, pastries, the revelation that they had prison sentences in common. Harold yielded. Why not? The guy was almost eighty and here was a younger woman claiming she ached for his body. Yolanda became a fixture around the Gardens. So did her dog, a part Dobermann named Sandy. King Clancy was assigned the task of caring for Sandy, walking it, feeding it, bedding it down, but the brute had too much Gestapo in its genes for ageing, frail King. Sandy was allowed to run wild at the Gardens. Yolanda was too.

YOLANDA CAME ALONG IN A PERIOD WHEN BALLARD WAS becoming vulnerable. Two men crucial to his equilibrium died in 1984; one was Bob Sedgewick, the Gardens' long-time lawyer and a steadying influence in both business and personal matters, and the other was Harry "Red" Foster, probably Ballard's oldest friend, reaching back to his flaming youth. Clancy was failing at the same time, growing old, unable to take road trips with the Leafs, still good for an anecdote but not for a song or a dance. He died in late November 1986, eighty-four years old, after an operation to remove his gall bladder. The death left Ballard isolated.

Partly by default, Yolanda stepped forward as Ballard's sidekick and confidante. That wasn't all bad news. Apart from the boost her presence gave to Ballard's self-esteem, Yolanda took an interest in keeping Harold alive. He was a diabetic and a binge-consumer of sweets. That was a lethal combination. Yolanda got Ballard on a diet, took sixty pounds off his overweight body. She threw a fancy eighty-fourth birthday party for him in 1987 (Steve Stavro's gift was a goose and a gander, ribbons identifying the birds as "Harold" and "Yolanda"). Though Ballard occasionally rebelled at Yolanda's smothering attention, she was his for better or for worse.

MICHAEL GOBUTY MIGHT BE IDENTIFIED AMONG THE "FOR worse." Gobuty, a man of some charm, began business life in his family's

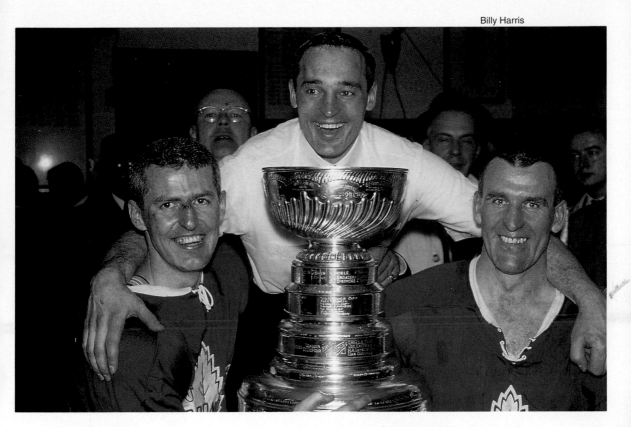

How sweet it was: celebrating the 1964 Stanley Cup with Gerry Ehman, Frank Mahovlich and Billy Harris.

Bob Nevin and Frank Mahovlich sip the champagne (above) while (below) Bob Baun, Ron Stewart and Billy Harris flash championship smiles, with and without teeth.

The Big M— Frank Mahovlich himself — gets in a guessing game with Montreal's Gump Worsley.

Captain George Armstrong asks for
the first kiss from the 1966-67
Stanley Cup.

Terry Sawchuk, on walkabout from his net, clears the puck against the
Montreal Canadiens.

John Anderson, Rick Vaive and Stewart Gavin. Vaive made his mark on the Leafs: captain and 299 goals scored.

The three players on the right — John Anderson, Rick Vaive and Bill Derlago — made a sweet offensive unit in the 1980s, but the team won no prizes.

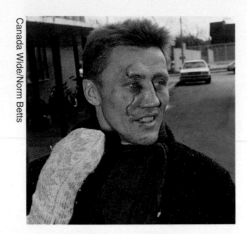

No, it isn't Frankenstein's monster after a bad day at the laboratory. It's Borje Salming after a cutting night on the ice.

Harold Ballard appears equally delighted with these two 1985 draft choices. He was right about the fellow on the left, Wendel Clark, but Ken Spangler played no NHL hockey.

Victoria Leather Jacket Co. of Winnipeg. Later he joined the consortium that owned the Winnipeg Jets, then of the WHA. He appeared to be riding high, but things went poorly for Gobuty in Winnipeg in the early 1980s, and he moved to Toronto, where he got into garbage-truck rentals.

Even in the rancorous days of the NHL–WHA rivalry, Gobuty had put himself on good terms with Ballard, a dextrous piece of work for "a Hebe from Winnipeg." Gobuty did it mainly by laughing at Ballard's jokes, showing respect, performing ingratiating numbers. When he arrived in Toronto, he continued to cultivate Ballard so masterfully, assuming many of King Clancy's former gofer tasks, sitting alongside Harold in the private box at the Gardens, that the usually cautious old man agreed to guarantee Gobuty's bank loans and lines of credit.

These guarantees, for ever-escalating amounts, were made largely over the dead bodies of Ballard's Gardens people, treasurer Don Crump and lawyer Rosanne Rocchi. Finally, when Ballard put his signature to a guarantee of a $2.15-million loan to Gobuty by the National Bank of Canada in October 1987, Crump put his foot down. Ballard, he announced, had no intention of staying on the hook for $2.15 million. The National Bank got very nervous. It asked Gobuty to return the loan. Sorry, said Gobuty, the cash had gone into garbage or somewhere. The National Bank sued the guarantor, Ballard, and it was in this lawsuit that Yolanda's role in the disagreeable business surfaced on the public record.

It seemed that in September 1987, a month before Ballard signed the National Bank guarantee, Yolanda was in receipt of a certified cheque for $75,000 from none other than Michael Gobuty. No one had previously mistaken Yolanda for a financial wizard—she had declared personal bankruptcy in August 1983, with debts of $592,500 and nil assets—but she was the mistress of the quick recovery. Oh, she said, the $75,000 was payment for some of her jewellery that dear Michael had admired and purchased. It had nothing to do with any influence she might apply to Harold on Michael's behalf. Ballard accepted the explanation. At any rate, he didn't kick Yolanda out of the Gardens suite. He needed her, and all of this—the reliance on Yolanda, the misguided guarantee for Gobuty—seemed to indicate that Ballard was seriously losing his formerly steely grip on events at the Gardens.

The judge in the lawsuit that the National Bank brought against Ballard chalked up the guarantee to Harold's "capacity to misjudge people." The judge was Douglas Coo of the Ontario Court's General Division, and his decision came at the end of a six-day trial in February 1993, long after Ballard's death. Coo held that "it was quite apparent Ballard had no faith in Gobuty as a businessman," but that Ballard signed the guarantee because "he was capable of making a mistake, as he obviously did here." Some mistake! Harold's goof meant that his estate got stuck with a judgment against it in favour of the National Bank for $3.5 million, covering the guarantee plus accumulating interest.

THE MUDDLE INTENSIFIED HAROLD, YOLANDA, AND THE Gardens' rupturing financial state. Ballard's kids got into it. Actually, as we'll see, they were never out of it from the time they were teenagers, but Yolanda's involvement added spice and anger to the mix.

Ballard's relations with his children, particularly after Dorothy Ballard died, seemed to grow long on volatility and short on affection. He was particularly rough on his two sons, on Bill who was a superb-enough businessman to make his own fortune in concert promotions, and on Harold, Jr., who was the youngest, artistically inclined, the most vulnerable. Both took their shots of public humiliation from Ballard. Still, from all of the kids' point of view, Harold was the only father they had, and at first they welcomed Yolanda as a companion for their sometimes dear old dad.

This attitude speedily deteriorated. Yolanda became too grabby, in the children's opinion, a gold-digger incarnate, and when she went to court in the spring of 1987 and had her name legally changed to Ballard, the young Ballards thought, what, this woman thinks she can replace our mother?

The struggle over Harold—Yolanda on one side and the three kids on the other—staggered from one wretched episode to another. In January 1988, Harold suffered a heart attack in Florida. Yolanda, pleading the best interests of her sweetie, set up barricades at the Miami Heart Institute to keep the Ballard children from him. And the same sad scenario was acted out at the Wellesley Hospital in Toronto the following summer when Harold's heart again weakened.

This confrontational stuff bottomed out in what may or may not have been fisticuffs in the Gardens suite on a day in September 1988. Yolanda claimed that Bill punched her. She laid assault charges. At the trial, Harold testified against his own son and in favour of Yolanda. He said he saw Bill give Yolanda a couple of fearsome whacks. But when Bill's lawyer, Clive Bynoe, cross-examined Harold Ballard, Harold came across as a confused old party who probably didn't see, couldn't have seen, given his position in the suite at the time, the alleged assault. Judge Walter Bell, hearing the case, brushed off Ballard's testimony as "of no use." But he convicted Bill, mainly on Yolanda's testimony, and fined him $500.

Such events could be dismissed as the continuing saga in the waning life of a man who had always courted turmoil and generated distress except for one crucial fact—money was at stake here, big money, the ownership of the Gardens itself.

THE RELEVANT HISTORY DATES FROM 1966. THAT WAS THE year Ballard, seeking to minimize inheritance taxes, established a holding company called Harold E. Ballard Limited. Through a trust agreement, he controlled the shares, but he vested their ownership in his three children. Over the years, the shares in HEBL came to represent, at their peak, about 80 percent of all Gardens stock. And the kids owned it. Here was a recipe for pandemonium.

By the late 1980s, Ballard wanted desperately to recover the HEBL ownership for himself. That was because he felt Molson's Breweries breathing down his neck. In 1980, Molson's had lent Ballard $8.8 million. Ballard needed the cash to meet the enormous interest charges on the money he had borrowed from the Toronto-Dominion Bank in the early 1970s to buy out the Gardens shares held by John Bassett and the Staff Smythe estate. In return for the $8.8 million, Molson's got generous repayment terms plus—here was the rub—an option to acquire 20 percent of Gardens stock in the autumn of 1990 and first right of refusal on Ballard's remaining shares. It was small wonder that, as the years moved to the end of the 1980s, Ballard was sweating.

"Harold made it clear," Donald Crump said a few years later, speaking from experience as the Gardens treasurer, "that there were two groups he didn't want to take control of the Gardens—his children and breweries."

To head off both groups, Ballard made a series of what he hoped were pre-emptive strikes. In January 1989, he bought from his daughter, Mary Elizabeth, her one-third share in HEBL for $15.5 million. Where did he get the money? He borrowed it from Molson's. That seemed strange, going deeper in hock to the brewery. But Ballard wasn't finished. In June 16 of that year, he transferred some of his personal Gardens shares to HEBL in exchange for HEBL shares plus cash, the whole package amounting to about $15.5 million. Four days later, he bought Harold, Jr.'s one-third share of HEBL for $21 million. Where did Ballard raise the cash for this purchase? From his favourite institutional lender, the Toronto-Dominion Bank, to the tune of the whole $21 million.

The financial jugglery left Ballard in two-thirds control of the holding company, HEBL. It also left him more beholden than ever to Molson's, more in its potential long-term grasp, since, as a condition of its loan to Ballard to buy Mary Elizabeth's shares in HEBL, Molson's took an option to acquire that share if the loan wasn't repaid at the end of 1990. And, of course, the jugglery left Ballard heavily in debt—to Molson's, to the Toronto-Dominion Bank, not to forget the National Bank and the $3.5 million it was claiming on the Michael Gobuty guarantee.

Tangled?

Yes, but, wait, it gets more Byzantine.

Two additional elements—one of possible familial retribution, one of fate taking its course—entered the picture.

For one, Bill Ballard brought a lawsuit in September 1989, claiming that his father had no right to Harold, Jr.'s share of HEBL because he, Bill, had a prior option on the shares. Bill moved in court to void the deal between the two Harolds. He planned to exercise his option to buy Harold, Jr.'s share, thereby giving him control over HEBL and over the Gardens. The motive here could be one of two—that Bill wanted to keep the Gardens in the Ballard name, a sane and healthy Ballard, himself, or that he wished to pay back his old man for past failures as a parent. Or maybe some of both.

And, the second element, nature making its final appearance in Harold Ballard's life, in January 1990, again in Miami, Ballard fell ultimately ill. His kidneys failed, his heart grew weaker. He was dying.

YOLANDA PROBABLY REALIZED THAT HER MAIN CHANCE AT whatever Harold would leave behind was running out fast. She made moves to marry Harold in death-bed nuptials. Rosanne Rocchi, the Gardens lawyer, headed that off. Yolanda sought to have herself declared Harold's guardian. Ballard's daughter intervened. Largely at Mary Elizabeth's instigation, an Ontario District Court Judge named Donna Haley appointed Bud Estey as Ballard's personal guardian. Estey was a former justice of the Supreme Court of Canada and an old Ballard friend. Judge Haley issued a couple of other orders that February. She declared Ballard mentally incompetent, and she appointed three other men as a committee to oversee Ballard's finances and to run the Gardens. The three, Ballard friends and Gardens directors, were Don Crump, Steve Stavro and Don Giffin. The trio—who would later split off in a two-against-one dispute over control of the Gardens—also served as executors of Ballard's will. Yolanda was frozen out. What was a girl to do? Yolanda eventually brought an action against Harold's estate for support. She placed the support at $300,000. Annually.

ON APRIL 11, 1990, HAROLD BALLARD DIED.

Ballard's will named the following beneficiaries: the Princess Margaret Hospital, the Wellesley Hospital, the Ontario Crippled Children's Centre, the Canadian Association for the Mentally Retarded, the Salvation Army, the Charlie Conacher Throat Cancer Fund, the Maple Leaf Gardens Scholarship Fund, Hockey Canada.

In sum, Ballard left behind the following circumstances:

A lawsuit instituted by his son Bill which threw future ownership of the Gardens in doubt and which seemed set to rival *Jarndyce* vs. *Jarndyce* in complexity and length.

An estate that was heavily freighted in debt.

The prospect that, even without Bill Ballard's lawsuit, the ownership of the Gardens could fall into hands which Harold himself would consider alien, perhaps into the hands of Molson's Breweries with the various options and rights it had obtained in return for its loans to Ballard.

A Gardens president and CEO, Don Giffin, named to the posts by the Gardens Board of Directors on March 12, 1990, who turned out, a year later, to be in the early stages of cancer.

Three principals at the Gardens, Giffin, Steve Stavro and Don Crump, who disagreed over hockey and business policy, Crump siding with Stavro and both opposing Giffin.

And a hockey team ending a decade in which it had never finished above .500, had missed the playoffs five times, and had become the punchline to all of hockey's terrible jokes.

Question: Why don't they serve tea at the Gardens?

Answer: Because all the mugs are out on the ice.

This was Harold Ballard's legacy.

22

The New Beginning

ALL OF THE MEN WHO SWEPT UP THE PIECES after Harold Ballard was gone—men like Don Giffin and Steve Stavro, even Terry Kelly, who, as we'll see, came to occupy a position with the Maple Leafs that is special in both its fact and its symbolism—all of these men, at one time or another, used the same peculiar phrase in describing their task at the Gardens. All of them spoke of "carrying on the Ballard tradition."

What they meant, of course, was the tradition of winning hockey that pre-dated Harold Ballard. They weren't referring to the more recent and purely Ballardian tradition of bungling, cheapness, ego-gratification and losing. The actions of Giffin, Stavro and Kelly through the early 1990s demonstrated that they had other things in mind, things like generosity and pride and organizational efficiency. But none was going to turn his back on Ballard. To Giffin, Stavro and Kelly, Harold wasn't such a bad guy. A bit rough maybe, but generous to charities, loved hockey, could be a very amusing companion. Ballard had owned the Gardens for twenty years. That piece of history couldn't be ignored. Nor could Ballard. Stavro and the others would honour him and his memory. They just wouldn't run the Gardens the way Harold did.

CONSIDER, FIRST, DON GIFFIN.

He was a self-made millionaire in sheet metal. He arrived in Toronto from his home town of Brockville, Ontario, as a teenager before the Second World War and apprenticed in the sheet-metal trade. By 1949, he had launched his own company, Giffin Sheet Metals, and it brought him success and money. With some of the money, he bought a summer home on Georgian Bay. His neighbour happened to be Harold Ballard. The two became friends and, to a degree, business associates. Giffin helped Ballard with the financing he needed to buy out John Bassett and the Staff Smythe estate, and in 1970, Ballard put Giffin, who gathered for himself almost 2 percent of all Gardens stock over the years, on the Gardens board. When Ballard grew incapacitated in the late winter of 1990, Giffin's status as the most senior director—as well as his own unconcealed ambition to succeed Ballard—made him the choice of the other directors as the Gardens' new president.

That's when Giffin began to act in a very un–Ballard-like manner. He put items like history and dignity on the Gardens agenda. He got the ball rolling in forming an alumni group among former Leaf players, welcoming back to the Gardens the heroes whom Ballard had turned away. He started the move to hoist Gardens banners honouring championship Leaf teams. He inaugurated a campaign of repair and refurbishment around the building. But all of these were mere prelude to the Giffin blockbuster. That came when Giffin went after something that had been missing from the Gardens for decades, a hockey man with credentials, a general manager with a track record for winning in the NHL. Giffin laid out serious money—almost a million dollars a year over a five-year contract—to get the best in the business. Giffin hired Cliff Fletcher.

CLIFF FLETCHER KEEPS OUT OF HIS COACH'S HAIR. He never does trades when his team is on a losing streak. He makes sure his players and their families are secure in the community where the team plays. These are some of the notions Fletcher has formed over his thirty-five years in hockey management. If possible, hire a colourful coach, that's another one. He hired Bernie Geoffrion in Atlanta, Bob Johnson and Terry Crisp in Calgary, Pat Burns in Toronto, good hockey guys but good with the press too, talkative and quotable. Fletcher has never felt overshadowed by these characters. He's probably never felt overshadowed by anyone. He likes colourful coaches who give great interviews. It saves him the trouble. Instead of talking to reporters, keeping the team in the news, he can stick to his office, work the phones, build a team, fill the seats, earn the profits.

Fletcher is an unflappable, silver-haired man in his late fifties. He's serious, but his face sometimes wears a whimsical cast. He goes first-cabin on everything, at work and in pleasure. His Toronto home is in Rosedale. His Florida home is on Singer Island. He collects Canadian paintings. He recognizes good wines and restaurants with accomplished chefs. He knows all about wielding authority. When he came to the Leafs in the summer of 1991, he asked for and got the big titles — chief operating officer, president and general manager (Giffin moved upstairs to board chairman). All of this responsibility, for both hockey and non-hockey matters, sits effortlessly with Fletcher. He has the right air about him — quiet, smooth, polished, just a little mysterious.

"Cliff Fletcher can come to a board meeting," says Terry Kelly, speaking as one of the Gardens' directors, "talk for ten minutes, tell us absolutely nothing, and we'll all agree unanimously that he gave a great report."

Fletcher learned his manner from the masters of hockey management, legerdemain and other such elusive skills. He started as a young guy in his home town, Montreal, running minor and junior teams for the great Canadiens manipulator, Sam Pollock. Then came four years in St. Louis as assistant to the equally cagey Scotty Bowman. In 1972, he landed the job as general manager of the expansion Atlanta Flames. He supervised the Flames' 1980 move to Calgary, and he put together the strong Flames teams of the late 1980s, two first-overall finishes, one Stanley Cup. After nineteen years running the show in Atlanta–Calgary, Fletcher took the Toronto offer to give himself one last grand adventure in hockey, maybe the biggest challenge of all, restoring a mighty team that had suffered terrible neglect.

Fletcher didn't waste much time changing the names and character in the Leaf lineup. In September 1991, he traded with Edmonton to get the All-Star goalie Grant Fuhr and the veteran goal scorer Glenn Anderson.

Six months later, in a deal that involved ten players altogether, he acquired Doug Gilmour from Calgary, giving up five guys, including Gary Leeman, who proceeded to make absolutely nil impact on the Flames' play. That trade was a steal. Another Fletcher trade, engineered a year later, in February 1993, was a surprise, giving up Grant Fuhr, whom everybody had welcomed as the ultimate solution to Toronto's goaltending problems, in return for the Buffalo Sabres' right-winger Dave Andreychuk. A puzzler of a deal? So it seemed, but it soon became apparent that Fletcher knew what he was doing.

In all matters around the Gardens, Fletcher seemed to know what he was doing. But, in his first year on the job, Fletcher himself must have wondered this: what in the world was Steve Stavro doing?

HE WAS BORN MONOLI STAVROFF SHOLDAS IN THE VILLAGE of Gabresh in Greek Macedonia. His dad, Anatas, went ahead to Toronto in 1927 and opened a grocery store in the east end. Seven years later, Anatas sent for his wife and two sons. That's when Steve, as he was to become in the Anglo world of Toronto, left Macedonia, but to this day, if you want to curry favour with Stavro, then show him you know a little Macedonian history, even second-hand tourist stuff. He's awfully proud of his heritage.

In Toronto, Steve worked his way through the family trade, groceries, and came out the other side with a simple but revolutionary idea: sell good product with no frills, no packaging, minimal service, fast turnover. Stavro opened his first store based on that premise in 1949 on Danforth Avenue. He called it Knob Hill Farms. The idea clicked. He opened more and larger stores. The stores, eight of them now, grew to humongous proportions; the one in Cambridge, Ontario, has a meat counter 517 feet long, 85 butchers, 42 checkout counters, railway cars that roll on to the floor, which covers 8 acres, to unload the produce. The Biggest Grocery Store in the World.

Naturally, Stavro became a very rich man. He has a wife, Sally, four daughters, and a shifting collection of homes, in Palm Beach (Harold Ballard had a heart attack there), in Kentucky (for the Stavro racing stable), in the country south of Peterborough, Ontario (where, in a manor house holding suits of armour and baronial furniture, Stravro indulges his affection for the Romantic tradition), and on Teddington Park Avenue in Toronto. The latter is a residence in the grand sense: forty-nine rooms, including a ballroom, backing on the eighteenth fairway of Rosedale Golf Club (Stavro isn't a member), gargoyles guarding the long circular driveway, former home of the late co-founder of Argus Corporation, Colonel Eric Phillips (who was a Rosedale member). When Steve and Sally entertain at Teddington Park, they don't kid around. Luciano Pavarotti once came to dinner, along with a lot of other people who paid a thousand dollars each for the privilege; the money went to a centre for Toronto's Italian community. On another occasion, referred to in this context as "glittering," the Stavros opened up Teddington Park for a banquet that celebrated the Opera Ball crowd.

If the above makes it appear that, somewhere along the line, Steve Stavro went high hat, forget the notion. He doesn't mind rubbing shoulders with people of different prominences, but he's a self-effacing, socially modest sort. He isn't reclusive in the Howard Hughes sense, but his guard, no offence intended and none taken, is usually up when he's around people he hasn't known for many years.

He knew Harold Ballard over three decades, ever since Stavro started the Eastern Professional Soccer League and invited Ballard to get in on it. The soccer league failed—probably the only Stavro enterprise that has bombed—but the connection with Ballard continued. It even survived a small flap when Stavro thought Yolanda had swiped one of his pens. Ballard invited Stavro on to the Gardens board in 1981, and it was in that role, and as co-executor of Ballard's estate, that Stavro worried that Don Giffin and Cliff Fletcher might not make the right fit for the Gardens.

ONE MAJOR OBJECTION THAT STAVRO HAD TO GIFFIN WAS that Giffin was drawing a salary of $300,000 to serve as head man at the Gardens. Since Giffin, Ballard's executor along with Stavro and Don Crump, was supposed to be running the Gardens for the benefit of all those charities named in Ballard's will, Giffin was in effect taking money away from the Crippled Children, the Salvation Army, and the rest. Stavro didn't care for that, nor for some of the other non–cost effective spending Giffin was indulging in—a 52 percent raise for all Gardens maintenance workers, for example.

As for Fletcher, Stavro thought he'd been handed too much authority. Run the hockey team, okay, but not the entire Gardens operation. The plan that Stavro advanced, before Fletcher was hired, was to bring in a business guy who would look after such matters as marketing, broadcasting rights, renting out the building for non-hockey affairs. Then the business guy would hire a hockey guy—Fletcher might be fine—who would report to him. Stavro had a specific business guy in mind, Lyman MacInnis, an accountant who had experience in the entertainment field with Anne Murray and with Labatt's. None of the other directors, except Crump, went for Stavro's plan, and at the meeting of the Gardens board on June 4, 1990, to consider hiring Fletcher, the six Gardens' directors present—Crump did not attend the meeting—voted 5–1 in favour of Fletcher. Stavro was the odd man out. Fletcher got the job.

In this mildly uneasy atmosphere, the Gardens muddled through its first post-Ballard year. Fletcher must have been glancing over his shoulder now and then at Stavro. Bill Ballard was still out there with his lawsuit, asking the courts to allow him to purchase his brother's, Harold, Jr.'s, one-third share in Harold E. Ballard Limited, which would give him a majority ownership of the Gardens. Giffin, seeking to beef up his own power, was aligning himself with Bill. Molson's Breweries, with its options on various ownership slices, was hovering over to one side. And Steve Stavro, the silent man with all the money, was biding his time, musing on his duty.

Then two things happened that helped to set the Gardens in a new direction.

First, in April 1991, Don Giffin had surgery to remove a cancerous lump under his arm. Giffin was seventy-five, he had cancer, he would die on March 20, 1992, he was no longer a force at the Gardens.

Second, Bill Ballard quit the battle. This was in the late summer of 1991. The reason Bill advanced for calling off his court challenge to Gardens' ownership was weariness. "I'm tired of fighting alone," he said.

And he sold his share in HEBL to the Harold Ballard estate for $21 million (the money came from another Toronto-Dominion Bank loan).

And, fundamentally, a third factor entered into the picture through these months of 1991. It was the Steve Stavro factor. Somewhere along the line, at some specific moment, Stavro made the decision to go all out in seeking control of the Gardens. His motivation wasn't money; he had enough of that. It wasn't public recognition; he shuns that. His choice—to get in or stay out—originated in a quality that wasn't much in evidence at the Gardens in recent years. The quality was altruism.

Stavro decided to bring stability to the franchise. Except that he never uses the word "franchise" when he talks about the Toronto Maple Leafs. In conversation, he is meticulous about his choice of the correct word. He calls the Leafs an "institution." He thinks of himself as the custodian of the institution and the representative of the Leaf fans. Does this sound too good to be true? Well, believe it, Stavro is the genuine article, a selfless, though business-like, hockey man. And, not so incidentally, his friends say he's getting an enormous kick out of his Maple Leaf life. "He's like a little kid with the team," Terry Kelly says.

To position himself for all of this fun and responsibility, Stavro had to make some important money moves from the spring of 1991 through to the early fall of that year. Principally he dealt with Molson's. Stavro lent the Ballard estate $20 million to pay off one of the pending Molson's loans; the payoff gave Stavro an option to acquire the Gardens shares affected by the Stavro $20 million. Then he entered into a separate deal with Molson's under which he agreed to buy at a future date—sometime in the mid-1990s—the remaining shares held by Molson's plus the various rights that Molson's held to take up Gardens shares. When all the financial dust had settled, ownership in the Gardens shook down this way: 60 percent held by the Harold Ballard estate, 20 percent by Molson's in trust, 20 percent by individual investors, with Stavro retaining options to acquire close to 80 percent of the ownership by the mid-to-late 1990s.

Stavro was in the driver's seat. Or, more accurately, the chairman's chair. As part of the deal in lending money to the Ballard estate, Stavro reserved the right to name new directors and the new CEO. So, at the annual Gardens shareholders' meeting on October 22, 1991, it was the Steve Stavro show. He tossed Don Giffin out of the chairman's job, dismissed the four directors who supported Giffin, confirmed Don Crump as a continuing director, introduced a group of four new directors, and got himself named chairman and CEO.

And what of Cliff Fletcher? Stavro had already made peace on that front. It came in a two-and-a-half-hour sit-down Stavro had with Fletcher in a room at the Royal York Hotel on October 4, a couple of weeks before the shareholders' meeting. Stavro approached Fletcher aware of several home truths: that Fletcher's contract contained a buy-out clause which would compel the Gardens to pay him in the neighbourhood of $1.5 million if he were replaced before July 1, 1994; that it was imperative for the Gardens to be seen at last as a business place of harmony and team work; that everyone around Toronto who took hockey seriously looked to Fletcher as the right man, the only man, to straighten around the hockey club, that the fans wanted Fletcher on the job. Pretty compelling arguments, Stavro agreed, and he let it be known that he was now a committed Fletcher person. He doesn't phrase it in precisely that way in explaining his pro-Fletcher decision. He phrases it in a way that more reflects his all-encompassing approach to Maple Leaf hockey. "The fans spoke," he says, "and I listened."

Fans. The word keeps coming up. When Stavro picked the four new Gardens directors, he looked for men who were, for starters, hockey fans. "Steve wanted to make sure the directors' box was filled on hockey nights," Terry Kelly explains. "That's the box in the golds over on the west side. There used to be empty seats in there in the past. Not any more. Empty seats don't show respect and support for the team." Another quality that Stavro apparently asked of his directors was that they not come out of the Toronto Establishment, that they not have names like Ted Rogers (of the cable-TV empire) or Thor Eaton (of the department-store empire) who were two of the Giffin directors. Instead, Stavro went for guys who were more like him, successful but men of the people. He chose Ted Nikolaou, head of the J.J. Muggs restaurant chain; Brian Bellmore, a lawyer, not from a large and storied downtown firm but the operator of his own practice; Ron Pringle, a

Coca-Cola executive; George Whyte, another lawyer and independent entrepreneur until early 1994 when he was appointed senior vice-president and general counsel with the Bank of Nova Scotia; and Terry Kelly, a criminal lawyer in Oshawa.

IN THE SPORTS PAGES, TERRY KELLY IS REFERRED TO AS "Superfan." That's fair. He spends about $20,000 a year knocking around the world in pursuit of sports events, a soccer game at Wembley, a featherweight boxing match in Belfast, cricket in South Africa, often many events in one day (his record is six soccer games, all between dawn and lights out, all in Scotland); nothing is too modest—a darts tournament in Preston, England—or too colossal—a soccer game between Mexico and Bulgaria in front of 114,000 people at Mexico City's Azteca Stadium. He revels in them all. He relishes what he calls the "electricity" of the competition.

All of this is true, this Superfandom, but it misses a large part of the point. Kelly is a curious man. He's a talkative man. Both of these characteristics serve him well in the criminal courts. And both form part of his motivation in pursuing sports around the world. He loves to get out there, to travel, to see strange towns, special events, to chat up the fella in the next seat at the baseball game in Tucson, Arizona. He accumulates local lore. He hears stories—and not just sports stories. Over the Christmas holidays of 1993, he set off alone on a five-day drive to minor-league hockey arenas in Ohio and Pennsylvania, out-of-the-way spots, a dip down to Wheeling, West Virginia. And along the way, he stopped off at the historic home in Fremont, Ohio, of Rutherford B. Hayes, nineteenth president of the United States. And he talked to a man in Johnstown, Pennsylvania, about the great event in the city's history, about the terrible flood of 1889 that cost 2,000 Johnstown residents their lives. Kelly, the man of curiosity, thought it was an amazing tale.

Kelly has brought this nature of his to Maple Leaf Gardens, and his is far from an inconsequential contribution. Kelly's the man—the director—who gossips with the sportswriters, glad-hands visiting dignitaries, shmoozes with the fans. He treats the Gardens as an adjunct of his own living room, and when he brings people into it, as, for example, when he conducted a tour of lawyers in town for a Bar Association convention on a January Saturday in 1994, he gave them a little of the building's awe and a lot of its new welcoming character.

Kelly is the last man to speak ill of Harold Ballard. It was Ballard who annually made the Leafs available to Kelly for team practices at the arena in Oshawa, occasions which Kelly used as fund raisers for local charities (in partial return for which Kelly served as a character witness at Ballard's trial). But Kelly makes a handy—and enlightening—symbol of the differences between the old and the new at the Gardens, between the Ballard and post-Ballard eras. It isn't just that the Leafs are winning now or that the days of Leaf jokes have vanished. It's that the Gardens has become again an open place, part of the community the way it used to be, something to be proud of, to talk about. A Terry Kelly kind of place.

23

A Different Team

HERE IS WHAT TORONTO HOCKEY HISTORY OF the last twenty years taught: a brave run at the beginning of the season, maybe a tentative challenge to the other teams around Christmas, but by February? After the All-Star Game? When the other teams were revving their engines for the playoff surge? Never mind. Never mind the Leafs. History said they'd go into a decline.

So, at the Gardens on the night of Thursday, February 11, 1993, Toronto was poised for the traditional fold. The signs were there. In the first game after the All-Star break, the Leafs had looked dreadful, losing to Tampa Bay, to an expansion team! That happened two nights earlier on the road. Now Vancouver was in town, the Canucks who had whipped the Leafs 5–2 on their last visit to Toronto on January 6.

"We watched them in their morning skate," Pat Burns would say later of the Canucks. "They looked a bit cocky."

The Leafs weren't feeling cocky. They were feeling slightly tense, partly as a result of a small contretemps around the dressing room. The team captain, Wendel Clark, who hadn't been playing great hockey anyway, seeming rather undisciplined in Burns' disciplined system, had hurt a rib earlier in the month. Burns wanted Clark to take therapy during the time off for the All-Star Game. Clark went on a Caribbean holiday instead. Burns was pissed off.

The omens for the Vancouver game were not good.

But this Leaf team was different. This Leaf team came out hard and checking against Vancouver. The tenacity produced an early goal. Dave Andreychuk got it, the right-shooting left-winger, a big guy, as tall as the CN Tower, the goal scorer whom Cliff Fletcher had got for the team only nine days earlier in the daring trade with Buffalo, Grant Fuhr for Andreychuk. The Canucks tied the game, still in the first period, but the Leafs kept pressing until Mike Krushelnyski put the Leafs back ahead on a power play before the period ended.

Vancouver had players who were massively gifted, Trevor Linden and the exceptionally fast Pavel Bure. The Leafs clamped down on both of them. Toronto winger Ken Baumgartner took care of Linden practically all by himself with his array of bumps, pushes and smacks. As for Bure, Todd Gill gave him one hellacious check that let Bure know he wasn't going to score on this night. Felix Potvin in the Toronto net, sharp, even brilliant, all through the game, allowed only two goals, and the Leafs were up 4–2 fairly late in the third period when Doug Gilmour scored a particular goal. It was a small work of art, a goal that proclaimed just what sort of team the new Leafs were. Gilmour, with the puck, began the play with a classic spinorama move that got him free at centre ice. He fed a quick pass to Glenn Anderson near the Canuck blueline, and the two dashed on a two-on-one break. Gilmour, going full tilt for the Vancouver net, took the return pass and, in one motion, quicker than an eye — certainly quicker than Canuck goalie Kirk McLean's eye — he popped the puck in the upper corner. The game ended a few minutes later, 5–2.

The following Saturday, Minnesota arrived at the Gardens for another game crucial to the Leafs. The Norris Division was tight and competitive this season. Detroit and Chicago boasted the teams with the most talent. But St. Louis had Brett Hull and a fabulous goalie named Curtis Joseph; Minnesota was strong on coaching, with Bob Gainey, and on discipline, with players who did what Gainey told them; and Toronto seemed risen from years of torpor and failure. The Norris playoff spots were available to all five clubs in any order, and every game between division teams counted for serious points.

The Leafs figured to have trouble with the North Stars, who had beaten them in their three previous 1992–93 games. But, no, on this Saturday night, the Leafs, especially Doug Gilmour, blew the Stars' doors off. The score was 6–1, and Gilmour set up each of the six Toronto goals. Next night, in Minnesota for the return match, the Leafs won again. They did it differently this time, trailing at one point in the game 5–1, and coming back for the kind of victory, 6–5 on Todd Gill's goal, that makes a team's spirits sing.

In the following three games, all at the Gardens, the Leafs beat Tampa Bay and Calgary and tied Boston. They flew to Vancouver, where the Canucks were anxious to do a little evening-up. It didn't work out that way. The Leafs had found a pace. They'd located an almost unassailable confidence. "Nothing rattled us tonight," Pat Burns said after the game. Toronto won it 8–1. Gilmour had three assists and broke Darryl Sittler's 1977–78 Toronto record of seventy-two assists in a season. Glenn Anderson scored a goal which gave him 1,000 career points. The Leafs on the bench jumped over the boards to congratulate Anderson. Referee Denis Morel, the spoilsport, called the Leafs for a delay-of-game penalty. Burns, a big smile on his face, told Anderson to serve the penalty. It was that kind of game for the Leafs, where the coach could fool around with the players.

The Leafs, staying on a tear through the late winter, won eight games in February, lost two, tied two. In March, not slacking off, they went nine wins, three losses, two ties.

The Leafs, this year, were different.

BUT WHO WERE THESE LEAFS?

Some had been around for a while. Todd Gill. Wendel Clark. And Mark Osborne, the large, often obstreperous, beautifully conditioned left-winger who played three years for the Leafs in the late 1980s, got traded to Winnipeg, then returned to the Leafs near the end of the 1991–92 season.

Some were players picked up in trades in the couple of years before

Cliff Fletcher took over. These tended to be guys who fell into the young-veteran category—in their late twenties, had paid some dues with other NHL teams. Peter Zezel was one; he arrived after a half dozen seasons in Philadelphia, St. Louis and Washington, a no-nonsense kind of centre who could score a little and check a lot. Bob Rouse and Dave Ellett were defencemen, Rouse out of Minnesota and Washington, not fast but a standup defender, and Ellett, six years with the Winnipeg Jets, an intelligent player and a dedicated leader. And then there was Mike Krushelnyski, a veteran of the Edmonton Stanley Cup teams and of Los Angeles, a big guy—all of these players had size—a centre who came from the play-tough, follow-orders, take-care-of-business school.

Some were players who emerged from Toronto's own draft. Felix Potvin and Nikolai Borschevsky and Dmitri Mironov. Mironov was the slowest to develop, a defenceman from Moscow with a huge shot and a certain indecisiveness. Potvin and Borschevsky qualified as large surprises. Potvin wasn't supposed to be ready for the big team so soon, only twenty-two years old, only a season out of the Chicoutimi juniors, only forty games in the American League. But he blossomed early—quick and alert and agile—and Cliff Fletcher was hardly nervous at all when he let Grant Fuhr go to the Sabres and placed the goaltending in the hands of the kid. And Borschevsky? He was small, came from Siberia, spoke no English, hadn't scored a whole lot of goals in his nine seasons with Dynamo Moscow and Spartak Moscow. But he, too, blossomed quickly, an almost instant goal scorer, a left-winger with guts and a heavenly touch around the net.

And some were players Cliff Fletcher traded for, guys picked to fill specific niches. Fletcher got Glenn Anderson from Edmonton and Dave Andreychuk from Buffalo, both wingers, to score goals. He got John Cullen from Hartford, a centre, to set goals up. He got Jamie Macoun from Calgary, a defenceman, to play aggressive and smart hockey on the blueline. He got Bill Berg from the New York Islanders, a left-winger, to annoy people, check them, infuriate them into penalties, to be a pest. He got Ken Baumgartner from the Islanders, a utility forward and an articulate, sweet-faced guy to act as—here, given Baumgartner's disposition and brains, is a seeming contradiction—the team's enforcer. And he got

Doug Gilmour from Calgary, a centre, to show the way to the playoffs and beyond.

THERE'S SOMETHING ELUSIVE ABOUT DOUG GILMOUR'S looks. With his hockey helmet on, he's got the face of a mean little kid. When he opens his mouth and shows all those missing upper teeth, he's a pale-faced Leon Spinks. One teammate gave him the nickname Killer because of a supposed resemblance—is this sick or what?—to Charles Manson. But put in his teeth and dress him up with a smile, and women find him cute and sexy. Amy Cable does. She's the gorgeous teenager, a former Gardens usherette and present model, who began sharing a mid-Toronto condominium with Gilmour in the winter of 1993.

Whatever way you describe Gilmour's looks, they were omnipresent in Toronto in 1992–93. Everyone wanted a piece of the guy, a TV commercial, a personal appearance, an endorsement. To find a player more popular in Leaf history, you'd have to go back, past Wendel Clark and Rick Vaive, perhaps on a level with Darryl Sittler, or maybe even farther back, rivalled only by Syl Apps and the heroes of the 1930s. Did any of those guys have to change his phone number eight times in a season? Doug Gilmour did in 1992–93.

Part of Gilmour's appeal lay in his size, just a little guy getting smaller as the season progressed. He started in October a pound or so over 170, but under the intensity of his play, his skin turned pallid by February, his cheeks and eyes sinking into dark holes by March, his weight dropping off to something closer to 155. This impersonation of the incredible shrinking man didn't affect Gilmour's game. It remained reckless, skilled and inspirational. He was the Leafs' best offensive player and the entire league's best defensive forward.

The man seemed to do everything the hard way, and when he didn't, bad breaks turned up to make things rough. His size worked against him coming out of junior hockey, and 133 players were picked in the 1982 draft before St. Louis gave Gilmour a look. But he established himself as a ferocious checker, then as a scorer, with forty-two goals in 1986–87. Just as he was hinting at star status in St. Louis, fate took a crack at him; a thirteen-year-old babysitter for Gilmour's daughter accused him of having repeated sex with her. A grand jury refused to indict Gilmour, but the babysitter's parents brought a civil suit against him. Gilmour countersued for libel and slander. And in the midst of the nastiness, with the lawsuits unresolved (both were ultimately dropped), the Blues decided they didn't care for the lousy publicity and hustled Gilmour out of town by trading him to Calgary for about one-tenth his value.

In Calgary, it was more good news–bad news. On the bright side, he confirmed his standing as one of the NHL's most rounded forwards, and he helped Calgary to its 1988–89 Stanley Cup. On the gloomy side, the Flames management, in arbitration hearings over Gilmour's salary, said that maybe Gilmour wasn't all that rounded, that maybe his skills were eroding. Gilmour was furious, demanded to be traded, and on January 2, 1992, he got his wish, a trade to Toronto, where things were—what else?—up and down. The down part occurred off the ice when his marriage broke up in the summer of 1992. The up part was on the ice where Gilmour, responding particularly to Pat Burns' coaching, made the case that he was possibly, as Don Cherry described him on *Hockey Night in Canada*, just before Cherry kissed Gilmour on camera, "the best hockey player in the world."

PAT BURNS COULD DELIVER THE LINE—"YOU WANT TO know who I am, Scumbag? I'm your worst nightmare!"— and make it stick. He's got the size, got the glare. The voice might need work, a little more baritone. But overall Burns can be a scarey guy. "Freeze, Asshole!" He could do that one too. In fact, he probably barked both lines a couple of thousand times in the fifteen years he was a cop in Gatineau, Quebec. Burns solved homicides, went undercover as a biker, got the goods on mob guys. That's scarey.

Burns grew up working class, the youngest of six children, in the St. Henri district near the Montreal Forum. Both parents worked for Imperial Tobacco. His dad died when he was a kid, and he moved with his mother and new stepfather to Ottawa. He played sports, but injuries to his arm and shoulder kept him out of the draft of junior hockey players. He turned to coaching and to police work. He rose towards the top simultaneously in both, a detective-sergeant with the Gatineau police, coach of the Hull Junior As. He came to a crossroads. The police wanted him to stick to policing. Wayne Gretzky, who owned the Hull Juniors, told him he had a future in coaching. Burns' wife just wanted to know when he was coming home. Burns opted for coaching and took a two-year leave of absence from the Gatineau police. His wife said goodbye, and moved out with the two Burns children. She didn't think Pat would ever come home.

It was Gretzky who turned out to have the right fix on Burns. In 1988, the Canadiens named him head coach: from a $30,000 cop to a $300,000 coach in the toughest hockey market in the world. The Montreal sports press rode Burns hard. They said his French was too rough and colloquial, that his manner was abrasive, that he discriminated against French-Canadian players. "The press in Montreal does it *National Enquirer* style," Burns later said. The hell with it, Burns would show them — and he did, 174 wins in four seasons, one trip to the Stanley Cup finals, one selection as Coach of the Year. But the racket from the press persuaded Burns that coaching might bring more peace elsewhere, and in May 1992, when Cliff Fletcher dangled the Toronto job, he seized it.

Burns established an early and indelible personality in Toronto. He was the guy who played country–western guitar and sat in with the Good Brothers. He was the sharp dresser, sometimes going for all-black ensembles just like one of his coaching idols, Jerry Granville of the National Football League. Burns was the guy who loved speed in his vehicles, in his Corvette, his Harley Davidson, in the power boat he kept on Lake Couchiching. He lived in a condominium on the Toronto waterfront, he had a girlfriend named Tina who was director of marketing for Monsieur Felix and Mr. Norton cookies, and he said things like "Being trained as a detective-sergeant, I'm trained in dealing with people who lie, cheat and steal."

Burns has always said that, contrary to reputation, he doesn't coach defensive hockey. "I coach hard work," he says. The players agree with that. "As a team," Mike Foligno, the rambunctious winger who came to Toronto from Buffalo, once said, "our whole reason for being here, our very existence, is to try to put a smile on the face of Pat Burns." Players who didn't work didn't play in games. It was very simple.

But the work had to have purpose to it, and Burns enunciated a series of tactics he insisted on, lessons, schemes, thoughts for the day. Each player must do his own job, not the other guy's. Don't play long shifts, fifty-five seconds maximum. Don't lose the puck at either blueline. Never leave the front of our own net open. Forecheck with one man and count on stopping the other team in the neutral zone. No Mario Lemieux stuff, the centre floating at mid-ice for a pass out of the defensive end. And so on.

It took the Leaf players a couple of months to catch on to everything that Burns was talking about. From late November to late December of the 1992–93 season, the team went on a horrible streak, just three wins in fifteen games. After a loss to Buffalo on December 20, 5–4 at Memorial Auditorium, Burns blew his stack in front of the press in the dressing room. Then he did two things. He stopped blowing his stack, and he decided to rely on his veteran players, despatching most of the kids and rookies to the minors.

The Burns message sunk in, and the veteran Leafs elevated their game through January, February, March, slumping off just slightly in early April when Gilmour got the flu, Andreychuk stopped scoring goals, and Potvin started letting them in. The glitches were temporary, and Toronto finished an astounding eighth overall in the league, with ninety-nine points, an all-time Leaf record.

Two of the seven teams that finished ahead of the Leafs were from their own division, Chicago and Detroit, and that meant the playoffs within the Norris promised difficult hockey. The Leafs drew the Red Wings in the first round.

ROSIE DiMANNO IS A *TORONTO STAR* COLUMNIST. HER beat is injustice. She complains. She kvetches. She whines about the indignities visited on her and other victims. This could be tiresome, but in Rosie DiManno's sharp, funny prose, it's entertainment.

On the Thursday after the Leafs' second loss in Joe Louis Arena, putting them down to the Red Wings, two games to none, DiManno wrote a front-page column that fingered Wendel Clark. Her point was that the Leafs had backed down to the Wings, let themselves get pushed around, that the team looked chicken out there on the ice, and that the biggest chicken of all was Captain Clark.

"He turned his back. He turned his cheek," the column began. "And when it was over, he shrugged."

This was rough stuff for the front page. Vicious even. The column appeared in the first edition of Thursday's *Star*. By the second edition, it had been pulled. There was no Rosie DiManno column. Nor was there any explanation for its disappearance. Surely not the vicious content? No editor ever pulled a column on account of viciousness.

Another question: did Wendel Clark read the column? If he did, perhaps it was the goad he needed. The Leafs won the third game, and Clark scored the winning goal. It wasn't a thing of beauty, just a lot of persistent jabbing at the puck during a scrum in front of the Detroit net, but if a guy was looking for vindication, Clark found it. Except, as he pointed out after the game, vindication didn't enter into his thought processes.

"If people judge your play, that's part of living in Toronto," Clark said. "You start taking that stuff personally, you go in the mental home."

Much of the series seemed to turn on this sort of thing—on self-worth, on pride, on a sense of one's own person.

Dave Andreychuk's pride, for instance. In his ten seasons with Buffalo, he scored big during the regular season, 348 goals, but vanished during the playoffs, 12 goals in forty-one games. He was doing the same unfortunate act for Toronto in the Detroit series. He went scoreless in the first two games, and the fans were spelling it "Andrey-choke." But in game three, he scored two goals, and in game four, an absolute thriller, he got another two, as Toronto won 3–2. No more "Andrey-choke."

Or Steve Yzerman's pride. Yzerman had a stunningly fine year for Detroit, fifty-eight goals and seventy-nine assists. If Doug Gilmour wasn't the most comprehensive forward in the NHL, Yzerman was. But he was having playoff troubles. When he didn't score, Detroit lost. That's what happened in game five which Toronto took in overtime, 5–4, on Mike Foligno's goal. Before the sixth game, Detroit's team psychologist, Kent Osborne, gave Yzerman a short piece of advice. "Lighten up," Osborne said. In the sixth game, a relaxed Yzerman scored a short-handed goal, checked Doug Gilmour almost to a stand-still, and led the Wings to a 7–3 win.

Or Gilmour's pride. Gilmour had hardly disappeared in the series. He'd scored two goals, assisted on six others, and his face recorded the obsessed gallantry of his play. It looked like the face of a man who'd come under the razor of a barber with the shakes. Cuts, knicks, patches of purple and mauve, and a long line of criss-cross stitching over the right eye. None of this restrained Gilmour in game seven. The Leafs were compelled to fight constantly from behind, and Gilmour was the principal battler. He set up Glenn Anderson for a nifty goal in the first period. In the second, he provided the groundwork for a goal by Bob Rouse from the right face-off circle. And in the third, at 17:17, with the Leafs trailing 3–2, it was Gilmour who took a feed from Wendel Clark and drove on the Detroit net for the tying goal.

Then came overtime. Then came more Gilmour. At 2:55, he snag-gled the puck in the Detroit end, slid a pass to the point where Rouse let fly a rocket that Nikolai Borschevsky's extended stick deflected into the Detroit net.

A triumph for Doug Gilmour's pride.

THE REASON THE LEAFS MET ST. LOUIS RATHER THAN Chicago in the second round of the playoffs was named Curtis Joseph. The Blackhawks finished in third place overall on the season, behind only Pittsburgh and Boston, and twenty-one points ahead of the Blues, who were the sixteenth and last team to qualify for the playoffs. But in their series, Chicago versus St. Louis, the Blues goalie, Curtis Joseph, stoned the Black Hawks, who went down in four straight.

Joseph had in mind doing similarly embarrassing things to the Leafs. In the first game, at the Gardens, he stopped an amazing sixty-two shots, and the Blues lost only when Gilmour scored just past the three-minute mark of the second overtime period. Game two was more of the same from Joseph, fifty-seven saves, and this time, it was the Blues who won it on a goal just after three minutes of the second overtime. In St. Louis for the third game, Joseph allowed three goals, but he was hot enough to stop another thirty-four shots, and St. Louis won again, 4–3.

For game four, Pat Burns instructed his big guys to do a clogging job in front of the St. Louis net. Block Joseph's view, whack his gloves, put him off his infernal composure. Mike Foligno spent much of the night swooping past Joseph's crease. So did Mike Krushelnyski. Since Krushelnyski is as large as some Saskatchewan towns, Joseph grew very annoyed. And it showed. "I lost my focus," he said afterwards. He also lost the game 4–1, the winning goal produced by Dave Andreychuk.

Back in Toronto for the fifth game, the Gardens felt like a suburb of Dubai— at 28° C, the day was the hottest May 11 for Toronto since 1911— and it was a night when the Leafs must have figured they had irretrievably shattered the Joseph mystique. They scored five goals, winner by Bob Rouse, and the fans in the Gardens put a fresh pronunciation on Joseph's name. "Joe-Sieve," they chanted. But—oops—Joseph got it all back in game six in St. Louis, stopping forty shots and beating the Leafs 2–1.

In the seventh game, for all the marbles, Andreychuk scored for the Leafs in the first period. Then the Blues scored on themselves, St. Louis defenceman Bret Hedican banking in a clearing shot off fellow defenceman Curt Giles. And then the Leafs turned utterly dominant. Felix Potvin allowed not a single shot to get past him. Wendel Clark scored two goals. Gilmour had one goal and assisted on two others. Every Toronto player checked hard and often. And the Leafs, 6–0 winners, were on the way to the Stanley Cup semi-finals against the Los Angeles Kings.

MARTY MCSORLEY WAS FEELING EXASPERATED, BELEAGUERED. Two and a half minutes to go in the third period of the first game at the Gardens, and here was his team, the Kings, behind 4–1 and on their way to being outshot in the period twenty-two to one. Just one crummy shot on the Leaf net in twenty minutes. So, McSorley, a defenceman, six-feet-two, 235 pounds, decided to take out his aggravation— and maybe light a fire in his team—on Doug Gilmour. He roared in behind the far-smaller Gilmour, laid a crushing elbow on his head, and as an afterthought, worked in a flick with his left leg that sent Gilmour cartwheeling across the ice.

Behind the Leaf bench, watching the attack on his star player, Pat Burns went wild. He charged down the aisle halfway to the L.A. bench, shouting his views of Barry Melrose's morals. Melrose was the Kings coach, a cool young customer — he chewed sunflower seeds and read *The Leadership Secrets of Attila the Hun* for coaching tips — and he seemed bemused at Burns' outrage. Melrose smirked.

"Go get a fucking haircut!" Burns bellowed at Melrose.

Burns had a point there. Melrose wore his hair patterned on the shag-with-an-attitude style of Billy Ray Cyrus. On the other hand, who was Burns to talk? His 'do was strictly Vegas, swept back from his forehead in swoops and valleys, don't spare the spray. Then there was Wayne Gretzky. He arrived at the game sporting two weeks of wispy moustache and goatee, a less hirsute D'Artagnan. Everybody was having a bad-hair night.

Except Doug Gilmour. He wore a conventionally medium trim on top, and all that showed on his face were two new welts, McSorley's contribution to the existing collection of bruises, lesions, scars and stitches. Gilmour also wore an expression of satisfaction. He'd scored the game's first goal and set up Glenn Anderson's winning goal on the night.

The second game represented pay-back time for the Kings' right-winger Tomas Sandstrom. Earlier in the season, during a game in Los Angeles in November, Gilmour had put a stick chop to Sandstrom. It broke Sandstrom's hand and took him out of the lineup for a month. Now, in this night's game, all tied at 2–2 with eight minutes to go, Sandstrom zipped a high shot on Felix Potvin's glove side that went in for the winner. Scoring well is the best revenge.

In Los Angeles, the Leafs made such egregious errors in game three — they allowed two short-handed goals on the way to losing 4–2 — that Burns gathered them together the next day in a room at the team's hotel in Santa Monica for a focus session.

"Do you people realize how close we are?" Burns asked. "How close to the whole thing? To the Stanley Cup? Just seven wins. That's all. So do you want to get it right now? It's up to you people. You have to decide how much you want it right now!"

The pep talk worked on Mike Foligno, Bob Rouse, Mike Eastwood and Rob Pearson. Those four weren't regarded as potential goal scorers in a key playoff game: Foligno, essentially a mucker; Rouse, a defenceman; Eastwood, a rookie who'd spent most of the season in the minors; and Pearson, a sophomore who was considered to be not quite playing to his full potential. But the four got the goals, and the Leafs won 4–2.

In game five, back at the Gardens, a Leaf who was supposed to score the goals, Glenn Anderson, got the big one. It came at 19:20 of the first overtime period, and it came when Anderson swung *à la* Joe Carter at a puck that was tumbling in a high arc in the area dead centre of the Kings' net. Anderson's stick caught the puck flush and zoomed it past L.A. goalie Kelly Hrudey. That gave the Leafs a 3–2 win and sent the series to Los Angeles, where Wayne Gretzky took charge in more ways than one.

It had started as the worst of all seasons for Gretzky. A herniated thoracic disk in his upper spine kept him away from hockey until January. When he returned, he started slowly, so slowly that he went sixteen games without scoring a goal, so slowly that the Kings, who had a record of 20–14–5 without him, won only five games of the next eighteen with him, so slowly that the fickle fans at the Great Western Forum chanted, "Refund! Refund!"

Early in February, on the road in Quebec City, Barry Melrose took Gretzky to dinner. Gretzky was feeling understandably down in the dumps. The two men ate Italian and drank some red wine.

"We want you to lead us," Melrose said. "We still think you're the best player in the game."

It took a while, but somewhere around early March, the old familiar, inventive, resourceful Gretzky began showing up at the rink. He closed out the season with sixty-five points in forty-five games. That wasn't up to the usual Gretzkyesque standards—he had averaged 2.26 points per game in his thirteen-year NHL career—but for a guy who began the season moving like Walter Matthau, it was almost miraculous. And in L.A.'s two playoff series against Calgary and Vancouver, Gretzky led the offence, eight goals and fifteen assists in twelve playoff games.

Against the Leafs, however, Gretzky seemed to be off by a notch. Maybe it was the ingrown toenail, an annoyance that meant he had to play a couple of games with a frozen foot. Maybe Doug Gilmour was giving him too much to handle. Maybe his mind was wandering to the restaurant he planned to open down the block from the SkyDome in Toronto. Whatever held him back, his sub-par play, measured against the Gretzky of the previous two months, remained the major puzzle of the Kings–Leafs games.

Until, that is, he scored the major goal in the series.

Game six had gone into overtime, tied at four, with Wendel Clark potting three of the Leaf goals. A minute or so after the overtime started, Gretzky's stick nicked Doug Gilmour in the face. It seemed an accident, but the nick cost Gilmour eight stitches. It cost Gretzky nothing, no time in the penalty box for drawing blood, because referee Kerry Fraser said he didn't see the contact. Now, a few seconds later, L.A. winger Luc Robitaille had the puck at the boards in the Leaf end. He intended to shoot, but changed his mind when he spotted Gretzky breaking for the net on the other side. Robitaille passed the puck across the goal mouth. Gretzky reached out, a piece of impeccable timing, and tipped the puck into the net.

"It may be the biggest goal I've ever scored," Gretzky said later.

He got that right. The goal sent the Kings back to Toronto, where they won the seventh game. They went on to lose to the Montreal Canadiens in the Stanley Cup final, but it had been a great year for the Kings, the best in the franchise's history.

In a sense, it had been a better year for the Leafs, back from twenty years in the wilderness, a team with brilliant players, a contender again.

24

Chasing the Summit

IT'S PROBABLY WRITTEN DOWN SOMEWHERE, A LAW, that hockey players' wives and girlfriends are required to look this way: about five-feet-eight and willowy; plenty of hair (colour optional), in sufficient supply that, with a flick of the head, it streams out behind in slo mo; eye makeup applied by the same person who does Princess Di's; legs that go on for days; high cheekbones; and a wardrobe of skinny black cocktail dresses held up by spaghetti straps.

This is the way it was — a proven fact that hockey players allow only gorgeous young women in their orbit — at the Toronto Maple Leafs Directors' Dinner Dance in the Imperial Room of the Royal York Hotel on the Sunday night before the 1993–94 regular season opened. The event, a first ever in Leaf history, showed one side of Steve Stavro's management style: treat the employees nice. On this night, treat the employees exceptionally nice. Make it a black-tie occasion. Uncork the champagne for the six o'clock reception. Bathe the Imperial Room in candlelight. Book a twelve-piece dance band. Serve a six-course dinner, Beef Wellington as the entrée and for dessert "Canadian Maple Mousse with Blue and White Sauce and Chocolate Hockey Stick." Invite practically the entire living Leaf family, back to the most senior surviving player (Red Horner). Include those who might be feeling alienated, a Smythe (Dorothea, Stafford's widow) and a Ballard (Mary Elizabeth, Harold's daughter). Hire a jokey master of ceremonies, Harry Neale of *Hockey Night In Canada*, and hand out prizes — a ring to each player from the 1992–93 team for winning the Norris Division, and the J.P. Bickell Memorial Trophy for the most worthy Leaf of the season (more about the Bickell and worthy Leafs later). And make each invitation for two: get the spouses and girlfriends into the room, especially the women attached to the current players. Perfume, sex, silk dresses that whisper, girls whose names are Cindi and Lauryn and Elle.

Gary Bettman sat beside one of the Cindis. Bettman was the newish commissioner of the NHL, appointed a year earlier, American and a lawyer, a guy who had come over from the savviest league in pro sports, the National Basketball Association. In the Imperial Room, he found himself stationed at the principal table, with Stavro and his wife, Cliff Fletcher and his wife, Wendel Clark and his date. The date could have passed for Lolita, almost prepubescently fresh but beaming something fatally mature in the expression. Wendel looked kind of original himself. He was wearing a black cowboy hat. He doffed it for dinner. He doffed his tuxedo jacket too, hung it on the back of the chair. Bettman seemed to think all of this was on the novel side, what was going on around him, seated in company that included a multi-millionaire owner, a cowboy captain, and a girl from a Vladimir Nabokov novel. Boy, was this the Maple Leafs of the 'nineties!

The speeches and presentations came between courses. "Remember this," Cliff Fletcher said, "you can't manufacture pride or tradition. They're the product of history." All the speeches were of that order, part company line, part pep talk. The J.P. Bickell Trophy was presented by Dr. Hugh Smythe, Conn's remaining son, and by George Gardiner, an octogenarian who was the oldest living former Leaf director. The reason these two elderly parties were chosen to hand out the Bickell may have been that they were among the few in the room who remembered the trophy's existence.

The Bickell, named for Conn Smythe's early associate, dated back to

1953, an in-house Toronto honour, awarded to the Leaf deemed by the directors to be "the most valuable player" in each season. Ted Kennedy won it, George Armstrong, Dave Keon, Johnny Bower (three times), and other such storied Leaf stars. But during his long reign, Harold Ballard placed the Bickell in virtual retirement. He handed it out just twice, in 1972 to his best buddy King Clancy (a choice that appeared to violate the trophy's "most valuable player" guidelines) and in 1979 to goalie Mike Palmateer. For the rest of two decades, as Ballard had done with other Leaf traditions and artefacts, he mothballed the Bickell. (It could have been worse—Ballard could have awarded the trophy to Yolanda.) And it wasn't until Steve Stavro began restoring the old institutions that, in 1993, it occurred to somebody to revive the Bickell.

For the first winner in fourteen years, the Leaf directors made a choice that was automatic. The winner, summoned to the stage in the Imperial Room by Hugh Smythe and George Gardiner, was the guy who recorded 127 points in 1992–93, finished second in the voting for the Hart Trophy, won the Frank Selke Trophy as the league's best defensive forward, racked up ten goals and fifteen assists in the playoffs, the superstar, the resident Toronto hockey idol—Doug Gilmour.

"All I can say," said Gilmour, looking disconcertingly small and bashful at the front of the room, "is I promise another year of effort."

That anticlimactic moment was supposed to end the formal part of the evening, but out of the crowd, on to the stage, up to the mike, unbidden and unscheduled, bounded the Boomer—Bobby Baun himself, a Leaf great, a Bickell winner in 1971, the man who scored a Stanley Cup goal on a broken leg.

"I'm an emotional guy," Baun said, leaning close to the microphone, his voice bouncing around the room, eyes glistening moistly. "And I'm telling you I haven't seen the kind of Leaf spirit like we've got here tonight for years. It's so great all I wish is that I could play for Pat Burns and win the Stanley Cup!"

The room broke into the most sustained cheer of the night, stomping and clapping, and when the noise finally died away, the twelve-piece band struck up a tune and the young players hit the dance floor, their arms around the girls with the flowing hair and the flashing legs.

ON OCTOBER 28, THE LEAFS WENT INTO CHICAGO FOR A Thursday game at the Stadium. Up until that night, Toronto hadn't won in Chicago for a period that covered four years and thirteen games. It didn't look as if the winless streak would end on this evening. The Blackhawks scored the first goal, and by the end of the game they would outshoot the Leafs by an awesome margin, forty-eight to twenty-four.

By all statistical probability, Chicago should have won, but the Leaf players hung in there. Nikolai Borschevsky tied the game in the second period off a nice setup from Todd Gill. Then, still in the second period, Wendel Clark did a number on the Hawks, scoring two goals, the first on a rebound off a Doug Gilmour blast and the second on a slapshot from the right circle after he'd taken a Gill pass. Kent Manderville rounded things off with a breakaway goal in the third period. And in the meantime, in the Toronto end, Felix Potvin allowed just two goals on those forty-eight Blackhawk shots.

The win was a record setter. It broke the Chicago Stadium winless streak. That was gratifying. But, far more sensational, it was Toronto's tenth consecutive win since the beginning of the season. The victories would end the following Saturday night when Montreal beat the Leafs at the Gardens. Still, the ten-straight wins put the team in the record books, the best start to a season any team had ever pulled off in NHL history.

GLENN ANDERSON SAID SHORTLY AFTER THE BIG GAME in Chicago, "It's all heart and desire that's getting us through because the talent we have is nowhere near what some other clubs have."

As a matter of documentable reality, the Leafs could count on only four players whose skill levels matched up with the very best around the league. The four were Gilmour, Potvin, Clark and Dave Andreychuk. Gilmour, more bravely intense than ever, played demon defence and consolidated his status as the NHL's second-best assists man after Wayne Gretzky. (As usual, Gilmour wasn't spared a dash of off-ice melodrama. This season, it was a crazed woman stalker, like the one who invaded David Letterman's house a few years ago or the one who shot the Philadelphia Phillies' first baseman Eddie Waitkus in a hotel room in the 1960s. Gilmour's "fan" settled for a few telephoned death threats in February and a couple of phantom appearances at the Gardens. Police put a protective cover around Gilmour and his friend, Amy Cable, but never got a lead on the elusive crackpot. "It really scared the crap out of me," Gilmour said. But he didn't miss a hockey game.) Potvin had two flat stretches, one in December and another towards the end of the season, but the rest of the time, depending largely on his lightning-quick catching glove, his play put him among the league's top half-dozen goalies. Andreychuk, with his size and reach, his great sense of purpose, his ability to stand in the slot, take all sorts of abuse and wait for Gilmour to get him the puck, kept on scoring goals, fifty-three of them for the season, fourth-most in the league. Clark was the grand surprise. He arrived in training camp in the best shape of his career, started fast, nineteen goals in the first twenty-one games, and, apart from lulls when his battered body may have gone balky, he never let up—forty-six goals on the year, a personal high for him.

Alas, in pure talent, especially in offensive terms, there was a sharp dropoff from the four main guys to the rest of the Leafs. If Andreychuk, Clark or Gilmour didn't score goals, who would? Nobody, as it turned out. Not one of the players who might be expected to produce—Anderson, John Cullen, Rob Pearson, Nikolai Borschevsky, Mike Krushelnyski—came through. As we'll see, injuries, particularly in Borschevsky's case, played a scarey part. Still, none of Anderson (who had twenty goals in 1992–93), Cullen (eighteen), Pearson (twenty-three), Borschevsky (thirty-four) or Krushelnyski (nineteen) hit the double digits in goals scored for 1993–94 until more than halfway into the season, and none scored twenty on the entire year, except Anderson who got his last goals after he was traded to the Rangers.

It was a dodgey way to stay in contention in the NHL, all the goal scorers among a tiny elite of players, and it wasn't the only deficiency the team had to deal with.

IT SEEMED LIKE A RUN-OF-THE-GAME CHECK, SOMETHING that Nikolai Borschevsky had absorbed a hundred times a season. A Florida Panther winger named Bill Lindsay gave him a quick smack. That was all. But, for a reason that Borschevsky couldn't fathom, this smack, in the first period of a game at the Gardens on November 3, lingered. A pain inside wouldn't go away, and Borschevsky felt waves of dizziness. He insisted on playing, finished the period, sat through the intermission, took two more shifts in the second period. That's when the Leaf head athletic therapist, Chris Broadhurst, stepped in. He didn't like the sound of Borschevsky's talk of dizziness. He guided Nikki to the dressing room and summoned two Leaf doctors, Michael Clarfield and Darrell Olgilvie-Harris. They checked out Borschevsky. Dizzy spells. Pain in the abdomen. Blood pressure down. Heart rate way up.

"We've got internal bleeding here," Clarfield said.

"Absolutely," Olgilvie-Harris agreed. "Maybe something in the spleen."

The two doctors paged a third medical man at the Gardens, Ray Mathews, the Leafs surgical consultant. They didn't know whether Mathews had come to the game. He had. He was sitting in the blues.

"Let's get to the hospital," Mathews said after he'd had his own look at Borshevsky. "Fast."

Borschevsky was admitted to the Western General at eleven that night. The staff ran tests. Two to four litres of blood had spilled into Borschevsky's abdomen, and his spleen, in the words of one doctor, "looked like it had come through a car accident." At one in the morning, Borschevsky was wheeled into the operating room. Surgeons removed his ruined spleen. He didn't play hockey again until December 22.

That was the worst Toronto injury of the season, the only one that threatened a player's future. "It was a life-and-death situation," Dr. Michael Clarfield says. "And that's no exaggeration." But Borshevsky was far from the only Leaf who lost time to the disabled list. Wendel Clark, in his most high-flying season, was gone for twenty games. A swollen ankle was to blame. Peter Zezel missed a serious chunk of the season (disk in the back out of commission). Rob Pearson did too (strained knee ligaments). And so did John Cullen and Mike Krushelnyski. Nor was Borschevsky spared after he returned from the spleen surgery. In a game against Ottawa in late February, a defenceman named Darren Rumble ran him into the boards. Separated shoulder. Out for another month. And in the same Ottawa game, Ken Baumgartner got into a fight. He bounced a punch off an Ottawa helmet. Uh-oh, dislocated thumb. Two months on the DL.

And the above list of casualties covers only the forwards. With the defence guys, the situation was worse. Toronto's six starting defencemen probably constituted the best-rounded blueline group in the league. Todd Gill and Dave Ellett had wonderful skills as puck handlers. Dmitri Mironov, who had seemed so dozey through the previous season, emerged as another zingy offensive operator. Jamie Macoun and Sylvain Lefebvre were more strictly defensive specialists, tough, reliable, good at playing within their capabilities and not committing errors, while Bob Rouse offered a little of everything: strength, promptness at moving the puck, hard checking. When these six defencemen played for the Leafs, all six together, the team had a phenomenal record—fourteen wins, three losses, four ties. The trouble was they played as a unit in only those twenty-one games. The rest of the time, one or two, or even three, of them sat out games with frustrating injuries.

Todd Gill's aching groin cost him twenty-six games, and just as he was returning nicely to a groove, back spasms took him out of action again from February 24 to March 26. Dave Ellett missed ten games in December with a sore leg. Rouse tore the cartilege in his right knee during a January 29 game against Pittsburgh and didn't return until March 7. Then it was Ellett's turn for more grief: a separated shoulder in a March 31 San Jose game that wiped him out until the playoffs. So it went. A bruised head for Mironov, followed by a couple of deep charlie horses, then a thirty-stitch cut from Brendan Shanahan's stick in a game against St. Louis on March 7. The injuries kept on coming, and by the end of the season, the valiant Sylvain Lefebvre was the sole defenceman of the basic Toronto six who made it intact through the season's eighty-four games.

The fact was, with all these bodies on the DL, the Leafs didn't have guys in reserve to fill the gaps. Pat Burns was called on to perform feats of improvisation that even he knew weren't long-term solutions. Borschevsky was out? Okay, on Gilmour's line, switch Andreychuk from left wing to right, and move Clark up from the second line to play the left side. Hey, great line, a goal-scoring line. But the second line? Ugh, now it was really feeble. Damn. And the power play suffered gruesomely when the offensive-minded defencemen went down with injuries. In a game against the Islanders on December 17, with the two principal point operators on the power play, Todd Gill and Dave Ellett, not available, Burns inserted Clark at the point. Not a good idea, as it developed. On one shift, with the Leafs at a man advantage and Clark in an unaccustomed role, Pierre Turgeon stripped Wendel of the puck at the Islander blueline and sent Marty McInnis away for an easy goal. New York took the win. And that sort of thing—terrible little setbacks brought on by injuries, lack of manpower, not enough strength among the reserves—kept happening all year.

On the other hand, enough marvellous things happened to give the Leafs a regular season that was just a tad off the lofty standard of the previous year.

Marvellous things?

The zoom out of the gate, ten-straight wins to start the season. Another stretch of excellence in January, unbeaten in eleven consecutive games. The maturing of two or three younger guys—notably Kent Manderville—into dependable niche players. Nights when all the elements of the Leaf style—shoot the puck into the offensive zone, bump the other team hard, drive on the net—coalesced into winning hockey. Cliff Fletcher's midnight-hour deal, right on the March 21 trading deadline, bringing Mike Gartner from the Rangers in exchange for Glenn Anderson. Gartner was a gem of a right-winger, long in the tooth at thirty-four maybe, but still one of the league's fastest skaters, still a prodigious scorer with the fifth-highest goal total in NHL history, still keeping the pace of his lifetime with thirty-four goals in 1993–94.

The result of all of this, the good and the bad, the wonderful and the disappointing, was a team point total on the season, ninety-eight, that was just one off the year before, one win fewer at forty-three, eight fewer goals scored, two more allowed, and a standing among the other teams that placed the Leafs fifth-best in the league, as against eighth in 1992–93. In short, the team was up with the elite and back in the playoffs.

IT WAS A NUTSY SERIES, LEAFS VERSUS THE CHICAGO BLACK-hawks in the first playoff round. The numbers tell the story. Chicago scored only ten goals in the six games the series lasted. Nine of the ten came in the two games Chicago won. Two Hawks scored seven of the ten, right-winger Tony Amonte getting four in Game three and defenceman Gary Suter drilling three in Game four. In three other games, the Hawks were shut out, all by 1–0 scores. If those statistics leave the impression Chicago was a fairly hapless offensive team, the impression is accurate.

But give Toronto credit. The big six Leaf defencemen, reunited at last, refused to allow Chicago room to operate in the four Leaf victories (though the six shared screwups in the two Chicago wins). Felix Potvin, rising out of his late-season slump, was brilliant on crunch occasions. Peter Zezel, who showed himself to be an ace at winning face-offs, led the forwards on a crusade of tough defensive hockey. Leafs were oppor-tunists when they had to be—as, for example, on a sweet pass from Dave Andreychuk to Mike Eastwood for the only goal in Game five—and lucky when luck was called for. The best illustration of the latter came when Game two, scoreless, went into overtime. Todd Gill had the puck at the point. He let fly a hard shot. Was he putting it on the Chicago net? Or was he aiming it for Wendel Clark, who was hovering to the right of Hawk goalie Ed Belfour? And did Clark, with the puck still in flight, give Belfour a small nudge? Put him off his concentration? Distract him? Neither Gill nor Clark was saying much after the game. Belfour was saying plenty. He said Clark should have been given a penalty for goalie interference. But nobody who counted, not the referee, was listening to Belfour. The puck had gone into the net, goal to Gill, victory to the Leafs, temper tantrum to Belfour.

But the major factor in Toronto's series victory—no surprise here—was Doug Gilmour. He checked. He scored goals (two). He assisted on others (six). And he set the stage for plays leading to yet other goals (two). These numbers meant he had a hand in ten of the fifteen goals Leafs scored in the series. And then there was Gilmour's incalculable inspirational value. Consider that in the sixth game he was playing hockey on a right ankle that ordinary people couldn't walk on. In the previous game, Gilmour found himself tangled with Gary Suter and came out of the mess with a severely strained tendon running up his right leg from the ankle. For Game six, a doctor stuck needles into

Gilmour's leg to freeze the strained area, and a trainer wrapped the ankle in an envelope of tape. Gilmour played. Just past the fourteen-minute mark of the first period, he faced-off against the best of all Hawks, Jeremy Roenick. Gilmour won the draw, slipped the puck back to Dmitri Mironov, who passed along the blueline to Dave Ellett, who fired a shot that bounced off Mike Gartner's right thigh and into the Chicago net. It was the only goal either team scored all night. It was enough. It was the work of Dougie Gilmour on one leg.

THE EXPRESSION THAT CROSSED THE FACE OF SAN JOSE defenceman Jay More was something like the look Joe Pesci wore in *Home Alone* after Macaulay Culkin thumped him for the first time. Is this allowed? That's what More's expression said. He was puzzled. It was fifteen seconds into the second game of the second-round playoff series between the Leafs and the Sharks, and Mike Gartner had put a crusher of a bodycheck on More behind the San Jose net. The Leafs were hitting us tonight? More and the other Sharks began to wonder. Things were going to get physical?

There were two reasons for the Sharks to ponder such questions. One was Toronto's behaviour in the first game of the series, when the Leafs played like pussycats and the Sharks won, no problem, 3–2. The other reason was the Sharks' own style, which normally discouraged bodychecking. When San Jose went on offence, bringing the puck out of their own end, they frequently adopted the old Russian swirling game, weaving in crossing patterns and swinging back into their own zone until they spotted an opening down ice. It was awkward for defenders to put the body on opponents who stuck to such elusive tactics. San Jose was a confounding team to play against.

But in Game two, Gartner's rattling check against More announced that, dammit, the Leafs would return to their own style. Hunt down the Sharks, knock them off the puck, pounce on San Jose blunders. Toronto managed all of that, and winning was a comparative breeze, 5–2.

But, wait a minute, San Jose? An expansion team? A mere three years in the business? What were the Sharks doing in the second round of the playoffs?

Well, true, they made the playoffs only by a hair, the last team in, the only team with a losing record, the one that had scored the least number of goals. But they had a couple of ageing Soviet legends, Igor Larionov and Sergei Makarov, to whom the Russian swirling style was as natural as sipping Stolichnya. And the rest of the Sharks, essentially no-names and kids, excelled on defence at the holdup game, just generally tugging, pulling and bumping opponents in the neutral zone. This was deliberate, patient and boring hockey. But it got San Jose into the playoffs and it astounded—or maybe mesmerized—Detroit in the first round, the flashy multitalented Red Wings who had finished the regular season with the fourth-best record in the entire league.

And the same San Jose methods, counterpunching hockey, again beat the Leafs in the third game of their round. That loss apparently prompted Wendel Clark to do for Toronto in Game four what Gartner had done in Game two. Clark crunched somebody. The victim was Shark defenceman Jeff Norton. The time was just past the ten-minute mark of the first period. Norton was loitering near the San Jose bench, and Clark hit him so precisely, so vividly, that Norton's head and neck snapped over backwards in a position that only pretzels adopt. When Norton's body rebounded upright again, Clark delivered another marginally less staggering hit. Nothing illegal about the check, nothing that called for a penalty. Just a Wendel Clark special, the kind of blow that exhilarated his teammates (and sent Norton to the dressing room for revivifying). By the end of the first period, the Leafs, a fire lit under them, were up 3–0. By the end of the game, it was 8–3. The hockey universe appeared to have assumed its proper order.

Oh yeah?

In Game five, the Leaf fire went out yet again. The players seemed unable to take the Sharks seriously for two games in a row. It was as if they expected the Sharks to roll over and accept their designated spot as the patsies of the playoffs. The Sharks declined, and with the Leafs in a non-threatening frame of mind, San Jose's two Russians skated as free and loose as Oksana Baiul. Makarov scored once on a breakaway, got another off a rebound of a big Larionov shot, while Larionov's gorgeous passing helped set up a couple of other goals. On the Leaf side, Doug

Gilmour, still taking the needle for his strained tendon, never quit—he made the plays for the two Toronto goals—but the other guys faded to black. Final score: San Jose 5, Toronto 2, and the Leafs, unbelievably, were a single loss away from elimination.

MIKE GARTNER, DURING HIS CAREER, COULDN'T SEEM to buy the big break. Fourteen years in the NHL, and he'd never come close to the Stanley Cup, never played for a team that got out of the second round of the playoffs. Scored six hundred goals, and the sportswriters hadn't once elected him to a First or Second All-Star Team. And—what a life—three times in the past five seasons, including this one, he'd found himself traded on deadline day, at the very last available moment, for a deal.

"Pack the car, honey," he had to tell his wife each March. "Get the kids out of school. Say goodbye to the neighbours. It's happened again."

Gartner wasn't a fellow who merited such lousy luck. A wonderful player, as those six hundred goals attest, but a decent man too—intelligent, articulate, so respected around the league that his fellow players voted him president of the NHL Players' Association.

So who, apart from the San Jose Sharks, could begrudge Mike Gartner's moment of fortune when he scored the goal at 8:53 of the first overtime period that made the Leafs 3–2 winners of Game six? It was hardly a piece of elegance, this goal, not a product of Gartner's enormous speed or his whipping shot. A pass by Doug Gilmour from behind the San Jose net ticked off the skate of Sharks defenceman Shawn Irwin and beamed on to Gartner's stick. He was standing close to the right goal post and had neither the time nor the room to arrange anything elaborate. He struck the puck with a motion halfway between a nudge and a poke. It ticked off another skate, San Jose goalie Arturs Irbe's, and proceeded, almost reluctantly, into the net. A lucky goal on a night when the Leafs seemed occasionally dispirited and frequently tired. But who more than Mike Gartner had a break heading his way?

GAME SEVEN, AND THE HINT THAT WENDEL CLARK WAS ON course for a hot night came early. For a couple of seasons, it had always been this way: if Wendel found skating room in his first couple of shifts, if he got his legs, if he felt the speed and made one or two hits, he knew he was going to have fun that night. And that was how it went at the Gardens in the seventh game against San Jose.

The Sharks didn't cramp the Leafs early on, didn't clog the neutral zone, and Wendel took advantage of the open spaces. Just before the nine-minute mark of the first period, seconds after Felix Potvin ripped a potential goal away from Igor Larionov, Clark seized the puck and tore down the right side, part Road Runner, part cannonball. Nobody, no force on earth, was going to stop this guy. At the top of San Jose's right face-off circle, Clark wristed a shot that travelled missile-like into the upper-right corner of the net. It was a raw, brutish goal, the rush and the shot seeming utterly inevitable.

This was a night when no opponent could resist Clark. He got another goal in the second period, again moments after Potvin stymied Larionov, the second goal coming from some fierce Clark banging at a loose puck in close. And he masterminded a goal in the third period when some refined Clark puck handling—here was another side of Wendel—sprung Doug Gilmour for an open wrist shot. That made it 4–1—the game ended 4–2 for the Leafs—on a night that Clark sensed early on belonged to him.

TO THE CURRENT GENERATION OF PLAYERS AND FANS WHO think Elvis is a figure skater, what meaning did the names Norris, Smythe, Patrick and Adams offer? Practically none. Jim Norris, Conn Smythe, Lester Patrick and Jack Adams may have built the NHL, but, now long dead, buried and forgotten, they belonged to the age of dinosaurs (the kind of thing, in animal form, that basketball teams get named after). And the new, hip NHL management under Gary Bettman decided at the beginning of the 1993–94 schedule to dispense with the four mouldy names as designations of the four league divisions in favour of more immediately identifiable titles of a simple geographical nature. Thus, there came into being the Eastern Conference, split into the Atlantic and Northeast divisions, and the Western Conference, made up of the Central and Pacific divisions. For playoff purposes, the top eight teams from each conference, regardless of division, would fight it out in best-of-seven confrontations until two finalists, a representative from each conference, met for the Stanley Cup.

Things proceeded in 1993–94 according to the best wished-for plan in the Eastern Conference, where the New York Rangers and New Jersey Devils went against one another in the conference final. The Rangers and Devils, both of the Atlantic Division, had finished the regular season with the two best overall records, not just in their conference, but in the entire league. Over in the Western Conference, which was demonstrably weaker on the year than the Eastern, the situation was more dangerously fluid. The top conference team, and fourth-best in the league, Detroit, succumbed, as noted, to the dull and lowly San Jose Sharks in the first round. The same thing happened to Calgary, Pacific Division champs, tied for third-best in the Western Conference, tied for sixth-best in the NHL, but gone in the first playoff round. There was a plethora of upsets until ultimately the Western Conference showdown matched Toronto (Central Division) and Vancouver (Pacific Division).

The Leafs, having finished the season second-best in the conference and fifth overall in the league, earned their spot, though heaven knows they shouldn't have experienced such angst in the early playoff rounds against the league's number-thirteen team (Chicago) and number sixteen (San Jose). Vancouver was another, more puzzling matter. The Canucks managed to play barely .500 hockey, with just one more win than loss. They seemed mediocre at most tasks, at scoring goals (thirteen teams scored more) and letting them in (fifteen teams allowed fewer), and ended up number fourteen overall among the NHL's twenty-six teams.

So how did Vancouver reach the Western Conference final, the NHL semi-finals, in the heady company of the Rangers, Devils and Leafs?

By a fortunate concatenation of circumstances. Or, as the Canucks' general manager and coach, Pat Quinn, might put it, by a clever GM's trade and a smart coach's rearrangement of lines.

The trade came at the tail end of the season and brought to the Canucks a pair of steady defencemen from St. Louis, Jeff Brown and Bret Hedican. These two guys gave Vancouver's formerly shakey defence instant balance and speed.

The line changes occurred even later, five games into Vancouver's first-round playoff series against Calgary when they trailed the Flames, three games to one. Quinn moved his second-line right-winger, Trevor Linden, to centre on the first line between Pavel Bure and Greg Adams. Anyone could have predicted that this line would do interesting things. Bure was merely the league's best goal scorer, with sixty for the season. Linden was a Doug Gilmour type, gifted in all phases of the game, except that Linden happened to be larger than Gilmour by five inches and fifty pounds. And Greg Adams was no slouch, big and a consistent scorer in the thirty-goal-per-year range. But the line turned out to be much more than interesting. It was as sensational as any threesome in the league, and led the Canucks to seven wins in their next eight playoff games. The streak eliminated the Flames, Bure getting the deciding goal in the second overtime period of Game seven, and brushed aside the Dallas Stars in the second round. It helped the Canucks, during this run of invincibility, that several players seemed to acquire a confidence they hadn't exhibited during the season and that the big guys on the team— Vancouver had plenty of them—started to throw their weight around in more effective ways. Bottom line: Vancouver, in the playoffs, operated at several notches above a .500 team.

But the team wasn't entirely goof-proof.

In the first game of the semi-finals against the Leafs at the Gardens, Vancouver's excellent goalie, Kirk McLean, went on a bit of a walkabout into the right corner behind his net and cleared the puck directly to Peter Zezel. Okay, that kind of thing happens, but not at 16:55 of overtime in a 2–2 Stanley Cup playoff game. Zezel gladly received the puck and popped it into the net that McLean had so generously left unattended. Actually, McLean's goof aside, Zezel and his linemates, Mark Osborne and Bill Berg, deserved credit for a hustling, resourceful play, one that Pat Burns had drilled into them. Osborne had shot the puck into the Vancouver zone from outside the centre line. This would normally constitute icing. But Berg, as per Burns's instructions, went hard after the puck, hoping to touch it before it crossed the icing line or to force McLean to play it. McLean played it. But Berg had hurried him, and Zezel was in hot pursuit to pick up

McLean's rushed clearing pass. Goof? Or heads-up play? Either way, it led to the winning goal for the Leafs.

GAMES TWO, THREE AND FOUR OF THE SERIES SUGGESTED that maybe the scores in these games were matters of perspective. The Leafs might like to think so since Toronto lost all three contests.

But, to illustrate the point about perspective, Doug Gilmour had three assists in Game two at the Gardens. Three assists? Well, one would conclude, a productive night for Dougie, and a certain Leaf win. Not quite. Each assist came on a power-play pass back to a Leaf defenceman, who fed the puck to the other defenceman on the point, who scored on a long drive. Not exactly finesse setups by Gilmour, who had no shots on goal for the night, who seemed to be forever steered harmlessly off to the wings on Leaf rushes. Gilmour wasn't a commanding presence in the game. Perhaps fatigue was at last wearing him down, the bum ankle, the months of lifting the Leafs on his shoulders. Score: Canucks 4, Leafs 3.

Another illustration of the point about perspective: Pavel Bure in Game three. Bure had already performed two or three feats in the second game that ought to be included in the all-time, all-world hockey highlights film. In one, he passed the puck from behind the Leaf goal by flipping it over the top of the net, over Felix Potvin, then raced out to accept his own high-flying pass. In another, he put a deke on Dave Ellett that left Ellett sliding in the direction of the parking lot on Church Street, then did the same to Potvin for a goal. But that was Game two. In Game three, which ended 4–0 for the Canucks in the first of three consecutive games played at Vancouver's Pacific Coliseum, Bure jumped on a couple of Toronto errors and flew on the Leaf net for two goals. Brilliant play by Bure? Not from Wendel Clark's perspective. "If those pucks had bounced left instead of right, Bure would never have had those chances," Clark said a day after the game. "He would have had shots and no goals, and people would have been saying he had a bad game. But he got the bounces. It's fate."

Fate? Perspective? What are you going to do? Suffer, if you're the Leafs. That's what happened in Game four. This was a tight-checking, highly defensive match. Leafs probably had a small advantage in play over the first fifty-seven and a half minutes. But it was hard to tell because most of the hockey was of the sluggish sort. Few dazzling breaks on either goal, not much open-ice action, no Pavel Bure making like Nijinsky (neither the dancer nor the racehorse). It was also a mean-spirited sort of night. In that day's *Vancouver Sun*, a columnist had revived the old *Frank* magazine rumours about Wendel Clark's sexuality, and at the game Vancouver fans got into the act by chanting—were these people ugly of soul or what?—"Wendy, Wendy" at Clark.

For the Leafs, that was only the moral low point. The hockey low point came at 17:35 of the third period, when, the game still scoreless, Vancouver's Cliff Ronning, probably the smallest guy on the ice and supposedly a checking centre in the series, dodged around Dmitri Mironov inside the Leaf blueline, skipped a pass to Sergio Momesso on his right, evaded Rob Pearson, took a return pass from Momesso, and, in the clear, shot the puck past Potvin. That goal, plus an empty-netter a couple of minutes later by Bure, beat the Leafs, 2–0.

This time it was Todd Gill who gave the game the official Leaf perspective: it was Kirk McLean's, the Vancouver goalie's, fault. "I thought we out-shot and out-hit them," Gill said afterwards. "But McLean's hot as a firecracker. If it wasn't for him, it would've been a different story."

Clark got into the perspective business too. "Yeah, I heard some guy called me gay again," he said. "I don't look on it as a negative to have that happen on the road. It means you're doing something to get noticed."

Doing what to get noticed? Wearing a ring in the left ear? Cruising Robson Street? One yearned for Clark to get serious. To say his sexuality was no concern of a bunch of strangers sitting in the Vancouver Coliseum, that the people with the "Wendy" chorus were homophobic and a tribute to no one except maybe the hysterical wing of the Reform Party. On the other hand, Clark had scored zero goals in four playoff games against Vancouver. What was the perspective on that?

WENDEL GOT A GOAL. IT CAME AT 12:19 OF THE FIRST period in Game five, and it was a Wendel sort of goal. He barrelled down the wing on a Leaf three-on-one, set on his mission, looking neither to right nor to left, no frills here, just ferocious determination, until he unloaded a thirty-five-foot slapshot past Kirk McLean into the Canucks' net. Wendel's goal put the Leafs ahead 3–0. That was the joyous news. Wendel's goal was also the last scored by a Leaf player in the series against Vancouver. That was news of a more deflating kind, news that signified an abrupt end to the 1993–94 season for Toronto.

In the second period, ahead by those three goals, suddenly, horribly, the deficiencies that the Leafs had laboured under all season went on shocking display. A microcosm of Toronto failures accentuated by the players' extreme fatigue.

Starting with this deficiency: if the big guys on the team didn't score plenty of goals — Clark, Doug Gilmour, Dave Andreychuk — who would? Same old answer: nobody. The situation got worse when even a big guy failed to produce; Andreychuk scored a mere five goals in the entire three-playoff series, none against the Canucks. And no one else on the roster could assume his job.

Injuries. Would they never allow the Leafs to stay whole? Gilmour's ankle was the killer. The best player on the team, its inspiration, and ever since the fifth game of the Chicago series, he'd been functioning at about 70 percent — or less? — of his normal level. Brave, he looked brave out there, the heart, the soul, but the games were measured in goals scored, and a gimpy Gilmour couldn't plot those. Nor was Gilmour the single casualty. Clark and maybe a couple of others played through horrendous pain, and late in the first period of Game five, a Sergio Momesso check sprained Todd Gill's ankle. So much for the squad of six Toronto defencemen.

And the shortage of dependable reserves still kept the Leafs desperate. Toronto had just the single strong centre, Gilmour double-shifting on one leg. The two remaining centres, Peter Zezel and Mike Eastwood, had their moments, particularly in defensive circumstances, but this was the Stanley Cup semi-finals, not a time for players who couldn't bring some attack to the battle. So it went among the reserves, Nikolai Borschevsky, for example, a wonderfully adept little guy, but not muscular enough to handle Vancouver players who had a ton of weight on him. Worse, Borschevsky took a fairly stupid retaliatory penalty on

Trevor Linden in the second period; it led to the Canucks' power-play goal that tied the game at 3–3.

The Leafs fought on. None of the Toronto players surrendered, not the handful of stars, not the guys with the spear-carrier roles. They tried hard, showed desire that would break your heart. The game went scoreless through the third period, through the first overtime. Then—so quickly, so permanently—a few seconds after the second overtime period began, Trevor Linden snapped the puck away from Sylvain Lefebvre, slipped it to Dave Babych at the Leaf blueline. Babych fired on the net. Potvin caught the puck. Dropped it. Greg Adams shoved the loose puck under Potvin's blocker. Goal. Series over. Leafs gone. For the second consecutive season, Toronto had flamed out in the Stanley Cup semi-finals.

"We just can't get over the hump," Pat Burns said later, looking more than ever like the man with no smile. "We tried two years in a row, and we just can't."

Now what?

25

Future Business

ON APRIL 5, 1994, STEVE STAVRO ANNOUNCED
the news, long in preparation, long anticipated, that he
was taking the final steps to make the Leafs totally his
business. Well, "totally" except for a few million dollars
of other people's money. Stavro may be a huge Leaf fan,
conspicuously supportive and a terrific administrator, but
he didn't become an extremely rich man by acting fast and loose with his
own money.

The steps that Stavro engineered to consolidate his control over the
Leafs and the Gardens encompassed the following:

He bought the percentage of the Gardens still retained by Molson's
Breweries, almost 20 percent, for $21 million. This completed the deal
that Stavro had initiated with Molson's in 1991 and closed out the interest that the brewery had first acquired in its relationship with Harold
Ballard almost fifteen years earlier.

He arranged to purchase from the Ballard estate its 60.3 percent
stake in the Gardens for about $75 million.

He formed a company called Maple Leaf Gardens Ventures which
would assume the above two ownership chunks in the Gardens, together
with all the loose stock that Stavro could pick up at a price of thirty-four

dollars per share. Maple Leaf Ventures was not purely a Stavro outfit. Far from it. MLG Ventures would be owned, 49 percent, by the Ontario Teachers' Pension Board (an entity with assets of some $34 billion); the Toronto-Dominion Bank, 20 percent; and Stavro, 31 percent. Under the agreement among the owners of Maple Leaf Gardens Ventures, in case anyone was worried that a bunch of school teachers would end up running the Gardens and the Leafs, controlling interest remained with Stavro.

All of this high-level manoeuvring wasn't accomplished without a few objections from the sidelines. They came from groups and people as disparate as Toronto Teamsters Local 847, the Public Trustee of Ontario, and two Gardens minority shareholders named Jim Devellano and Harry Ornest. The basic quibble these opponents raised centred on the many hats worn by Stavro. He was the incumbent Gardens chairman of the board. He was a co-executor of the Harold Ballard estate (along with Don Crump and Terry Kelly). And he was the big winner in the new ownership arrangement.

Were there conflicts of interest here? Was Stavro, wearing his Ballard-executor chapeau, giving Stavro, in his MLG Ventures head gear, a deal that was rich for Ventures but not so rewarding for the charities who were the beneficiaries of Harold's will? And had Stavro, now in his chairman-of-the-board hat, pegged the Gardens stock, thirty-four dollars per share, at a level significantly below current market value?

The Teamsters wondered about such questions because its membership included Gardens employees who might expect aid under a term of Ballard's will that promised scholarships to help in the education of kids whose parents worked at the Gardens. The Public Trustee was concerned, too, since part of its legislated mandate was to look out for the interests of charities in line to receive benefits from any estate, specifically, in this case, from Harold Ballard's estate. As for the two minority shareholders, Jim Devellano, a senior V.P. for the Detroit Red Wings, owned about 1 percent of the total Gardens stock, and Harry Ornest, a former owner of the St. Louis Blues, held close to 3.6 percent of the outstanding shares, and both of them figured their stock was worth considerably more than the thirty-four-dollars-per-share pittance that Stavro was offering. To back up their beliefs, all of these parties—Teamsters,

Public Trustee, Devellano, Ornest—invited the courts and the Ontario Securities Commission to take a close look at Stavro's machinations.

Stavro, in the meantime, proceeded full speed ahead. The NHL was on his side; the league governors were so overjoyed to have a strong man like Stavro take complete charge in Toronto that they rushed to vote approval of the Maple Leaf Gardens Ventures ownership. And enough other minority stockholders threw in their lot with Stavro, at the offered thirty-four bucks per share, that, by early May 1994, Ventures had accumulated 90.2 percent of all stock. That amount, any amount over 90 percent, entitled Ventures, barring court action, to buy up all outstanding shares and take the company private.

While Stavro was getting on with his business in the summer of 1994, consolidating power at the Gardens, other members of the Leaf family were hardly idle. Wendel Clark, for example. He was undergoing a mild trauma. That's because Cliff Fletcher was doing his general manager's number with more daring and intensity than any GM in the league. Fletcher traded Clark to Quebec.

"Well, what are you gonna do?" Clark said, shrugging but looking stricken, standing in front of his apartment in the Annex, getting ready to stroll two blocks south to his local, the Madison Avenue Pub, for a consoling brew. Clark, always the classy fellow, took the trade as part of hockey business, left behind a tear or two, and moved on from the city where he'd been the stuff of heroism.

One could see the trade coming, not necessarily of Clark, but the unloading of a major Leaf star to get a solid second-line centre. That's what Fletcher pulled off, acquiring Mats Sundin from Quebec, a big kid (only twenty-three to Clark's rapidly-ageing twenty-seven) and a proven goal scorer. And that didn't finish Fletcher's tinkering. When the day of reckoning had passed, June 28, the Leafs had acquired a tough defenceman, Garth Butcher, and a promising forward, Todd Warriner, (both from Quebec) and the veteran goal-scoring centre, Mike Ridley (from Washington), while surrendering the defensive defenceman Sylvain Lefebvre and the young forward prospect, Landon Wilson (both to Quebec) plus forward Rob Pearson (to Washington).

Fletcher had more to do. Renegotiate a raise for Pat Burns. Buy out a couple of incumbent centres, John Cullen and Mike Krushelnyski. Handle the probable departure of defenceman Bob Rouse. Lure the apparently wondrous young Swedish defenceman Kenny Jonsson to North America. So much to accomplish. Planning. Retooling. Stepping the team up a notch from semi-finalist to finalist. A Stanley Cup. Business.

BY EARLY IN THE THIRD PERIOD OF A GAME AT THE Gardens on a Thursday night, January 13, 1994, the Leafs looked as if they were headed towards sure defeat. Dallas was up on them 3–1, and the Stars were always stingy about surrendering a lead. But halfway through the period, Dave Andreychuk, in the slot as usual, deflected a Todd Gill drive from the blueline into the Dallas net, and fifty-five seconds later Mike Eastwood got his first goal of the season on a setup from Mark Osborne. Tie game. In overtime, Glenn Anderson took a goalmouth pass and, showing graceful art, lifted the puck over goalie Darcy Wakaluk, who had gone into a defensive slide. Leafs 4, Stars 3.

"I think we should go over there," Steve Stavro, speaking in his soft voice, said to the other directors. What Stavro meant was that the directors should make the trek across the ice from their box on the Gardens' west side to the Leaf dressing room on the east side, drop in on the players, tell them how splendid the comeback win was this night.

"Ah, well, Steve," Terry Kelly said, "you know how Pat Burns feels about that."

Stavro smiled.

Kelly said, "Every time we visit the dressing room, Pat thinks it gives the players the idea they've already won the Stanley Cup."

"We'll go over anyway," Stavro said.

And they went, Stavro and Kelly and the others.

Stavro likes to show support, likes to let the players know that the guys in the suits care about them. In the spring of 1993, when the Leafs travelled to Los Angeles for games in the semi-finals series against the Kings, most of the directors went on the trip to the coast. It wasn't lost on anybody that the Hollywood racing season was on, that Stavro the ultimate horse man might like to take in a day at the track between hockey games. No way, Stavro said. Nobody from the Leaf contingent, no director, not even the boss, was going to the track on this trip.

"We'll be at the hockey practices," Stavro told the other directors. "It's business for the players, and they've got to see it's business for us too."

Serious Toronto Maple Leaf business.

Acknowledgments

MANY WRITERS HAVE WRITTEN BOOKS THAT DEAL ALL OR in part with the Leafs. I have read, enjoyed and learned from many of these books, and I'm especially indebted to the following excellent writers: Scott Young, Trent Frayne, William Houston, Earl McRae, Allan Turowetz, David Cruise and Alison Griffiths, Bruce Dowbiggan, David Shoalts, Scott Morrison, James Lawton, Dick Beddoes and Brian McFarlane. I'm grateful to the present and past Leaf players who gave me their time and memories. Their names and words appear in the text of the book, but Billy Harris deserves special mention. After all, he qualifies as both a Leaf player and an author of his own wonderful book about the team. The redoubtable Terry Kelly was extraordinarily generous with his help and his reminiscences. So was Rick Boulton. And my great thanks go to the master researcher, Mary Rutherford.

Index